PUBLIC
POLICY

Peter Woll

UNIVERSITY
PRESS OF
AMERICA

Library of Congress Catalog Card Number: 81-40886

Again, after a decade, for Bob and Cindy

Contents

Preface

The American political system is surrounded by myths and misconceptions about how public policy is formed. Elite theorists suggest that there is an elite class that makes the decisions affecting our lives. Group theorists hold that public policy is and should be controlled by pressure groups. Voters often feel that the political party of their choice shapes policy. Before Watergate, the "imperial presidency" overshadowed Congress as a policy force. Congress is valiantly trying to reassert itself. The role of the courts and the bureaucracy in policy formation remains mysterious to most people. This book attempts to unravel the complexities of the policy process.

The book concentrates upon the role of major political institutions in policy-making: interest groups, political parties, the presidency, Congress, courts, and the bureaucracy. The formal and informal context within which these institutions operate is covered. The capability of each institution to affect public policy is assessed, in an attempt to answer the question: where does the real power to make public policy reside in the political system?

Hopefully, this book will be useful to all students of public policy, whether in special public policy courses or in more generalized courses in American government where the connections between institutions and policy-making are examined. It should be of particular value to those seeking a supplement to books that primarily discuss substantive issues of public policy.

I am particularly indebted to Michael Danielson who gave the book a careful reading and made many valuable suggestions. The constructive criticism and encouragement of Rochelle Jones is deeply appreciated. I would like to thank Jim Murray and Robert H. Binstock for their support and suggestions throughout the writing and production of this book. Michèle Borgers gave me generous support in the final stages of the book. And, finally, I want to acknowledge with thanks the skill, speed, and good humor of Linda McDaniel and Trudi Rogers who typed the manuscript.

1

The Context

of Policy

Formation

The 1960's and the early 1970's witnessed a tension in the American political system that had not been seen for many decades. Suddenly people in all walks of life seemed to be questioning the viability of our political institutions. Watergate caused unprecedented disillusionment with government. But long before Watergate the public policy outputs of the system were not meeting the expectations of many segments of the community. Blacks were not content with what they felt was the unduly slow progress being made toward equality with whites in jobs, schooling, housing, and in many other areas. Strong reactions were registered against the government's Vietnam policy by groups of college students, housewives, businessmen, and ad hoc peace groups drawn from other parts of the community. Counterreactions in support of the government were undertaken by the "hard-hats," and other more conservative elements of the community. It seemed that no matter what policies the government advanced it received the wrath of some elements of the public. In civil rights, for example, attempts by the government to enforce various provisions of the Civil Rights Act of 1964 were opposed by conservative elements in all parts of the country, at the same time that blacks were equally unhappy with what they considered to be the lack of government action.

Political demonstrations have always been an important tactic in our system. The 1960's witnessed the use of demonstrations by an unusually large number of groups. Martin Luther King, Jr. led the poor people's march on Washington, and either led or inspired numerous other demonstrations in the cause of equal rights for blacks. Large numbers of students, both white and black, joined in civil rights marches and sit-ins. Civil rights demonstrations often led to violence, as did demonstrations against the Vietnam war, which were so prevalent among the campuses of the nation's colleges and universities. The extent of the anti-war demonstrations shook the administrations of Johnson and Nixon, and led the latter to attempt to set up an extensive system of intelligence activities to counter what President Nixon and his staff felt to be subversive activities. Testifying before the Watergate committee, former presidential counselor John Ehrlichman brazenly justified the administration's breaking and entering into the office of Daniel Ellsberg's psychiatrist as necessary to preserve national security against Communist threats from within and without the system. This is but one reflection of the thinking of the Nixon Administration in response to anti-war activities.

Although the government's civil rights and Vietnam policies produced the most dramatic public reactions, governments at all levels were also being besieged by conservationists and other environmental action organizations and individuals to enact legislation and to put into effect administrative regulations to preserve and purify the nation's natural resources. Moreover, consumer advocate Ralph Nader led a concerted attack upon government to force it to implement policies to protect the interests of consumers. The environmental and consumer movements have made inputs into government in a relatively conservative fashion, lobbying Congress, the bureaucracy, and using the courts to achieve their goals.

Governmental institutions are supposed to be responsive to the demands made upon them. These demands, however, are never one sided, but always reflect the conflicting interests of the community. The governmental process is continually involved in bringing about compromise among the diverse interests of the politically active elements of society. This does not mean that public policy is or should be formulated merely by balancing conflicting interests. Government must exercise leadership, which may mean going beyond the desires of the various elements of the community that make demands upon the government. In many cases the president, for example, formulates foreign policy on his own initiative and sometimes in opposition to the wishes of powerful groups. Most presidents espouse free trade regardless of the fact that there is very strong pressure from some segments of industry for protective tariffs. This is not to suggest that the president is always free from domestic pressures in the foreign policy area, or that these pressures do not profoundly influence him. Consistent United States support for Israel reflects in part presidential response to a powerful group within the domestic constituency.

POLITICAL ELITES

The existence of political leadership does not necessarily imply rule by an elite. Elite rule is by a definable class, from whom leaders are drawn. Gaetano Mosca pointed out in *The Ruling Class:*

Among the constant facts and tendencies that are to be found in all political organisms, one is so obvious that it is apparent to the most casual eye. In all societies—from societies that are very meagerly developed and have barely attained the dawnings of civilization, down to the most advanced and powerful societies—two *classes* of people appeared —a class that rules and a class that is ruled. The first class, always the less numerous, performs all political functions, monopolizes power and enjoys the advantages that power brings, whereas the second, the more numerous class, is directed and controlled by the first, in a manner that is now more or less legal, now more or less arbitrary and violent, and supplies the first in appearance, at least, with material means of subsistence and with the instrumentalities that are essential to the vitality of the political organism.[1]

Although there is little doubt that throughout American history minorities have controlled the formulation of public policy, it is difficult to generalize about the composition of the class from which leadership in both the public and private realms has been drawn. A common generalization is that we have been ruled by WASPS, Anglo-Saxons of superior wealth and education. There is little doubt that Protestants, if not always WASPS, have tended to dominate positions of leadership in government and industry; however, their economic background has varied. For example, as one looks at the American presidency it is true that every president until John F. Kennedy was a Protestant; however, all presidents were not from wealthy backgrounds. And, of course, the machine politics of the developing urban areas in the nineteenth century that depended upon the votes of immigrant groups produced leaders that were not drawn from the WASP sections of the community.[2]

Recognizing the fact that of necessity governmental power is

---

[1] Gaetano Mosca, *The Ruling Class* (New York: McGraw-Hill, 1939), p. 50. The Italian edition of this work first appeared in 1895, and was subsequently revised in 1923. Italics added.

[2] For a discussion of elite theory see Chapter 2.

exercised by a minority of the population, the real issue is the extent to which political leaders are responsive to the interests of the community. The lack of political skills, financial resources, and specialized knowledge about important issues of public policy on the part of the general electorate has inevitably resulted in giving to government policy-makers a great deal of discretion. At all levels of government the interests of pressure groups, as articulated by their leaders, have been given great weight in public policy decision-making. This was especially true before the rise of Nader-like public interest pressure groups.

PUBLIC POLICY AND
PRIVATE POWER

Public policy and private power have always been closely linked at the national, state and local levels of government. The "public interest" has often been defined as a reflection of private interests within particular spheres of public policy. During the nineteenth century, while the rhetoric of laissez-faire capitalism supported the idea that that government which governs least is best, private economic groups continuously obtained government subsidies and favors to solidify their power, increase their opportunities, and profits. What one author has called "the saturnalia of spoils and plunder that passed for politics after the Civil War,"[3] was vividly portrayed by Mark Twain in *The Gilded Age*.[4] Outright bribery was common, particularly at the state level. One extreme example occurred in New York, where Vanderbilt and Gould were in competition for railroad subsidies from the New York Legislature. Not satisfied with relying upon ordinary bribery, Gould appeared in Albany with $500,000 in greenbacks, which he proceeded to distribute among the legislators.[5] Elected officials as well as bureaucrats held substantial interests in private enterprise, and conflicts of interests were an accepted fact of political life.

For most of the nineteenth century it would not be an exaggeration to say that public policy served the economic interests of

[3] Edgar Lane, *Lobbying and the Law* (Berkeley and Los Angeles: University of California Press, 1964), p. 24.
[4] Mark Twain, *The Gilded Age* (Hartford, Conn.: The American Publishing Co., 1873).
[5] Lane, p. 24.

selected groups in the private sector. The railroads benefited most from governmental largesse, through extraordinary grants of public lands, and state guaranteed loans for railroad construction, most of which were not paid back. Both federal and state governments were involved in this unprecedented giveaway to the railroad industry. Hundreds of millions of acres of land were transferred, and loans estimated at approximately $¾ billion were made. In comparison to government subsidies for the railroads, subsidies achieved in the form of protective tariffs were minuscule. It was not until the end of the nineteenth century that the forces of populism and progressivism succeeded in extracting from state and federal governments public policies designed to control the extraordinary influence of private economic interests upon government (for example, through the passage of lobbying laws requiring disclosure of information concerning the lobbying activities of pressure groups), and to control the unbridled economic discretion of industrial firms. The passage of the Interstate Commerce Act of 1887 was a victory for populist forces seeking to establish governmental control over the practices of the railroad industry. This was followed by the Sherman Act of 1890, designed to curb unreasonable restraints of trade, and hence, the burgeoning monopolies in major economic sectors. In the early twentieth century these laws were extended by new legislation to strengthen the capabilities of government to deal with problems of economic regulation, and to extend the authority of government over the economy.

The entry of the government into the field of economic regulation added a new and difficult dimension to public policy. The political forces behind the passage of statutes giving government agencies authority to regulate industry mandated that the agencies should act in the "public interest." This public interest was clearly to be different from those of the private groups being regulated. But it was impossible to define clearly by statute exactly what constituted the public interest as opposed to the interests of private groups. The 1887 Interstate Commerce Act was more specific in regulating the practices of railroads than most subsequent statutes, but it also contained many vague provisions that had to be subsequently defined by the Interstate Commerce Commission. Statutory ambiguity essentially meant that the dominant forces in the political constituencies of the agencies involved in regulating economic groups would determine the policy outputs of government in their respective fields. They supplied the expertise and political clout that virtually guaranteed them control over the policy-making process.

The fate of government regulatory commissions was well-predicted by Attorney General Richard S. Olney in 1892 in a letter to a railroad executive:

My impression would be that, looking at the matter from a railroad point of view exclusively, it would not be a wise thing to undertake to abolish the [Interstate Commerce] Commission. The attempt would not be likely to succeed—if it did not succeed and were made on the ground of the inefficiency and uselessness of the Commission, the result would very probably be giving it the powers it now lacks. The Commission, as its functions have now been limited by the courts is, or can be made of great use to the railroads. It satisfies the popular clamor for a government supervision of railroads, at the same time that the supervision is almost entirely nominal. Further, the older such a Commission gets to be, the more inclined it will be found to be to take the business and railroad view of things. It thus becomes a sort of barrier between the railroad corporations and the people and a sort of protection against hasty and crude legislation hostile to railroad interests. The Commission cost something, of course. But so long as its powers are advisory merely, for the reasons just stated, it strikes me that it is well worth the money. The part of wisdom is not to destroy the Commission, but to utilize it. . . .[6]

It was difficult indeed for the democratic populist forces to achieve effective regulation of the railroads when faced with hostility from such powerful individuals as the attorney general, as well as the majority of judges then on the Supreme Court and the lower judiciary.

Even at the end of the nineteenth and early twentieth centuries, politicians would, from time to time, take popular stands in favor of strong regulation of business in order to gain votes. This was particularly true among populist leaders in the Midwest. And although many of these politicians were genuine in their anti-business stance, they were never able to sustain at the national level sufficient votes in Congress to produce strong "public interest" policies. Congress, then as now, was controlled mainly by conservative politicians who had seniority and who were the chairmen of powerful committees. The important business of Congress has always been conducted in these committees. This system automatically produces conservative men in key congressional posts, because in

---

6 Richard S. Olney to Charles C. Perkins, cited from James M. Smith and Paul L. Murphy, *Liberty and Justice* (New York: Alfred A. Knopf, 1958), pp. 292–93.

order to achieve seniority, congressmen generally must come from "safe" districts which are controlled by one party over a period of years. Traditionally, powerful committee chairmen have come from the South in the Democratic Party, and from the Midwest and West in the Republican Party. These men often represent rural constituencies. The seniority rule has not always prevailed in Congress. As Nelson W. Polsby and his associates have pointed out, a rigid seniority system did not exist in the House of Representatives until after World War II. Even then the seniority rule was not always rigidly followed, and it has only been in recent years that the system was rarely if ever violated.[7] Nevertheless, whether the House of Representatives was dominatd by the Speaker or committee chairmen, its locus of power remained conservative. The Senate at the beginning of the twentieth century was an even more conservative force than the House of Representatives. It was not until 1913 that senators were popularly elected. The essentially conservative power-base of Congress made the passage of strict legislation to control business interests highly unlikely.

THE DELEGATION OF POLICY-MAKING POWER BY CONGRESS

A major attribute of our political system is the delegation of policy-making authority by Congress to the president and administrative agencies. Congress delegates this authority for both practical and political reasons. From a practical standpoint, Congress simply does not possess the expertise to cope with the complex policy matters which come before it. Such expertise requires large and expert staffs that deal with policy areas on a continuous basis. Congress does have staff, and individual congressmen, particularly long-term committee chairmen, have a high degree of expertise; however, neither the staff nor the personal skills and knowledge of the legislature are equivalent to the expertise of the bureaucracy. For example, the chairmen of the Appropriations subcommittees that deal with defense are highly knowledgeable individuals, but scarcely a match for the Pentagon. The ever-growing scope and complexity of the federal government,

---

[7] Nelson W. Polsby, Miriam Gallaher, and Barry Spencer Rundquist, "The Growth of the Seniority System in the U. S. House of Representatives," *The American Political Science Review* 63 (September, 1969): 787–807.

reflected, for example, in its highly technical and mammoth budget, continues to frustrate congressional attempts to keep in touch with governmental policy-making activities outside of Congress.

A major political reason for the delegation of policy-making authority is that within Congress it is difficult to secure an agreement on concrete terms to be used in legislation. When the members of Congress cannot agree on definite policy statements, they have tended to shift the burden of making concrete decisions to administrative agencies acting as agents of the legislature.

Both the practical and political reasons for congressional delegations of broad grants of authority are important. However, the example of Great Britain, where extensive delegation has taken place from the House of Commons to the bureaucracy, but where there is no issue of political disagreement because of the domination of the legislature by the majority party, suggests that it is really a practical impossibility for any legislature, regardless of how cohesive it is, to set forth the terms of public policy in a sufficiently concrete way to limit administrative discretion in law-making.

Congress attempts to control its delegated authority through the exercise of legislative oversight. Powerful congressmen generally keep in close touch with administrative agencies that deal with the same policy areas that are under the jurisdiction of their committees. Constant communication on important decisions may occur between legislators and administrators. Key congressmen and congressional staff become, in effect, part of the administrative process. Conversely, many administrators are deeply involved in the congressional process, by drafting legislation and giving advice to congressmen on what legislation should be enacted. Congress and the bureaucracy in this way work together not only to formulate public policy but to administer it.

DEFINING THE
PUBLIC INTEREST

One of the fundamental historical tenets of our constitutional democracy is that the legislative representatives of the people should be the ones to shape domestic policy. Congress is supposed to have a limited role in foreign policy-making, which is a primary responsibility of the president. In the domestic field, the broad delegations of authority by Congress clearly reduce its ability to control the content of public policy. By defining "the public interest" in broad and nebulous terms, Congress is allowing policy to be made by administrators on the basis of the inputs from the constituencies of administrative agencies. This, in turn, often results in policy-making outputs being swayed by powerful pressure groups that supply the major inputs of the administrative policy-making process. In terms of practical politics, whether or not a public interest exists depends upon its articulation by those who have power in the political process, whether pressure groups or individuals. The public interest never exists in the abstract. There is always disagreement about what constitutes the public interest in any given area of public policy. This is what makes the democratic process competitive and necessitates compromise among opposing points of view before policy decisions can be reached. Each of us may, in his heart, feel that he knows exactly what constitutes the public interest in any given policy field. But the more specifically one defines the public interest the greater the disagreement with others. It is necessary to accept the fact that the public interest in reality is what is defined as such after the governmental process has taken into account and compromised divergent viewpoints.

THE ROLE OF THE PUBLIC
IN POLICY-MAKING

A major difficulty that exists within the democratic process regarding the definition of the public interest is that often very few groups and individuals participate in the process of defining the public interest in particular policy areas. The broader electorate does not have the information, motivation, or time to involve itself in every area of public policy. Ideally, democratic theory posits that government decisions will be made only after those affected have a chance to express their viewpoints, and after a compromise of opposing interests has been made. In fact, democratic society is not nearly as open as this ideal suggests. Particularly in foreign policy, critical decisions are often made by small cliques of governmental officials, headed by the president, without adequate consultation with Congress or with outside interest groups. How does the public have a chance to participate in such vital decisions? For example, those critical decisions made by many administrations that gradually led to the deep involvement of the United States in the Vietnam war were not a matter of public record; even key congressmen were kept in the dark or misled about many of the important steps involved in escalating the American commitment to the war. This has led Congress in recent years to attempt to curb presidential authority to undertake military action without congressional consultation. Early congressional support for the Gulf of Tonkin Resolution soon gave way to strong opposition in votes opposing actions of the president to escalate the war. By the early 1970's the House and Senate were voting to limit funds for military operations in Vietnam unless authorized by Congress. In 1973 Congress forced the president to stop bombing Cambodia, and passed the War Powers Resolution that curbed his military discretion.

The effects of the Vietnam war upon the foreign policy decision-making process remain to be determined. Certainly in the past, although sporadic attempts have been made by the legislature to curb presidential authority in this area, no permanent mechanism has been devised to limit the power of the chief executive. The major difference between democracies and authoritarian or totalitarian states in this area of decision-making is that once the decision is made in a democracy the public can register its reaction at the polls. Although considerable damage may already have been made in the view of the majority of the electorate, the fact that it can change the occupant of the White House is at least a check, if only after the fact. The president does not follow public opinion in the foreign policy area, because in this policy sphere as in many others, there is usually little public opinion expressed until the government embarks upon a visible course of action, such as sending arms to Israel, troops to Vietnam, or reducing troop strength in Europe. Public opinion always follows rather than leads the president in foreign policy-making. Usually presidents have been able to shape public opinion to support foreign policy decisions. This has been particularly true during wars, when appeals to patriotic sentiments often brought about an outpouring of support for government actions. But in recent years the feeling of "my country, right or wrong" is diminishing as the public is bombarded with information from the mass media that is critical of government action revealing the danger of general support for the policies of political leaders.

In the domestic policy arena, the processes of governmental decision-making may be equally closed to the public at large. Domestic policy-making is often in the hands of individual congressmen and administrative agencies that are not in the public view. They are always known to powerful pressure groups, however, whose economic interests are affected by the decisions that are made. Demands are made known to governmental decision-makers through a relatively narrow spectrum of interest groups, not through broader public participation. Domestic policy formation is often a specialized process, that tends to exclude all but the highly motivated, skilled, monied, and powerful. In the domestic as in the foreign policy areas, the public interest is defined by specialized groups. If more of the public at large could be involved in the process of policy formulation then the public interest would be defined differently. But so far the mechanisms of our democracy have not been able to bring wider public participation into the processes of policy formulation.

THE RISE OF PUBLIC
INTEREST GROUPS

The decade of the 1960's and the early 1970's witnessed a new phenomenon in American politics, the expansion of interest groups that had as their primary goal the promotion of broad public rather than narrow private interests. Ralph Nader's Center for Study of Responsive Law, Common Cause, and various ecology action groups are typical of these public interest pressure groups. They differ from most pressure groups in that they do not have a direct economic motivation for the policies which they are promoting. Before such groups developed, most pressure groups were economically motivated, although in the area of civil liberties and civil rights groups such as the NAACP and the American Civil Liberties Union were public interest pressure groups in the same sense as these more recent groups. All were formed because their sponsors recognized that in order to change public policy, political pressure had to be brought to bear upon government decision-makers. This is best accomplished through the formation of groups, rather than on an individual basis. Although Ralph Nader originally operated very successfully as an individual, he soon formed a group himself and attempted to expand his political base. Public interest groups represent an attempt to counterbalance in the private sphere the power of private corporations.

The success of public interest groups in recent years supports the argument that the way to get things done in the political process is to organize. These groups have been particularly effective in using the courts to overturn or to delay governmental decisions that they consider to be unfavorable to the interests that they represent. Ralph Nader and his organization have used not only the courts, but he has also gained access to Congress and administrative agencies. He has been able to achieve a remarkable number of important changes in public policy from these branches. Nader's book, *Unsafe at Any Speed*, helped him to prod Congress into passing the Motor Vehicle Safety Act of 1966, which created an administrative agency to establish standards for motor vehicle safety. In 1967, using a Department of Agriculture report on filthy conditions in state-regulated meat-packing plants, Nader was able to call congressional attention to the need for stricter federal regulation. This resulted in the Wholesome Meat Act of 1967, which requires states to establish inspection programs with standards equal to federal requirements pertaining to interstate commerce in meat. In those states failing to tighten their regulatory restrictions, federal inspection would supplant state supervision. As Nader began to move more rapidly and to gather public support for his undertakings, toward the end of the 1960's much more legislation was inspired by the demands he made upon Congress. The Natural Gas Pipeline Safety Act of 1968, the Radiation Control for Health and Safety Act of 1968, the Coal Mine Health and Safety Act of 1969, and the Comprehensive Occupational Safety and Health Act of 1970 are laws that Nader and his organization helped to pass.

Nader has also been very effective in changing administrative policies through direct pressure upon the bureaucracy. In particular, "Nader's Raiders" swarmed down upon the FTC in 1968, finding a weak and ineffective agency in which some officials, Nader alleged, if they came to work at all, spent part of their time sleeping and drinking on the job. The revelations of Nader's Raiders were instrumental in reinvigorating the FTC and making it a stronger proponent of consumer interests. In 1969, Nader's Raiders descended upon the FDA, and revealed that the agency had approved cyclamates, and monosodium glutamate as food preservatives, without restriction. Adverse publicity resulting from these findings caused the FDA to ban cyclamates from soft drinks and prohibit the use of monosodium glutamate in baby food.

Although Nader's consumer-oriented organization has been the most successful in bringing about policy changes from government, other public interest groups have been successful in forcing administrative agencies to pay careful attention to such problems as conservation before they rendered decisions affecting the environment. Lawyers from all public interest groups have been active in taking class action suits to the judiciary in attempts to force national and state governments to adhere to standards of due process and equal protection of the laws in the delivery of public services. Until the Supreme Court upheld the use of the property tax to finance public education in *San Antonio* v. *Rodriguez* (1973), far-reaching implications for public policy stemmed from cases that were filed by public interest groups challenging the local property tax as the basis of financing public education. A number of state and federal courts had held that the use of the property tax to determine the amount of money spent for public education from one district to another was unconstitutional because it violated the equal protection clause of the fourteenth amendment. Since the property tax leads to unequal distribution of funds within states for public education, school children do not receive the same treatment from one part of the state to another. Although the Supreme Court did not uphold the decisions of these lower courts, the door is still open to broad challenges in other areas of public service, in which it can be claimed that equal treatment is not given within or among state jurisdictions, because of unequal financing of government programs.

The rise of public interest groups is an important force counteracting the majority of pressure groups that are primarily economically motivated. The leaders of these groups accept the viability of the democratic process, and believe that mobilization of political resources can bring about change within the system. They do not propose any radical alterations in the structure of government either at the national or state levels. If anything, they are conservative, believing that Congress should reassert its authority, and accept responsibility for dealing with critical issues of public policy rather than delegating blanket authority to administrative agencies for this purpose. Moreover, they support the concept of the independent judiciary, and readily use the courts to check the actions of other branches of the government. Some of these groups, particularly Common Cause, hope to change the system by bringing about an expansion of electoral participation. This reflects their faith in the capability of electoral politics to produce meaningful policy changes. Nothing better represents the folklore of American democracy than this attitude. Of course, the leaders of all these groups are sophisticated enough to understand elite theory, group theory, and the general workings of the political process. But they do not believe that governmental decision-making is necessarily described exclusively by any one of these models. They thoroughly believe in and support *citizen participation*, and recognize the mobilization of citizenry as a potential political force of great magnitude.

THE CONTEMPORARY
POLICY-MAKING PROCESS

The policy-making process is a complex mechanism involving all levels of government, and a wide range of political institutions that shape the demands and supports of government. Political scientists are fond of conceptualizing the political process in terms of what they call a political *system*. Demands and supports are made upon and given to all levels of government by individuals and groups seeking to achieve certain public policy goals, or outputs. Government, by definition, is the only legitimate authority that can make public policy decisions. This is determined by the Constitution that sets the formal rules for the system. Public policy, as opposed to private policy, has a compulsory effect upon those at whom it is directed. As a minimum condition of democracy, those affected by the public policy decisions of government should have an opportunity to make their demands known.

Specialization

Perhaps the most outstanding feature of the policy process is its specialization. A basic premise, first of our constitutional system, and later of democratic theory as it evolved in the nineteenth century, was that if given a chance men are rational political beings, capable of interpreting their interests in relation to government policies. "Political man" in theory is analogous to "economic man" in the theory of capitalism. Just as economic man is supposedly capable of making rational choices in the market place, political man chooses rationally in the political market place. Democratic theory, supporting the idea of participation in the formulation of public policy, is naturally predicated on a belief in man's capacity to make rational political judgments. Otherwise there would be little point in having public participation in government. The increasing specialization of the policy process, however, means that there are formidable barriers to broad public participation in policy formulation. Just as economic man cannot participate broadly in the production of goods, political man cannot be involved in the formulation of all policies. But, as economic man makes choices after goods are produced, so political man should be able to make a choice among political policies that affect him even if he did not take part in their formulation. Under such circumstances the conditions of democracy would be met.

Modern democracy is characterized by limited public choice among government policies as well as by selective participation in the determination of policy. The public, even if it had perfect knowledge about what government is doing, would not have access to the means to control all government decision-makers. This is in part because the policy process at the governmental level is highly fragmented among different legislators, legislative committees, administrative agencies, courts, and executives. And every part of the government has a different private constituency, from which the major policy inputs upon government are made. "The public" cannot be in every constituency at once. Only the president has a national constituency. But control over the presidency does not mean control over other parts of the government that have the authority to make public policy. The president has only limited power over the vast machinery of government with which he must deal. Therefore, the election of one man as opposed to another as president is not going to make any difference in many public policy spheres. The glowing promises made by many presidential candidates are more often than not incapable of being fulfilled.

Fragmentation

The fragmentation of the policy process is caused by many factors. The scope and complexity of governmental activities require functional specialization and a division of labor. This is reflected in congressional committees, and even more importantly, in the bureaucracy. Originally the constitutional system itself fragmented the policy process through the separation of powers and the system of checks and balances. This gave to each branch of the government a certain amount of independent authority that could be exercised without being checked by coordinate branches. Each branch of the government was to assume an outsider's role in making demands upon coordinate branches for policy outputs within the jurisdiction of those branches. For example, the president acts as an input upon Congress and vice versa when each is striving to get something from the other. All parts of government become, at one time or another, interest groups to advance their particular goals by putting pressure on other parts of the government. Administrative agencies are constantly pressuring Congress which, for its part, often makes demands upon administrative agencies.

Although the courts do not assume an active role in making demands for policy changes, they are themselves frequently the focal point of intense controversy regarding policy decisions. The strong reaction to the Warren Court's decisions expanding the rights of accused criminals, forcing reapportionment, desegregation, and loosening obscenity restrictions illustrates the way in which the judiciary becomes deeply involved in the political process. Reactions to these decisions helped to elect President Nixon, and produce the Burger Court, which has diluted many of the precedents of the Warren Court.

THE PROBLEM OF
INDIVIDUAL CHOICE

Where can one find direction in the maze of the policy-making process? How can an individual possibly affect the important decisions which government and private groups make that may shape his life? The major vehicles of public participation are interest groups and political parties. Interest groups represent the more specialized concerns of the public, while political parties encompass a broader spectrum of interests. How many people feel that their interests are being adequately represented in government through interest groups and political parties? Even those interest groups with the most cohesive type of membership, such as the American Medical Association, scarcely represent the views of their members in the political process. Each individual has multiple interests that cannot be reflected by often conflicting groups. The public policy that an individual favors depends upon the role with which he identifies. As the manager of a corporation, he may favor policies that will free his firm from government restraints in such areas as pollution and deceptive business practices in advertising. But as a consumer, and as a person who breathes air and is affected by pollution like any citizen, he will favor exactly the opposite policies as he identifies with his consumer and public roles. Theoretically, individuals should do a cost-benefit analysis in analyzing public policies in terms of their own interests. Probably many people do this in a haphazard way. But very few people have the tools and information available to see the true consequences of different kinds of public policies, nor have they determined for themselves exactly what policies on balance will benefit them the most. The multiplicity of public policy options available, and the complexity and far-reaching nature of the consequences of government action, make rational political choice for the individual virtually impossible. Unfortunately, the difficulty of making rational political choices extends to the most sophisticated governmental decision-makers as well as to the average citizen. The debacle of the Vietnam war, undertaken upon the advice of "the best and the brightest" in David Halberstam's phrase, illustrates that political fallibility is not a monopoly of the average citizen.[8]

Some of the Vietnam planners, such as Robert McNamara, attempted to apply vigorous and systematic decision-making methods to carrying out the war. The results were disastrous. Although scientific decision-making can be accurate when dealing with natural phenomena, and determining, for example, how to send an astronaut on a round-trip to the moon, political problems are not so readily susceptible to scientific solutions. Political choice is always to some degree subjective. Public policy generally represents a compromise of clashing viewpoints. Recognizing the impossibility of determining the substantive content of the public interest, democratic constitution-makers, political scientists, and theorists have concentrated upon insuring that certain procedures are followed before government can act. Our Constitution is basically a procedural document, establishing the machinery of government but not determining its outputs. The only way in which the Constitution shapes the substantive content of policy outputs is to prohibit government from abridging certain fundamental rights and liberties of citizens.

UNITY THROUGH LEADERSHIP

The basic reality of the American political system is its pluralism, and the major question for the future is whether or not pluralist politics can deal adequately with pressing issues of public concern. Is there any way to devise in our system an acceptable means to bring greater unity to the pluralist forces of the community without at the same time destroying the very fabric of democracy? This dilemma was discussed in different form by James Madison in *The Federalist, No. 10*, where he took the view that although faction is inherently an undesirable force within a political community, there is no way to stamp it out without at the same time destroying freedom. He noted that "liberty is to faction what air is to fire, an aliment, without which it instantly expires. But it could not be a less folly to abolish liberty, which is

---

[8] David Halberstam, *The Best and the Brightest* (New York: Random House, 1972).

essential to political life because it nourishes faction, than it would be to wish the annihilation of air, which is essential to animal life, because it imparts to fire its destructive agency."

Although most political institutions buttress our pluralist system, the presidency and the Supreme Court have at critical junctures been able to act decisively to break political stalemates often resulting from pluralist democracy. The presidency has been a major force throughout history, capable of taking independent action to overcome divisive forces within the community. Indeed, it can be argued that if it were not for the presidency there would be no United States of America in the sense in which we know it today, because it was President Lincoln's bold and innovative utilization of the authority of the office that was instrumental in preserving the Union.

The Supreme Court, too, because of its power and independence, has been a major force during its active periods in formulating policies in the public interest without regard to political considerations. The Warren Court was perhaps the most innovative court in American history in this regard. Desegregation, reapportionment, an expansion of the rights of accused criminals, a lessening of governmental authority to censor the press and media, were all major public policies emanating from the Supreme Court. Until the Supreme Court took a stand on these issues it was impossible for the pluralist forces of the community to take needed action to meet the demands of those seeking what they considered to be their constitutional rights. In these areas the electoral political process, including the office of the presidency, was not able to exert forceful leadership.

What are the implications and potentialities of the presidency and the Supreme Court as vehicles to overcome divisiveness in a democracy? At what point must a political system be able to produce concrete and uncompromising decisions? This is one of the great dilemmas of the modern democratic state. A government capable of exercising independent leadership is also capable of becoming, under certain circumstances, dictatorial and undemocratic. And when the president, for example, assumes the cloak of a "constitutional dictator"—to use Clinton Rossiter's phrase—those interested in preserving democracy become extremely worried about the extent of presidential authority. At such times it is the efficiency rather than the inefficiency of government which concerns people. With the memory of the World War II presidency fresh in his mind, Clinton Rossiter wrote in 1948 that:

There can no longer be any question that the constitutional democracies, faced with repeated emergencies and influenced by the examples of permanent authoritarian government all about them, are caught up in a pronounced, if lamentable trend toward more arbitrary, more powerful, and more efficient government. The instruments of government depicted here as temporary "crisis" arrangements have in some countries, and may eventually in all countries, become lasting peace-time institutions.[9]

During periods such as World War II the tendency is for the presidency, under broad delegations of authority from Congress, to assume extensive discretionary power in both the domestic and foreign policy spheres.

Whether leadership is exercised by the presidency or by the Supreme Court, there is little doubt that decisions which are made without attention to the intensity of political demands and interests produce strong negative political reaction. Sometimes such feedback can endanger the political stability of the system itself. This was certainly true regarding reaction to the decisions of the president escalating the Vietnam war. Although strong criticism of the Supreme Court has been present with respect to many of its decisions expanding constitutional rights, particularly under the equal protection clause of the fourteenth amendment in the areas of desegregation and reapportionment, never has such feedback severely shaken the very foundations of the system. Curiously enough, it was positive reaction to many of these Supreme Court decisions, particularly with regard to desegregation, that produced violence because of the heightened expectations of civil rights groups that government should, in accordance with the decrees of the Court, be more responsive to their demands.

The dilemma is this: people want effective leadership, provided it agrees with their viewpoint. But by definition, leadership involves going beyond the process of political compromise. The fact that the president does not have to compromise with Congress on many issues gives him the leeway to be an effective leader. Courts at all levels also have a great deal of political independence, and although they operate within the framework of highly developed procedural rules, nevertheless they are far more independent decision-makers than elected representatives. This is particularly true of the Supreme

---

[9] Clinton Rossiter, *Constitutional Dictatorship* (New York: Harcourt Brace Jovanovich, 1963), p. 313. This book was first published by the Princeton University Press in 1948.

Court. By 1972 the judiciary was embarking upon new innovations in public policy requiring equality of treatment under the equal protection clause of the fourteenth amendment in the delivery of public services. Federal and state courts rendered decisions requiring that the delivery of city services could not discriminate from one section of the city to another. Courts also mandated, using the equal protection and due process clauses of the Constitution, that mentally retarded and handicapped individuals must be given access to public education. These are examples of judicial decisions that have potentially dramatic effects on the course of public policy, but none of them were made on the basis of a broadly based democratic political process.

As we attempt in this book to unravel some of the complexities of the policy process, it will be important first to consider some of the more prevalent explanations of how policy is formed, and how it should be formed. We have already touched upon this in our discussion of certain aspects of the theory of our constitutional system, as well as the role of elites and pressure groups. In seeking to evaluate the political process it is important to have a frame of reference. After disposing of this theoretical discussion, we will turn to an analysis of the various components of the policy-making process, including, on the input side of the equation, the role of political parties, pressure groups, and public opinion. The adequacy of the institutions of government as policy-making instruments will also be covered as we look at Congress, the presidency, the judiciary, and the bureaucracy as conversion mechanisms within the policy process. Although we may be able to solve the riddle of how policy is formulated in the American political system, it will be far more difficult to make any kind of definitive judgment about what changes are desirable for the future. These will depend upon the subjective values of the observer, although there are certain minimum conditions that always must be preserved if a political system is to remain viable.

2

Models of the

Policy Process

There are five major models that are most frequently used to explain how public policy is formulated. These reflect in varying degrees both abstract theory and actual practice. The initial governmental process for the formulation of policy was formally set forth in the Constitution, and this "classical model" of policy formulation has been cited most often in textbooks and other general descriptions of our government to explain how the system "works." Although political processes have been vastly altered since the framing of the Constitution, there is no doubt that many of the devices created by the Framers have had a profound and lasting effect upon the way in which policy is made. Other models used to explain the policy-making process are: (1) group theory; (2) the liberal democratic model, in which political parties play a central role in policy-making; (3) elite theory; and (4) systems theory.

THE CLASSICAL MODEL

An important premise of the constitutional system is that government should not be capable of acting without taking into account different political interests that were to be represented in the three branches of the government. The separation of powers and the checks and balances mechanisms were designed to require a broad consensus among the branches of government before public policy could be developed and implemented. This consensus was made more difficult to achieve because each of the elected parts of the government had a separate constituency. The House of Representatives had a locally based constituency, while the Senate was chosen by state legislators and the president through an electoral college system designed to insulate the presidency from direct popular demands. The Supreme Court was to act independently of coordinate branches, and exercised the

21

power of judicial review over legislative and executive actions. Although the Court's power of judicial review was not explicitly stated in the Constitution, it was clearly implied, as can be seen, for example, from Hamilton's discourse in *The Federalist, No. 78.*

Establishing separate constituencies within Congress, and between the legislature and the presidency was to assure that the House, Senate, and Chief Executive would represent different interests and would not be motivated to act in unison. Each branch, having a will of its own based upon its constituency, was also given the necessary constitutional means to resist encroachments from other branches. This is the system of "checks and balances" under which the Constitution has created overlapping powers among the branches of the government enabling them to check each other in some matters. At the same time each branch has sufficiently independent authority to insure that it will not become subordinate to other branches of the government.

There was a division of opinion at the time of the framing of the Constitution regarding which branch of the government would be potentially the most powerful and significant, and the extent to which the powers of each branch should be extended or limited. No one wanted the weak Congress of the Articles of Confederation, and at the same time, among many, there was a fear that excessive power would be granted to the executive. Serious consideration was given at the Constitutional Convention to having the president elected by the legislature, a proposal which, if adopted, would greatly weaken the executive in the environment of American politics, then as now. If the president had to have the confidence of the legislature in order to remain in office, a weaker system of executive leadership would have resulted. Constant division and bickering in the legislature would guarantee rapid turnover in the executive branch. This was avoided by guaranteeing to the president a fixed term of office, during which he could not be removed except by the difficult process of impeachment by a majority and conviction by a two-thirds majority, respectively, of the House and Senate.

Policy-making Power in Congress

The Constitution never defined the term "public policy." Public policy consists first of legislation, which under the original constitutional scheme was to be the exclusive province of Congress, but which today is formulated to a great extent by the bureaucracy under grants of authority from

Congress. Legislation can be defined as rules of conduct that have general applicability, prospective effect, and become operative against individuals only through further proceedings of enforcement or adjudication. Legislation is the first stage of policy-making. Second, policy must be given concrete effect, and this is done by executive enforcement and adjudication by administrative agencies or the courts. The policy-making power of government, then, involves the exercise of all functions of government—legislative, executive, and judicial. Since the Constitution distributed these functions among the three branches, all parts of the government are involved in policy-making. At the time of the framing of the Constitution, however, legislative authority was most closely identified with the primary policy-making power of government. There was little doubt that Congress was to be the dominant institution in the policy-making process.

The whole concept of popular sovereignty in the Western political tradition requires that the most fundamental powers of government be carried out by a legislature representative of the people. The executive is to see that the laws are faithfully executed, not to formulate them. The courts are to act as impartial, independent judges of cases and controversies that involve issues of law formulated by the legislature, or pertaining to the Constitution, unless the legislature has failed to act. The judiciary is not to have supremacy over the legislature.

The concept of parliamentary supremacy, which has been firmly embedded in England since the Glorious Revolution of 1688, finally brought about a recognition that Parliament was to be supreme over the king. This belief shaped future developments in England and America. Before the drafting of the Constitution in 1787, the powers of colonial and state legislative bodies reflected the tradition of legislative supremacy. Many of the Framers of the Constitution, particularly Alexander Hamilton, wanted a strong executive and were able to go a long way in this direction by establishing a separate, independent presidency. However, the principle of legislative supremacy remained an important component of the Constitution.

In *The Federalist*, James Madison called attention to the extensive inherent powers of the legislature in arguing for a strong executive. Above all, he suggested that a legislature united through a majority would be virtually able to control the other branches of government unless some constitutional means was devised to curb the power of the legislature. Establishing a bicameral legislature impeded the possibility of majority control, because each part of the legislature served different constituencies, which reduced the possibility of a common interest binding a majority of the two houses together. The presidential veto power could also check ill-conceived legislative action. Moreover, the Constitution requires extraordinary majorities for legislative action in approving treaties, proposing amendments, and convicting an impeached president.

Constitutional Powers
of Congress

The Constitution, while attempting to place constraints upon the unbridled action of majorities in the legislature, nevertheless recognized that Congress would remain the key institution in government to exercise legislative authority, and therefore policy power. The most fundamental premise of our constitutional system is that the authority of government is to be limited by the terms of the Constitution. Legislative authority was to be limited by the enumerated powers of Article I, which sets forth the boundaries of congressional action. Although the enumerated powers themselves seem at first glance to be fairly specific, for example, the powers of Congress to control commerce among the states, declare war, and tax and spend for the general welfare, these and other parts of Article I require definition. Article I also contains the "implied powers" clause which gives the legislature the authority to enact laws that are "necessary and proper" to carry into execution these enumerated powers. Whether the Constitution was to be interpreted loosely or strictly was a matter for judicial determination, and this was finally settled in the historic cases of *McCullough* v. *Maryland* (1819), and *Gibbons* v. *Ogden* (1824). In the former case, Chief Justice Marshall, after noting that no constitution could possibly contain every detail regulating government action, pointed out that the American Constitution contained only the broad outlines of government. Article I set forth the powers of government in a very broad fashion, for "the sound construction of the Constitution must allow to the national legislature that discretion, with respect to the means by which the powers it confers are to be carried into execution, which will enable that body to perform the high duties assigned to it, in the manner most beneficial to the people." In the *McCullough* case one of the issues was whether or not Congress could incorporate a bank, given that nowhere in the Constitution is such specific authority granted. Marshall's opinion clearly held that such a power could be inferred from Article I's specific grant of authority to regulate.

The *Gibbons* decision fortified the *McCullough* doctrine of implied constitutional powers by holding that the commerce clause grants Congress authority under certain circumstances to regulate intrastate as well as interstate commerce. As the result of these and many other decisions that liberally interpreted the powers of Congress under the Constitution, the boundaries of congressional authority have never been stable, nor have they always been very clear. How far Congress can go depends upon political demands and support for particular actions, and Supreme Court interpretation of the extent of legislative power. After Marshall, the Court often judiciously avoided political controversies and thus saved itself from unequal combat with the legislature. During the early New Deal period a conservative Court locked horns with Congress and refused to budge from a position that interpreted legislative authority under Article I far more strictly than President Roosevelt wished. Key pieces of New Deal legislation were found to be unconstitutional, frustrating the president to the point of recommending a "court-packing" scheme in 1937, the principal component of which was that he would have the authority to appoint one new justice for every one over the age of 70. A well-timed change in position on the part of Justice Roberts shifted the balance of power and avoided the need for a final showdown between the president and the Court on the issue of judicial independence from the president.

The Marshall Court established the predominant trend in the interpretation of the authority of Congress under Article I. Marshall adopted a "loose constructionist" stance, liberally interpreting the authority of Congress, which allowed for a vast expansion of the powers of Congress. From the latter nineteenth century through the early New Deal, however, the Supreme Court adopted a "strict constructionist" position in some fields, limiting in particular the authority of Congress and state legislatures to regulate large areas of economic activity. The early New Deal court, however, marked the last time in which the strict constructionist viewpoint with specific regard to Article I powers of Congress represented the position of a majority of the Court. Today, Article I does not limit congressional authority.

The Scope of Executive Power

Exactly what was to constitute executive power was not spelled out in detail in Article II. In the sphere of foreign policy the president was to be the primary figure in the government conducting foreign relations. As Justice Sutherland said in *United States* v. *Curtiss-Wright Corp.* (1936):

Not only, as we have shown, is the federal power over external affairs in origin and essential character different from that over internal affairs, but participation in the exercise of the power is significantly limited. In this vast external realm, with its important, complicated, delicate, and manifold problems, the president alone has the power to speak or listen as a representative of the nation. He *makes* treaties with the advice and consent of the Senate: but he alone negotiates. Into the field of negotiation the Senate cannot intrude: and Congress itself is powerless to invade it. As Marshall said in his great argument of March 7, 1800, in the House of Representatives, "the president is the sole organ of the nation in its external relations, and its sole representative with foreign nations."

Although the nature of executive power over foreign affairs was clear, what constituted executive power in the domestic arena was not. The president is to be Commander-in-Chief and Chief Executive. He is to see that the laws are faithfully executed. He has the power to request the opinion in writing, on any matter relating to their duties, of the principal officers of the executive departments, and he appoints these officers (public ministers). Nothing more is said about his executive power in Article II. His veto power is really a "legislative" power, as is his power to recommend legislation to Congress. These powers enable the president to check Congress.

The Constitution adopted the Hamiltonian view that executive power should reside in the hands of one man, rather than a group. As Hamilton argued in *The Federalist, No. 70* ". . . energy in the executive is a leading character in the definition of good government." And, ". . . a feeble executive implies a feeble execution of the government. A feeble execution is but another phrase for a bad execution; and a government ill executed, whatever it may be in theory, must be, in practice, a bad government." He went on to argue that the primary way to instill energy in the executive was to make the office unified, and to give it a set term. The president thus became the sole agent of executive power, and was given a four-year term during which he could not be removed except after impeachment and conviction.

The Judiciary and Policy-making

The judicial power, as defined in Article III, essentially involved the settlement of cases and controversies arising under the Constitution, statutory law, treaties, and common law. The various categories of cases under the jurisdiction of the federal courts was defined with a great deal of precision. Although the Framers recognized that the president would be involved in formulating public policy, sometimes independently in the area of foreign affairs, and in both the foreign and domestic areas with the cooperation of Congress, there was no early recognition that the Supreme Court and lower courts might be a major force in the policy-making process. The views of Hamilton in *The Federalist, No. 78* may be taken as indicative of the general tenor of feeling about the judiciary:

Whoever tentatively considers the different departments of power must perceive that, in a government in which they are separated from each other, the judiciary, from the nature of its functions, will always be the least dangerous to the political rights of the Constitution; because it will be least in a capacity to annoy or injure them. The executive not only dispenses the honors, but holds the sword of the community. The legislature not only commands the purse, but prescribes the rules by which the duties and rights of every citizen are to be regulated. The judiciary, on the contrary, has no influence over either the sword or the purse; no direction either of the strength or of the wealth of the society; and can take no *active* resolution whatsoever. It may truly be said to have neither force nor will, but merely judgment; and must ultimately depend upon the aid of the executive arm for the efficacious exercise even of this faculty. [Italics added.]

Hamilton was arguing for the necessity of an independent judiciary, and therefore emphasizing the weakness of the judicial branch could have been in part designed to assuage the apprehensions of those in the states who might have been fearful of the possibility of an overly dominant judiciary. At the same time Hamilton recognized that the courts would have the right to pronounce legislative acts void. In an argument that foreshadowed that of Marshall in *Marbury* v. *Madison* (1803), Hamilton states in *The Federalist, No. 78*:

There is no position which depends on clearer principles than that every act of a delegated authority, contrary to the tenor of the commission under which it is exercised, is void. No legislative act, therefore, contrary to the Constitution, can be valid. To deny this would be to affirm that the deputy is greater than his principal; that the servant is above his master; that the representatives of the people are superior to the people themselves; that men, acting by virtue of powers, may do not only what their powers do not authorize, but what they forbid.

. . . The interpretation of the laws is the proper and peculiar province of the courts. A constitution is, in fact, and must be regarded by the judges as a fundamental law. It must therefore belong to them to ascertain its meaning as well as the meaning of any particular act proceeding from the legislative body. If there should happen to be an irreconcilable variance between the two, that which has the superior obligation and validity ought, of course, to be preferred; in other words, the Constitution ought to be preferred to the statute, the intention of the people to the intention of their agents.

Had Hamilton wished to deemphasize the potential power of the judiciary, he would not have brought up the argument that the courts have the authority to review and declare unconstitutional acts of Congress. It seems to contradict his previous point that the judiciary is inherently the weakest of the three branches of the government. The power of judicial review was not identified by Hamilton as a policy power. The implication was that the Constitution clearly sets forth certain principles which the courts would have to apply in ruling upon legislation, and that this judicial power did not involve a great deal of discretion. The courts would simply apply the letter of the law to the situation at hand. Regardless of what was believed at the time, of course, this authority has at critical times in our history produced important changes in public policy. In recent years the most dramatic effects have been felt by the states. It is safe to assume that the extensive role of the judiciary in shaping public policy was not foreseen by the Framers of the Constitution.

The main structural characteristic of the judiciary emphasized in the classical model was the necessity of independence from the other branches of the government, and from the people. Of course, this independence was tempered by the fact that the president appoints, by and with the advice and consent of the Senate, justices of the Supreme Court. Moreover, Congress has the authority to control the appellate jurisdiction of the Court, which determines the cases that can reach the Court on appeal from lower judicial bodies. The concept of independence is based upon the premise that "political" considerations should not enter into judicial judgments. Hamilton, in The Federalist, No. 78, particularly emphasized the fact that if the judiciary were dependent upon Congress or the president, it would not be able to exercise freely the vital function of judicial review. This would mean that the coordinate political branches would be able to enact any laws that they saw fit, regardless of constitutional considerations to the contrary. Apart from upholding the integrity of judicial review, the independence of the judicial function is rooted in common law theory and has been an integral part of the Anglo-American political tradition since the great struggle between Sir Edward Coke, the Lord Chief Justice of England, and the Crown in the latter sixteenth and early seventeenth centuries. The theoretical premise justifying this is that the determination of justice is based upon skilled judicial interpretation of the law, into which political considerations do not enter except under carefully prescribed conditions determined by the judges themselves.

The Bureaucracy and Policy-making

Today administrative agencies are the focal points of governmental policy-making. But they were not in 1787. It is understandable that nothing was contained in the Constitution relating to the structure and functions of the bureaucracy. However, many indirect inferences can and have been made from the provisions of the Constitution regarding the nature of what has become a fourth branch of the government.

First, agencies are established by Congress under the provisions of the enumerated powers of Article I and the "implied powers" clause. Occasionally, agencies have been established by executive order, but this has been under a grant of delegated power from Congress. The "organic power," which is the power to create and abolish agencies, is entirely contained in Congress. There is no way in which this authority can be inferred from Article II. When the Constitution is viewed in this light, the bureaucracy is always an agent of Congress, unless the legislature chooses to set up different arrangements. For example, it may decide, as it often has, to make agencies responsible to the president. But from the standpoint of the formal distribution of authority in our government, it is a common mistake to assume that the bureaucracy is "the executive branch" and entirely accountable to the White House. As an extension of the organic power, Congress also determines conditions of appointment, removal, and the general organization of the administrative branch. Because the executive power resides solely in the hands of the president, Congress cannot theoretically exercise what are clearly executive functions. Thus, although it can determine the conditions of appointment, it cannot itself appoint individuals to administrative posts. Nor, of course, can legislators formally serve as administrators. The area of removal is similar to that of appointment in terms of the formal powers of Congress. Congress can set the conditions of removal, but cannot itself remove administrative officials except by impeachment and conviction. All of this is in the formal realm, and does not in any way prevent Congress from informally determining appointments, removal, and even directing the day-to-day activities of administrative agencies.

Article II gives the president seemingly very few powers over the administrative branch. He can request the opinion in writing of the principal officers of executive departments, appoint ministers, and he must see that the laws are faithfully executed. Some of the Framers of the Constitution, such as Hamilton, had a clear-cut view that the president would in fact be the chief executive, meaning that the entire executive branch would be beholden to him for employment, and, consequently, entirely responsible to him for administrative decisions. This Hamiltonian view actually reflected reality during much of the nineteenth century when the spoils system was in effect. A good part of the personnel of the administrative branch changed hands with changing presidential administrations. The spoils system did not mean, however, that the president could in fact control those whom he had appointed, and therefore it did not imply that the president actually controlled the entire administrative branch. It merely meant that the limitation of the merit system upon the power of the removal of the president, which began in 1883 with the Pendleton Act, was not present.

The courts are involved with the administrative process through the exercise of judicial review of certain administrative actions. Excepting those rare instances where a constitutional issue is involved, it is entirely up to Congress under the Constitution to determine the scope of judicial review of administrative decisions. This stems from the basic constitutional authority of Congress to set up the agencies and also from its power to determine the appellate jurisdiction of the federal judiciary, including the Supreme Court. The courts can and have totally ignored Congress where they feel that important constitutional issues are involved (see Chapter 7). The courts always have the power, or at least the potential, to overturn administrative action, but frequently they choose not to exercise this power. Due to the scope of administrative decisions and their complexity, the courts generally defer to official expertise.

The bureaucracy exercises legislative, executive, and judicial functions under grants of authority from Congress. To make the reality of this fact conform to the rhetoric of the Constitution, the legislative and judicial powers of the bureaucracy are usually referred to as "quasi-legislative" and "quasi-judicial." The fact that agencies possess all three basic functions of government poses serious problems for the symmetry of the constitutional system. As James Madison stated in *The Federalist, No. 47*, "the accumulation of all powers, legislative, executive, and judicial, in the same hands, whether of one, a few, or many, and whether hereditary, self-appointed, or elected, may justly be pronounced the very definition of tyranny." A common objection raised about the powers of the bureaucracy is that agencies in fact do represent the accumulation of the three functions of government. An agency that has rule-making power (quasi-legislative power) as well as the responsibility of adjudicating cases and controversies arising under its rules is not conforming to constitutional criteria that requires the exercise of legislative and judicial functions in separate branches of government that can check and balance each other. This dilemma is in part reduced by the Administrative Procedure Act of 1946, which requires the separation within the agencies of those who initially perform judicial functions from those who make policy. However, ultimately agency policy-makers control the outcome of cases within the jurisdiction of the agency.[1]

The Effects of the Classical Model

One purpose of the constitutional policy-making model was to limit and control the policy-making power of the national government. The elaborate system set up for this purpose does not function today in accordance with the intentions of the Framers. The growth and the power of the presidency and the bureaucracy, in particular, have distorted the original balance of powers. This is not to suggest that limitation of governmental power was the only concern of the Framers. The whole purpose of the Constitutional Convention in the first place was to produce an instrument that would set up an effective national government capable of dealing with national problems, while at the same time respecting the sovereignty of the states in certain spheres. There were proponents at the Convention of a far more powerful national government than was finally established. Constitutional provisions for the supremacy of the national government

[1] See Chapter 8 for a fuller discussion of these issues.

within its own sphere, and the creation of a strong independent presidency reflected the influence of these men. The political realities of the period, however, did not allow for the creation of a national government without limits.

The Framers had hoped that no public policy could be finalized before the legislative and executive branches had their say. Moreover, under certain circumstances, a policy would be subject to the scrutiny of the Supreme Court upon judicial review if one assumes that the Framers considered this to be an inherent judicial prerogative. Each public policy was to be like a puzzle, the pieces of which were dispersed in the hands of the legislative and executive branches. Public policy could not be put together unless each branch contributed its piece. And, the Supreme Court could ultimately decide the acceptability of the puzzle under the standards of the Constitution. No one part of the government was to be able be put into effect until the president agreed. But policy-making was identified as a legislative function, and legislation could not be put into effect until the president agreed. The policy-making proved to be more than a legislative function, involving executive and judicial actions. The president, the bureaucracy, and the Supreme Court make important public policy decisions without being significantly checked by coordinate branches. The president uses his powers in both the domestic and foreign policy spheres to act independently. Both the president and the bureaucracy have been given what amounts to discretionary authority to formulate legislation under broad delegations from the Congress. The Supreme Court is almost by definition a policy-making body when it passes upon important constitutional questions, and one has only to observe the landmark decisions of the Warren Court to appreciate the policy-making power of the Supreme Court when it has a majority of activist judges.

Specialization of the
Policy Process
The fact that the policy process has become highly specialized within government also renders the checks and balances system much less effective. Specialized policy-making essentially means that the power to make the final policy decisions has been delegated throughout government to particular units that have the expertise to deal with particular spheres of public policy. Within the legislature this division of labor in the policy process is reflected in the committee system, and outside of

Congress, in administrative agencies and specialized staff agencies attached to the White House.

The specialization of the governmental policy process is complemented by specialization in the private sector where pressure groups have particular interests and expertise in those policy areas that affect them. Although one of the major purposes of the constitutional system, according to the arguments of Madison, in *The Federalist, No. 10*, is to reduce the capability of interest groups and political parties to control the apparatus of government, the specialized nature of the policy process in both the governmental and private spheres has produced a contrary result. Although political parties are weak instruments of public policy (see Chapter 4), interest groups in alliance with congressional committees and administrative agencies often shape the nature of public policy. This leads us to a discussion of the second model of the policy process, commonly called group theory, which seeks to explain how our system works in terms of the interaction of government with pressure groups.

THE GROUP THEORY MODEL

Group theorists start with the assumption that in the political process people do not function as individuals but through interest groups. Public policy decisions are always made on the basis of the interaction of interest groups. An interest group is very broadly defined as an organized or unorganized group of people with a common interest. In the political sphere, an interest group is one which shares common public policy objectives and generally agrees on the means of achieving them. Since individuals can function only as members of interest groups by definition, the group theorists emphasize that group politics is a natural and desirable part of the democratic process.

Madisonian View of Groups

The sanguine view of interest groups held by the group theorists has not always been part of the American political tradition. Indeed, the folklore of American democracy seems to be based more upon Madison's viewpoint of interest groups as expressed in *The Federalist, No. 10*, than upon the views held by group theorists. Madison implied that both interest groups and political parties were "factions," and he defined a faction as ". . . a number of citizens, whether amounting to a majority or a minority of the whole, who are united and actuated by some common impulse of passion, or of interest, adverse to the rights of other citizens, or to the permanent and aggregate interests of the community." Interest groups were thus defined as representing positions that could not possibly be identified with the national interest, because they reflect only the narrow interests of a small minority. Recognizing that it was impossible to stamp out factions without destroying the basic freedoms necessary for the operation of the democratic process, Madison suggested that the constitutional model establish procedures which would prevent any faction, whether a majority or a minority, from gaining control of the apparatus of government. If the faction is a minority, it must compromise its interests in order to be part of the majority required for the enactment of legislation. If a majority, a faction would be more difficult to control, but would nevertheless be limited by provisions in the Constitution requiring extraordinary majorities and by the checks and balances system. The president, for example, can always veto legislation passed by a majority in both houses of Congress and his veto cannot be overridden without a two-thirds vote in the legislature. The Supreme Court can always hold ill-advised acts unconstitutional. Madison also pointed out that the scope of the government, including such a large territorial area with many states, would make it difficult for factions that exist at the local level to control the national government. Moreover, factions in one state would have little if any influence in other states.

Origin of Group Theory— John C. Calhoun

The essential point where Madison's view of faction differs from that of the group theorists is in his original definition that faction is an evil rather than a positive force in the political community. The group theorists have always held that "factions" represent genuine and positive political interests that should be taken into account by government in the policy process. Indeed, one of the main dangers in majority rule is not that factions will control, but rather that the power of the majority will override legitimate minority interests.

This viewpoint was one of many eloquently expressed by John C. Calhoun, in *A Disquisition on Government*, published in 1853, shortly after his death. Calhoun was interested in constructing a theory of government that would assure that minority interests, such as were represented by the Southern states during his time, would not be ignored by the national government. Calhoun suggested that all societies are divided into a number of different interest groups, and that the interests of each group are equally legitimate and should not be arbitrarily dealt with by government any more than government should arbitrarily deal with the individual. The political interests of the individual are naturally subsumed within the various interest groups of the community. To Calhoun and modern interest group theorists, democracy means group rather than individual participation in public policy formulation. If every person's interests are represented by groups, then the formulation of public policy by groups automatically represents the interests of individuals.

Calhoun was opposed to the development of majority rule and party government. He felt that the division of the country into two major political parties would inevitably produce a major and minor party, the former dominating the political process completely. Moreover, as the parties developed he felt that they would become more and more detached from the broad interests of the community, and would reflect essentially the viewpoints of party elites. As he explained this process:

The government would gradually pass from the hands of the majority of the party into those of its leaders, as the struggle became more intense, and the honors and emoluments of the government, the all absorbing objects. At this stage, principle and policy would lose all influence in the elections; and cunning, falsehood, deception, slander, fraud, and gross appeals to the appetites of the lowest and most worthless portions of the community, would take the place of sound reason and wise debate.[2]

As the party leadership becomes further and further removed from the true interests of the community, the possibility of revolution inevitably increases.

Calhoun's views of the nature and role of political parties suggest a definite conflict between group theory and that branch of democratic theory based upon the idea that the only way in which effective democracy can be realized is through party rule. Moreover, although the constitutional model is not based upon the idea of party rule and is in fact designed to limit the potential power

---

[2] John C. Calhoun, *A Disquisition on Government* (New York: Political Science Classics, 1947), pp. 41–42.

of majorities and to control the influence of parties in government, Calhoun was not satisfied that the constitutional policy-making model sufficiently took into account the diverse interests of the community. He felt that the classical model set up a government in which the numerical majority would determine policy outputs. By numerical majority, he did not necessarily mean a majority of individuals, but also a majority formed on the basis of compromises among diverse interest groups. This interest group majority could dominate the branches of the national government and force its will upon the rest of the community. He proposed as a substitute for the constitutional model a system of "concurrent" majority rule. The concurrent majority differs from the numerical majority in that in the former each interest group essentially determines for itself whether or not to reject or to accept a government policy affecting it. Calhoun never worked out the details of this system, but clearly it implied that in their spheres of interests minority groups would be able to determine government policy. Accepting the premise that all legitimate political interests are represented by groups, the concurrent majority system would bring about the greatest possible freedom for the political interests of the community.

Calhoun was writing at a time when the South was struggling to maintain its interests in a government where it was outnumbered by the states of the North and West. The concurrent majority system that was so eloquently expressed in theory by Calhoun was very similar to the doctrine of nullification which had gained favor in the South, although not in the rest of the country. Under that doctrine each state, acting independently, could veto legislation that it did not feel was appropriate to it. The states were considered to be the major political interest groups.

Modern Group Theory

The most important expression of group theory in modern terms is that of David B. Truman, whose book *The Governmental Process*, published in 1953, has had a profound and lasting effect upon the way in which political scientists view the policy process.[3] Drawing upon the works of other group theorists, particularly Arthur F. Bentley's *The Process of*

---

[3] David B. Truman, *The Governmental Process* (New York: Alfred A. Knopf, 1953).

Government,[4] which appeared in 1908, Truman asserted that all policy is the result of group interaction and that this is the only realistic way that one can view the political process. Although he did not go so far as to suggest that Calhoun's concurrent majority system is in fact in operation, the tenor of Truman's work is in this direction. Moreover, like Calhoun he suggests that group determination of public policy is the most democratic method of government in channeling legitimate political demands to government.

"Potential" Groups

An important part of the group model of policy formation is the concept of the "potential" interest group. This concept is based on the idea that by definition there always exist within society potential political interests submerged below the surface which can be activated when people sharing those interests are brought to a condition of awareness about the need to take action. It might be possible, for example, to view some of the groups that organized to resist the expansion of the Vietnam war as formerly potential groups whose political awareness had not reached the stage necessary for political activism. As long as interest groups remain potential rather than actual they do not make direct inputs upon the political process. The possibility that they might organize, however, must always be taken into account by decision-makers. Thus, the group theorists suggest that even potential groups exert some influence upon the policy process.

The theory of potential interest groups conveniently solves the problem that is often raised with regard to the group model, that some interests are always far better represented in government than others. The group theorists do not deny this; however, they state that if one accepts the existence of potential groups then in fact all interests of society by definition are taken into account in one form or another by the institutions of government. It is primarily through the electoral process that potential groups presumably are able to exert influence, because politicians are constantly seeking to find the critical mass necessary for their election. There is always a great deal of guesswork among candidates regarding the representative feelings of their constituents. These feelings

---

[4] Arthur F. Bentley, *The Process of Government* (Chicago: University of Chicago Press, 1908).

cannot be determined simply by looking at the positions taken by the leaders of pressure groups, for group leaders do not always reflect the views of the membership. Moreover, the fact that members of one group generally identify with a number of other groups, means that the feelings of individuals are always ambiguous with regard to the official policy positions taken by the groups with which they identify.

In reality, it is very difficult to accept the views of the group theorists that potential interest groups solve the problem of lack of representation in government for those whose views are not reflected in the positions taken by the leaders of powerful organized interests. For example, it was not until Ralph Nader and others began to represent the interests of consumers and to organize consumer groups, that the government took consumer interests seriously. The concern of the government in recent years with environmental matters is also due to the rise of organized pressure groups, such as the Sierra Club, that counterbalance the power of private corporate interests.

Defining the "National Interest"

Interest group theory requires political pluralism. The group model is premised upon the idea that the "national interest" cannot be clearly identified apart from the interests of the groups in the political community. This seems almost true by definition, if one defines groups in such a way that they take into account the political interests of all individuals. However, no government decision can represent the views of all groups in society, but must compromise among competing interests. Under such circumstances, how are those given the responsibility to make final decisions to determine what is correct and proper or in the public interest?

Assuming equal access to government among groups whose interests are at stake, it seems reasonable that one can fall back upon the concept of a procedural ethic to produce the national interest. That is, if every relevant interest has its "day in court," the final decision made, as long as it takes into account the views that have been expressed by the groups involved, can be considered the closest approximation to the national interest that is possible in any democratic society. Even the group theorist, however, might not accept this view, because unless the interests of potential groups can also be taken into account in the policy-making process, what emerges cannot be considered the optimum national interest.

The national interest must be more than the sum of the interests of the organized groups of the nation. But by saying that the interest of potential groups must be taken into account, the group theorist is really adding such a mystical dimension to his theory that he is allowing for a national interest to be articulated apart from the interests of identifiable groups. Since no one can really know what constitutes a potential interest group, appealing to such a concept in making a public policy decision is tantamount to the invocation of the national interest. When President Nixon stated that the "silent majority" of the American people was supporting his decisions on Vietnam, as well as in certain domestic areas, he was, in the terms of group theory, appealing to a vast potential interest group whose needs had to be taken into account. But in reality no one can know what the "silent majority" is. In fact, the president was embarking upon a course of action that he considered to be in the national interest, regardless of the articulated views to the contrary of many organized groups.

Imperfect Mobilization of Political Interests

Apart from the concept of potential interest groups as a limitation upon excessive power on the part of organized pressure groups, the group model also has developed other concepts that explain why the interaction of groups does not lead to the domination by "factions" of the policy process. The most important of these is what Schattschneider once called the "law of the imperfect mobilization of political interests." [5] Based upon the fact that individuals are always members of more than one group, this law states that overlapping group membership makes it impossible for any one group to claim the total loyalty of its membership.

For example, a Veterans Administration (VA) doctor has a group identification both with the American Medical Association (AMA) and with his employer. On the important issue of socialized medicine the AMA and the Veterans Administration are in many important respects opposed to each other. The former has traditionally favored as much freedom of choice as possible for those delivering and receiving medical services, and has supported limited

---

[5] E. E. Schattschneider, *Party Government* (New York: Holt, Rinehart and Winston, 1942), pp. 32–34.

government involvement in medicine. The Veterans Administration has generally been an example of socialized medicine in practice, although on a limited scale. Both the AMA and the VA are interest groups that have vigorously pursued their viewpoints before Congress, the president and throughout the political system. Neither group, however, can completely claim the loyalty of doctors working for it on this particular issue, because of the conflicting identifications and values that they will hold as a result of simultaneous membership in the two groups.

For group theorists, the existence of overlapping group membership is considered to be the greatest check upon the domination of a particular policy by factions. However, a strong argument can be made that this check is ineffective because interest groups do not have to claim the total loyalty of their membership in order to be highly effective in the political process. In fact, the official positions of these groups on political issues are shaped primarily by leaders, not by the membership. Interest group leaders are more often than not able to convince policy-makers that they reflect the views of their group. This can be a serious limitation upon the effectiveness of the law of the imperfect mobilization of political interests as a check upon group power.

Countervailing Power

Another concept advanced by the group theorists explaining the limited nature of the power of groups is the theory of countervailing power. The essence of this theory is that the power of one group will balance that of another, and throughout the political system groups will tend to check and balance each other. For example, the power of industrial firms will tend to be balanced by that of labor unions, and this will mean that neither set of groups will be able to get its way in the political system. Originally advanced in the economic realm by John Kenneth Galbraith in the early 1950's,[6] it soon became evident that the theory worked neither in the economic nor in the political sphere. The tendency of interest groups is often not to counteract each other, but rather to operate together for mutual benefit. In the economic sphere, for example, the wage demands of labor unions are frequently happily met by business firms who simply pass the burden on to the consumer in the form of higher prices.

In the political sphere countervailing power is also more myth

---

[6] John Kenneth Galbraith, *American Capitalism* (Boston: Houghton Mifflin, 1952).

than reality. Each area of public policy has a set of interest groups that are concerned with it. This set operates within the framework of a political subsystem, in which the particular interests make demands and give supports to various parts of the government that act as conversion structures for the specialized policy area. For example, in the armaments field, the Defense Department in conjunction with the Armed Services and Appropriations committees in the House, as well as parts of the presidency, act as the focal points of demands from the armaments industry. Policy is formulated within this system, even though the effects of the policy have a profound impact upon the community as a whole. The interest groups within the subsystem check and balance each other to some extent, but they are mutually agreed upon the need to expand the pie so that their piece can be even larger once it is divided. In terms of the political system as a whole, the interests are in effect in collusion to expand the amount of money appropriated for their sphere relative to other areas. Within their subsystem, however, they are in conflict, but this countervailing power does not effectively limit their operations in terms of the political system as a whole.

Constitutional Checks

Another important way in which interest groups are supposed to be limited is, of course, by the classical constitutional model. Checks and balances, provisions for extraordinary majorities, and the general pluralistic character of the governmental apparatus itself are supposed to make it very difficult for any faction to gain overall control. But in many cases the very structure of government designed to limit and control factions has enhanced their influence. This is because of the many access points that have been established by the Constitution in the formal structure of government to which interest groups can go to influence policy. In the original scheme these access points were the three branches of the government taken as a whole. An interest group could under those circumstances more readily negate public policy than influence the government to make an affirmative decision. The policy process was not as highly specialized and delegated to small units of the government as it is now. At the present time, the highly specialized nature of policy formulation means that the administrative branch, in conjunction with specialized policy committees in Congress, can make both affirmative and negative policy decisions. Pressure groups now go to these groups to get their way. Regardless of what caused the fragmented nature of our policy-making process, this fragmentation vastly increases pressure group influence in both the positive and negative sense over what it would be if our government policy was formulated on the basis of a cohesive majority in Congress led by the president.[7]

On balance, it is difficult to rest easy with the assurances of the group theorists that the pluralism of our system is nothing more than a reflection of a healthy democracy. Perhaps we cannot find the national interest, but it is difficult to believe that it does not ever exist apart from the interests articulated by groups. The concept of potential groups seems excellent in theory, but almost impossible to identify in practice. The groups that are best organized, and that have the most resources and access to government decision-makers, exert the most power in the political system. The mystical concept of potential interest groups does not explain this away. Those who go along with Calhoun's theory of concurrent majority would support the idea that the most powerful interests have the greatest say in policy-making. In fact, Calhoun felt that this was the only way in which a political system could be held together. The more powerful interests should be given a larger voice in public policy formulation simply because of their power and position in the community. This does not produce irresponsible government, but rather government responsible to narrow interests.

Another limitation upon the democratic nature of group politics is that pressure groups tend to be run by elites, who are often given very broad boundaries within which they can make decisions. Interest group participation in politics means elite control, rather than the formulation of policies by the memberships of the groups. This is pointed out not because there is anything wrong in such a system, but merely to emphasize that interest group politics does not overcome the extraordinary difficulties that our system has in bringing about a realization of the democratic ideal.

THE LIBERAL
DEMOCRATIC MODEL

The definition of faction in *The Federalist, No. 10* encompassed both political parties and interest groups. Presumably the leaders of both parties and interest groups

---

[7] However, even where cohesive majorities rule, pressure groups may determine public policy. See Harry Eckstein, *Pressure Group Politics* (Stanford: Stanford University Press, 1960).

were considered equally as scoundrels. They were seeking to advance their own interests, and to do this hoped to gain control over the instruments of governmental power. The usual distinction that is made between parties and interest groups is that the former seek to place personnel directly into the elected offices of government, whereas the latter attempt only to influence those who have decision-making authority. The politician becomes directly involved in the formulation of policy, whereas the interest group leader attempts to shape it to benefit what are usually the economic interests of the group. Parties are not supposed to operate on the basis of selfish economic interests, whereas interest groups are. The contrasting expectations about elected politicians and interest groups suggests not only a difference in the roles they are to play, but a more exalted position for parties within the political system. Parties are to help define the public interest.

In the liberal democratic model of party government, the party definitely assumes the position superior to interest groups. It is an integral part of the government, acting as the primary force shaping public policy. At the same time, parties bridge the gap between people and government by providing the electorate with rational policy alternatives at election time. Ideally, the party model of policy-making is predicated on the existence of a two-party system.[8] The model assumes further that the individual voter is a key element, rational and desirous of making political choices based upon his interests.

Party government at its best has been called "government by discussion." [9] This phrase was coined before the advent of the modern public relations approach to political campaigns and elections. Also, it was based upon the party model as it operates in Great Britain, where perhaps more sober discussion of political issues takes place than in the United States. Regardless of whether the model is appropriate to our system, it was given serious attention by American political scientists in a major report in 1952 entitled "Toward a More Responsible Two-Party System," which recommended that steps be taken to strengthen party government in America.[10]

---

[8] For the best elaboration of the ideal party model of government see Sir Ernst Barker, *Reflections on Government* (London: Oxford University Press, 1942).

[9] Ibid.

[10] "Toward a More Responsible Two-Party System," supplement to *American Political Science Review* 44 (September, 1950).

Stages of Discussion

In the system of government by discussion, four stages of "discussion" occur. First, it is the responsibility of each major political party to formulate and to sharpen issues of public policy for debate and consideration by the electorate. The first stage of discussion occurs within the party organization, among the activist elements. An important premise of the party model is that the parties have a virtual monopoly over the presentation of major political issues. The demands of the political system are to be channeled first to the parties and then to government. This helps to bring about consistency, continuity, and visibility to public policy deliberations. Interest groups are not supposed to circumvent political parties by approaching government decision-makers directly. Moreover, the party model assumes a disciplined party organization in which the "parliamentary party," that is those members of the party who are also members of the legislative body, have total control over the ratification of legislation.

Once the parties have agreed internally on the important issues that are to be presented to the public, at the appropriate time elections occur and the voter is given a chance to make his decision on the basis of the different presentations of the parties. Presumably this extends the arena of rational debate from the parties to the electorate. If the parties have approached their task responsibly, rational choice by the electorate is far more likely. All relevant information is given to the voter, serious debates occur among different party candidates, and in the end the electorate makes its choice between one party or the other. Remembering always that party discipline is part of this model, once the majority chooses a party the legislature is automatically dominated by that party. The next stage of discussion then shifts to the legislature and cabinet, which in the British system is selected by the majority party of the legislature.

The final stage of discussion occurs within the legislature and the executive to refine the issues that have been presented to the electorate. The leadership of the majority party directs the discussion and determines finally what matters will be subject to legislative debate. No decision on public policy is made without extensive consideration by the legislature, and even after it is made and put into effect it can be subject to constant criticism by both the opposition and the government parties.

In light of the electoral system existing in the United States at the present time, and the political environment in which it functions, the party model seems totally abstract and academic. The constitutional system itself, with its separation of powers and its discouragement of parties, impedes the development of meaningful party government. The diversity of political interests throughout the community, and the fact that parties are state rather than nationally controlled, makes parties something quite different from the deliberative bodies within the party model.

Goals of Party Government

Party government is one way in which democracy can be made meaningful in a large complex society. It is a feasible alternative to domination of the policy process by interest groups. It enables broad considerations of public policy to be taken into account over the narrow economic interests of most specialized groups.

However, when Americans go to the polls and choose one party candidate over another, the reason for their choice is not always clear. There are multiple causes for voter selection. Sometimes policy considerations enter; often the personality of the candidate is a prime factor, as is party identification. The ideal party model is never fulfilled, as the voter is not given the opportunity to make a choice between competing policy packages. Specific issues of public policy may lead him in one direction or another, but the way in which electoral campaigns are conducted makes it very difficult for even the most intelligent voters to sort out what the real issue differences are between the two major parties.

Wherever policy power lies, it seems clear that it does not reside in an entity called "the political party." The party model does little to clarify the way in which policy is formulated. The realities of American politics are simply not conducive to party rule at the national level. At the state and local levels party organizations have frequently been able to develop and maintain that discipline necessary to shape policy outputs. State and city political machines are a well known phenomenon of our history. But the political machine does not mean party government in the sense in which it is used in the party model. It does not imply two party competition, but rather domination by one faction. It does not mean that different policy choices are given to the electorate, but that policy is determined by the inner circle of the party.

THE ELITE MODEL

The liberal democratic model of policy-making is based upon the premise of individual rationality in the arena of policy choice, as well as upon individual capability to make his voice heard. Elite theory suggests that all political and other institutions of society are inevitably dominated by small groups of skillful individuals who know how to manipulate the instruments of power for their own purposes. Elite theory, unlike group theory, does not deny the role of the individual, but rather assumes that individuals are divided into two classes: leaders and followers. The leaders have the means and the motivation to gain control over the avenues of power in the political system. Their motivation may be based upon greater ideological commitment than is generally present among the masses, or in the case of economic enterprises, a heightened concern for wealth, position, and power within the private economic sphere. Elite theory accepts the premise that there are large numbers of people who for psychological reasons simply do not wish to exercise leadership. This does not mean they may not be highly skilled, although skill and expertise lead to power if those who possess it wish to use it in this way. But often highly skilled individuals simply wish to be left alone, and delegate to others the responsibility for making political and economic decisions affecting their lives.

The concept of elite control over the apparatus of government is as ancient as political theory itself. Moreover, there are many descriptions of the way in which elites work, and the nature of the elites themselves. Robert Dahl, for example, has advanced the theory of polyarchy, stemming from his famous study of community power entitled *Who Governs?* [11] A polyarchy is a mixture of elite rule and democratic consent. Defining democracy as full participation by enlightened citizens in the policy process, and autocracy as domination of the policy process by a single individual, polyarchy falls somewhere between the two, closer to democracy than to autocracy. Like many American political scientists, Dahl does not wish to accept the full implications of elitist theory which deny the viability of democracy. In polyarchies, democratic procedures are maintained, such as elections and political opposition to the elites in power. Moreover, competition among elites is always present. These facts tend to mitigate the power of any one elite. They

---

[11] Robert A. Dahl, *Who Governs?* (New Haven: Yale University Press, 1961).

bring about circulation of elites, which is a vital principle in the maintenance of democratic leadership.

Exclusive Governmental Elites

The implications of elite theory for the policy process are well-summarized by C. Wright Mills in an essay published in 1958 entitled "The Structure of Power in American Society." [12] First, he suggested that such theories as countervailing powers, checks and balances, and by implication even the concurrent majority theory, do not really operate at the top decision-making levels. There, decision-making is concerned with the major issues of international and national politics having to do with war and peace. All other issues, mostly concerning the slice of the pie that particular interest groups are going to get from government, he defined as existing within the middle level of politics. It seemed to him then, as it does to many now, that the major issues are those that should be most debated and reasoned before adoption. For example, it would be Mills' argument that the decision to involve our forces in Vietnam was in no way subjected to the normal political processes used at lower levels. It was exclusively an elite decision.

Although many elite theorists have suggested that it is the elites of interest groups that interact with the elites of government to produce public policy, the thrust of Mills' argument is that in many instances this does not take place. Frequently, interest groups are irrelevant in the processes of major decision-making, which may be the exclusive province of government leaders. Interest groups, however, can be important in determining policy outcomes at the middle level of the political system. And many of these middle level decisions have an impact on the community as a whole, even though they may not be immediately a matter of life and death.

Mills suggests that the existence of a power elite destroys all of the premises upon which the other models of policy-making are based. He particularly feels that the concept of the rational electorate, as projected in the liberal democratic model of democracy, no longer has meaning in our political system. The "public-at-large" is a phantom. As Mills describes the classical model:

---

[12] C. Wright Mills, "The Structure of Power in American Society," *The British Journal of Sociology* 9, no. 1 (March, 1958). Reprinted in Irving Louis Horowitz, ed., *Power, Politics, and People* (New York: Ballantine, 1963).

The people are presented with problems. They discuss them. They formulate viewpoints. These viewpoints are organized and they compete. One viewpoint "wins out." Then the people act on this view, or their representatives are instructed to act it out, and this they promptly do.

Such are the images of democracy which are still used as working justifications of power in America. We must now recognize this description as more a fairy tale than a useful approximation. The issues that now shape man's fate are neither raised nor decided by any public-at-large.[13]

Collusive or Competitive Elites?

One of the great questions raised by elite theory is whether or not those who make the decisions for our society are collusive or competitive. Without agreeing totally with Mills, the premise can be granted that most political and economic decisions of necessity are made by small groups of leaders. Does this mean that they operate on the basis of a conspiracy against the broad masses of people and for their own interests? The various studies of community power structures indicate that both political and economic decisions are indeed made by relatively small and carefully placed groups of people. But even within local communities, there are often contrasts between the political and economic elites, suggesting that the simple paradigm of the "elite" versus the "masses" is false. There is a circulation of political elites at both national and community levels. This does not affect whether or not the decisions made by such groups are at any particular time responsive to the broader public interest. But elite circulation reduces the possibilities of the exercise of arbitrary power by a small group of political leaders over the broader community. Circulation of the elites does not answer Mills' criticism of our government that the major political decisions are made outside of the control of the general public and beyond the reach of all but a tiny minority.

Implications of Elite Theory

If we grant the premise that political power is controlled by elites, and, moreover, that interest groups are dominated by elites, how is elite policy-making to be made politically responsible? What does political responsibility

---

[13] Ibid.

mean in the context of elitist control? The Mills concept of a political elite holds not merely that decision-making is controlled by small leadership groups, but also that there is continuity of both political and economic elites. The elites represent certain characteristics, classes, economic positions, and skills, that are separate and distinct from those possessed by the general masses. Many elite theorists argue that we are inevitably going to be dominated by individuals who have these attributes, and who therefore control the avenues to power. Political leaders may have to operate on a basis of a very broad consensus, but this really does not limit government in those day-to-day decisions that may be so crucial in shaping public policy. Even more importantly, government leaders are relatively free to make major decisions in those critical spheres of foreign and military policy, where secrecy and speed often prevail in decision-making, which makes public participation, even through representatives in Congress, virtually impossible.

When elitism and leadership are identified as one and the same thing, there is no inconsistency between the concept of elitism and democratic theory. For example, if in certain spheres we elect our elites, then they are at least ultimately responsible to us. Is the presidency an elitist institution? Only if it is consistently under the control of individuals who possess certain definable characteristics that separate them from members of the community at large. For example, if the president must represent a particular religion, then in this sense the institution is elitist because all do not have access to it. If candidates must have wealth, this too limits the office to a small group. But the mere fact that the president makes decisions, often alone, that aren't directly the result of a broad range of inputs from the political community, does not make the institution elitist.

THE SYSTEMS MODEL

All of the previous models of policy formulation have focused upon one aspect of our political system to explain how public policy is or should be formulated. The constitutional model emphasizes the interaction of the three branches of government; the group theorists, the role of pressure groups both organized and unorganized; the party model, the role of parties and the electorate; and the elite theorist, the dominance of the system by a small, carefully defined group of leaders whose characteristics can be predicted. Systems theory is unlike any of these in that it explains the political process in terms of a wide variety of sources of power. Within the framework of system analysis all of the previous models can be encompassed in one way or another. The systems theorists state that public policy is determined on the basis of a wide range of political forces, and that particular policies are the result of different combinations of factors. For example, whereas the interest group theorist states that all public policy is basically the result of the interaction of groups, the systems theorist would say that in some areas this is true and in others it is not. In the area of foreign policy, the president alone may make decisions that cannot possibly be explained on the basis of interest group interaction.

The systems theorist views political life as "a system of interrelated activities." [14] Every part of the system is connected with every other part, and together this interaction produces the ultimate forces determining public policy. In the systems model, public policy is produced solely by government, which has the authority to make binding rules and regulations upon the community. Interest group and elite theorists do not always clearly define public policy in this way, and often suggest that important public decisions are made in the private sphere.

The policy system can be viewed in both macro-systemic and micro-systemic terms. Macro-systemic analysis views the political system in terms of the larger units within it that affect the governmental process. Political parties and interest groups become the major source of inputs upon government, making demands and giving supports to the legislative, executive, judicial, and administrative branches which act as "conversion mechanisms," taking into account the demands and supports in making public policy determinations. Moreover, the branches of government themselves become sources of inputs when they make demands and give supports to coordinate branches of the government. All parts of the political system are interconnected in such a way that it is difficult to make general statements about the focal point of political power. This becomes more possible when micro-systemic analysis is employed, and the system is broken down into subsystems for the purpose of analysis.

---

[14] David Easton, "An Approach to the Analysis of Political Systems," *World Politics* 9 (April, 1957). The systems approach is outlined in this article, and it has been expanded by Professor Easton in two books: *A Framework for the Analysis of Political Systems* (Englewood Cliffs, N.J.: Prentice-Hall, 1965) and *A Systems Analysis of Political Life* (New York: John Wiley & Sons, 1965).

Policy Subsystems

Subsystems consist of subsets of inputs and conversion mechanisms drawn from the system at large. Generally, in particular spheres of public policy, such as agriculture, defense, and communications, there are sets of interests involved in the input side of the systems equation making demands upon specific parts of the government that have undertaken the responsibility to formulate policy in their respective spheres. For example, in the communications area the Federal Communications Commission (FCC) is a key government mechanism setting policy. It receives specialized inputs from the interest groups concerned. Taken together, the FCC and the groups in the industry which it regulates form a policy subsystem. Often the subsystem will include as part of the conversion mechanism congressional committees that control legislation and appropriations. In the defense field, for example, the Armed Services committees and the Defense Appropriations subcommittees in both the House and Senate are an integral part of the government decision-making mechanism. Inputs flow to these committees, as well as to the Defense Department and the president, and taken together, all three form the conversion mechanism for defense policy.

Political subsystems exist because of the specialized nature of the policy-making process. The scope of governmental activities is far too broad to allow participation in policy formulation by all elements of the system. Therefore, it is only natural that those most affected by decisions will be the primary source of inputs. The concept of subsystems is similar to the idea of the concurrent majority in group theory. The only difference is that the emphasis is not placed entirely upon "groups," although they clearly form the central core of political subsystems. This is particularly evident if one accepts the view that there are both public and private interest groups. Administrative agencies and even congressional committees can be considered as interest groups when they make demands upon the policy process. The implication of subsystem policy formulation is the same as that of formulation through concurrent majorities. That is, policy is formulated within the sphere of specialized interests. The general public does not as a whole involve itself in the formulation of policy. Nevertheless, the outputs of subsystems affect more than those who fall within the narrow policy sphere. Therefore, although subsystem formulation of policy is democratic within certain limits, it is not necessarily responsive to the public interest.

The systems approach helps to break down the policy process into its component elements, and aids in the identification of the forces that shape public policy. For each policy sphere, and even for each issue of public policy, there are different sets of inputs and governmental conversion structures. Once these are identified, the channels of influence and the points of power within the political system are revealed.

CONCLUSION

None of the models that are most commonly used to explain how public policy should be formulated, as well as how the government works in practice, fully reveals all of the dimensions of the policy process. Those who like neat and tidy theories to describe government can only be disappointed in the American political process. Constitutional, group, liberal democratic, and elite theories are all accurate to some degree, but none by itself encompasses all of the complexities of government. Systems theory offers the broadest description of how political processes work by identifying the component parts and suggesting the ways in which they interact.

3

Interest Groups and

Policy Formation

The group model of policy formation suggests that interest groups are the focal point of the policy process, subsuming all of the legitimate political interests of the community. An interest group, as defined by group theorists, has shared attitudes concerning the goals it wants to achieve, and the methods for reaching its objectives. Interest groups can be both public and private. The Defense Department is as much an interest group lobbying other branches of the government for its own purposes as is General Motors Corporation. Most discussions of interest groups exclude the public realm, and thereby eliminate an important dimension. Both public and private groups often seek the same kinds of objectives, focusing upon solidifying their position and increasing their power within government.

THE CONTEXT OF
GROUP ACTION

The activities of both public and private pressure groups are affected by a number of factors. The constitutional structure was based upon the premise that factions should be discouraged. The mechanisms of government, especially the separation of powers and the checks and balances system, were designed to make it impossible for any one faction to dominate the policy process. However, the Constitution established a pluralistic structure of government, which means that public interest groups, in the form of governmental branches with contrasting objectives, are built into the governmental mechanism. The three branches of government are motivated to achieve different goals in response to contrasting constituencies.

Private interest groups are able to exercise influence by gaining access to many parts of the government. The establishment of the bureaucracy with broad policy-making powers leads to the most intense political pressures being focused upon administrative agencies. The first ingredient, then, in the context of pressure group operation, is the pluralism of our governmental structure, reflected in public interest groups, which enables private groups to gain more access to the policy-making process than would be the case in a more unified government.

The Effects of Federalism

Madison argued in *The Federalist, No. 10* that the federal structure would tend to isolate and to reduce the power of pressure groups. But the federal structure can only add to the pluralistic nature of the political process and expand the role of groups. First, it creates a large number of governmental pressure groups at the state and local levels which would not exist in a unitary form of government. State and local governments have their own power bases, and exert strong pressure upon the national political process for particular policy goals. Today, states maintain paid lobbyists in Washington, and many of the larger cities also have lobbyists whose sole responsibility is to look out for legislation and other government activities affecting the interests of the urban areas which they represent.

Federalism tends to increase the power of private groups. In contrast to Madison's argument in *The Federalist, No. 10*, the fact that state and local governments control many spheres of public policy means that insofar as private groups can exert pressure over them, they can control the policy process. A pressure group may be geographically "isolated" within a state, but this does not mean that its policy power is reduced. In fact, it will probably be increased because if it exerts power over the state government, or over city governments, its influence at the national level may also be heard more than would otherwise be the case. Private groups can use their state power as leverage in the national realm.

Constitutional Protection of Interest Groups

The constitutional system, in addition to expanding and encouraging interest group activity, protects the rights of private groups to organize and petition government for a redress of grievances. These first amendment rights mean that the government cannot take action which would curb the normal activities of interest groups. The issue was confronted head-on in the case of *United States* v. *Harriss* (1954), when the Court was asked to rule upon the constitutionality of the Federal Regulation of Lobbying Act of 1946.[1] This act required the registration with the Clerk of the House and the Secretary of the Senate of all persons "attempting to influence the passage or defeat of any legislation by the Congress. . . ." In the registration form the lobbyist was to give his name and address and that of his employer, how long he had been employed, how much was paid, by whom, and for what purposes. He was to list the names of any newspapers and periodicals in which he caused publications to appear in order to influence directly or indirectly the passage or defeat of legislation. The terms of the act were very broad indeed, and vague enough so that on appeal to the courts the plaintiffs argued that it violated the constitutional requirement of definiteness in the criminal realm.

In its opinion, the Supreme Court ruled that the statute could be upheld provided its provisions were interpreted narrowly to regulate only those directly involved in lobbying for or against pending or proposed legislation before Congress. Chief Justice Earl Warren made it clear that any attempt by Congress to enact broader restrictions upon the activities of pressure groups would be a violation of the first amendment. Justices Douglas and Black felt that even the Federal Regulation of Lobbying Act, narrowly construed, could "easily ensnare people who have done no more than exercise their constitutional rights of speech, assembly, and press." The majority, however, felt that some limitation upon these rights was justified if Congress was to exercise its legislative function in a rational and deliberative way without undue attention to the demands of pressure groups. In the words of Chief Justice Warren:

Present-day legislative complexities are such that individual members of Congress cannot be expected to explore the myriad pressures to which they are regularly subjected. Yet full realization of the American ideal of government by elected representatives depends to no small extent on their ability to properly evaluate such pressures. Otherwise the voice of the people may all too easily be drowned out by the voice of special interest groups seeking favored treatment while masquerading as proponents of the public weal. This is the evil which the Lobbying Act was designed to help prevent.[2]

---

[1] 347 U.S. 612 (1954).
[2] Ibid.

As long as Congress does not suppress pressure groups, but merely circumscribes them and requires that publicity be given to direct lobbying efforts, the requirements of the Constitution are met.

Lack of Disciplined Parties

Another key part of the context within which interest groups operate is the general lack of disciplined political parties in the United States. In many countries political parties represent very narrow interests just as pressure groups do. Under such circumstances they are factions in the Madisonian sense. In our political system the lack of disciplined parties is a reflection of the diversity of political forces in the nation. There is no way that disciplined parties can develop out of political pluralism and the fragmentation of power in the constitutional system. The lack of disciplined parties is not so much a cause of the increased importance of interest groups, as an effect of interest group pluralism.

Laissez-faire Capitalism

Although the Constitution in one strand of the folklore of American democracy discourages a reliance upon interest groups as the best inputs to shape public policy, the dominant attributes of economic, political, and social development have fostered pluralism. The philosophy of laissez-faire capitalism is analogous to political group theory. The belief that if individuals or groups pursue their own self interests and thereby produce what is economically in the public interest is directly equivalent to the interest group theory that the interaction of pressure groups will bring about the closest approximation of the public interest that is possible in a free society.

The capitalistic ethic was never fully believed or carried out. It was often used merely for propaganda purposes and as a support for the aggressive and often ruthless activities of private enterprise. Nevertheless, the theory of capitalism seeped into the crevices of the political system at many points by osmosis. It has had a strong impact in both the economic and political realms. As groups transferred their practices in the economic sphere to the area of political action, it was only natural to think that the best policy would be produced through group competition.

The ethic of capitalism lends strong support to the idea that pressure group competition should be the primary procedure for the formulation of public policy. This ethic is different from group theory in several important respects. It does not recognize the counterbalancing role of government against the forces of the private community. It suggests rather that the only legitimate interests are those in the private realm, and that government should be no more than a reflection of the powerful groups of society. Minimal government was the capitalistic ideal. Government was to intervene only to maintain the rules of the game and to provide minimum needs such as national defense.

Today, parts of the government are the captives of private interest groups, making government in those areas (for example, the "military-industrial complex") clearly subservient to the private sector. Although government dominated by private power might seem to conform to the capitalistic ethic, in fact this development creates serious dilemmas. Laissez-faire did not mean that government was to be controlled by private enterprise, but rather that government itself was to be virtually nonexistent. When any particular sector of the private economy controls government for its own purposes it clearly can upset the balance of competition and make the concept of the invisible hand a farce. Many industry groups do not want laissez-faire at all, but wish to use the instruments of governmental power to curb competition. Large enterprises seek to become even larger and gain monopolistic control if possible. When government acts as a countervailing force to these monopolistic tendencies, as when it enforces the antitrust laws, it is helping to preserve competition. Thus, we have the seeming paradox that the only way in which the capitalistic ethic can be maintained in practice is through a violation of one of the premises of the theory underlying the capitalistic system—namely that government should not be involved in regulating the competitive interaction of economic groups.

Rise of Voluntary Associations

Pluralism is shaped not only by the way in which economic groups interact with each other and relate to government, but also by the tendency of individuals in other spheres to organize associations to represent noneconomic interests. Alexis de Tocqueville wrote in *Democracy in America* that the tendency of Americans to form associations for virtually every conceivable purpose was one of the most notable characteristics of our society:

In no country in the world has the principle of association been more successfully used or applied to greater multitude of objects than in America. . . .

A citizen of the United States is taught from infancy to rely upon his own exertions in order to resist the evils and the difficulties of life; he looks upon the social authority with an eye of mistrust and anxiety, and he claims its assistance only when he is unable to do without it. This habit may be traced even in the schools, where the children in their games are wont to submit to rules which they have themselves established, and to punish misdemeanors which they have themselves defined. The same spirit pervades every act of social life. If a stoppage occurs in a thoroughfare and the circulation of vehicles is hindered, the neighbors immediately form themselves into a deliberative body; and this extemporaneous assembly gives rise to an executive power which remedies the inconvenience before anybody has thought of recurring to a pre-existing authority superior to that of the persons immediately concerned. . . . In the United States associations are established to promote the public safety, commerce, industry, morality, and religion. There is no end which the human will despairs of obtaining through the combined power of individuals united into a society.[3]

De Tocqueville was emphasizing the proclivity of Americans to organize their activities through groups. In many cases these groups perform functions similar to that of government today. Self-reliance and individualism did not mean that the individual stood by himself but rather that he organized with his fellows to meet whatever challenges he faced. As it became increasingly evident that voluntary associations could not by themselves handle the complex problems that were arising in nineteenth-century industrial America and that government would have to be expanded, the vast array of private groups formed the reservoir for the major inputs of an expanded political process. In de Tocqueville's terms, both interest groups and political parties were examples of voluntary associations in the society that he studied.

Voluntary associations had obvious limits in attempting to deal with political problems. They could not exercise the authority of the state unless it was delegated to them, and therefore had no legal power of compulsion. The problems of society required an expansion of the apparatus and workload of governments at all

---

[3] Alexis de Tocqueville, *Democracy in America*, vol. 1 (New York: Vintage Books, 1954), pp. 198–99.

levels. Only government could bring a common approach to problems within its jurisdiction. Only government could deal with the increasing demands on the part of interest groups and the public for new services, and regulation of various parts of the private sector. The expansion of government necessarily meant increasing specialization and diversity, reflected in the committee system in the legislatures, and in the expansion of national, state, and local bureaucracies.

The growth of the bureaucracy, in particular, added an important new dimension to the context in which interest groups had to function. Generally, the bureaucracy expanded the representation of various political interests in government as administrative agencies sought to reflect the views of the dominant groups within their constituencies. Many parts of the bureaucracy were established for the sole purpose of representing private interests, as in the case of the Departments of Agriculture, Commerce, and Labor. Insofar as these kinds of departments were delegated responsibility to formulate public policy, their outputs directly reflected the inputs of private interest groups. The "public interest" was identified by administrative departments and agencies with the promotional needs of private economic interests. For this reason the expansion of government did not always establish a countervailing force to private interest, but rather reinforced the power of the larger interests, usually at the expense of smaller and less influential groups.

Development of Procedures
for Decision-making

In the absence of disciplined parties, and a rational issue-oriented electorate, a procedural ethic was devised to deal with the problem of how to formulate a public policy that was different from the concept of majority rule and party government. It also differed from the mechanism of concurrent majority, which would give each group a veto over legislation affecting its interests. The basic procedural ethic employed was drawn from the Anglo-American legal tradition, and involved giving those parties affected by government policy decisions some kind of hearing before a decision was made. The effects of the legal profession upon the American government have been profound. From the beginning, lawyers have tended to be the most well-represented profession in Congress, and this, in turn, has not only shaped the nature of the legislative process, but also has affected key points within the bureaucracy through legislation. Just as congressmen consider certain parts of the judicial procedural ethic appropriate to their own deliberations, they also feel that the agents of Congress, those in administrative agencies exercising quasi-legislative and quasi-judicial functions, should employ such procedures if feasible.

The judicial procedural ethic utilizes selected ingredients of the judicial process. As is done in court proceedings, the first stage of decision-making involves holding a hearing in which those parties directly affected by the decision are given the opportunity to testify and present their views. These views may be recorded formally in a written record of the proceedings. The judicial decision-making model requires that the decision of the judge (and jury, if a jury is used) be based upon the record. This strict requirement, however, is not followed in the legislature or by the bureaucracy. The record that is compiled may or may not form the basis for the conclusions made by legislators. Both in Congress and the bureaucracy the fact that this procedural ethic is followed enhances the access of pressure groups. They are the ones that have the expertise, the time, and the money to testify on behalf of their own interests. Their voices are the ones that are most loudly and frequently heard. To the extent that both congressional and administrative procedures are judicialized, the public interest is defined in terms of narrow rather than broad inputs.

In line with preceding considerations it should also be pointed out that the courts make their important policy decisions on the basis of judicial procedure which emphasizes relatively limited group inputs. Courts are far more limited than Congress or the bureaucracy in the procedures they can employ. They cannot initiate cases, but must wait for legitimate cases and controversies to be brought to them. Their rulings must be written, and based upon the record of the proceedings and the relevant issues of statutory or constitutional law that are involved. Limitation of procedure does not prevent the courts, particularly the Supreme Court, from making far-reaching policy decisions. These decisions, however, do not flow from cases brought by individuals, but rather by groups. The groups may, like the NAACP or the American Civil Liberties Union, represent individuals in the judicial process. But individuals by themselves rarely have the necessary resources to gain access to the courts and to exhaust the judicial process, which is often necessary before a final policy decision can be made.

Although the procedural ethic of the judiciary requires expertise on the part of decision-makers in the area of procedure only, in the policy process outside of the courts decisions are often made by experts in the area of policy under consideration. This expertise is gained through specialization. Specialization occurs in congressional committees, their staffs, and administrative agencies, buttressed by specialized inputs from pressure groups.

The nature of the policy process means a diminished role for electoral politics as an influence upon policy-makers. The average man, whether he is aware or not of issues of public policy, cannot register his views meaningfully at the ballot box. In the broadest sense, elected politicians can gain an awareness of the public pulse by observing electoral behavior, but the nature of the political process excludes voting as a major input of government. If this is true, what influence does the average voter have? He does not get to testify before congressional committees, or to make his views known before administrative agencies. He does not involve himself in the judicial process. Often he does not even bother to go to the polls to register his preferences at election time. Politicians are well aware that they can be defeated if they do not meet the expectations of those in their electoral constituencies who do vote. But there is simply no way for the elected politician to know what voters are thinking, or what motivates them to vote one way or the other. The entire electoral process becomes guesswork, both on the part of candidates and voters. Neither knows the policy preferences of the other, nor how the other is really going to act regardless of statements that are so often made setting forth policy positions of the candidates on the one hand, and public opinion on the other. In this atmosphere of electoral uncertainty, the real decisions and channels of influence flow from constituencies to elected officials through the elites of powerful groups.

In general, the most accurate statement that can be made to summarize the nature of the policy process is to say that it involves the reconciliation of group interests at all levels and in every branch of government. Under certain circumstances the operation of the presidency is an exception to this rule. In the foreign policy area, decisions are often made on the basis of a very narrow range of inputs that does not include private pressure groups.

PRESSURE GROUPS
IN OPERATION

There is a constant circulation between those occupying positions in government and those in the private sector. It is very difficult to describe the world of private pressure groups as being apart from government. Virtually all private groups have their "representatives" located at some point within the political process. Legislators may have direct interests in private corporations. For example, throughout recent history many legislators have had direct interests in the oil industry, and have sponsored legislation favorable to oil interests. The late Senator Robert S. Kerr was an oil and gas millionaire, and president of the Kerr-McGee Oil Industries. He and other legislators coming from constituencies in which the oil interests were very powerful consistently supported legislation to increase profits for the oil industry. One of the major reasons that the oil depletion allowance has been a constant part of the Internal Revenue Code is the number of legislators who have direct interests in the oil industry.

Influencing Government Appointments

Apart from having direct representatives in the legislature, private pressure groups seek to place their own representatives in administrative agencies that regulate them. By exerting pressure on the president and the Senate, which must give advice and consent to presidential appointments, powerful pressure groups can often control the appointment process. A particularly famous case in this regard was the senatorial rejection of the Truman appointment of Leland Olds for a third term on the Federal Power Commission.

Olds had a reputation as a diligent public servant, one who did not bend readily to the pressures of the oil industry under the jurisdiction of the FPC. He was in favor of federal regulation of the price of natural gas, and at the time of his reappointment nomination the Congress was involved in a heated controversy over what was termed the Kerr Bill which would have removed certain powers of the FPC over the natural gas industry. Olds was Chairman of the FPC, and he had vigorously opposed the weakening of the powers of the commission in testimony before the Senate Committee on Interstate and Foreign Commerce. Partially for this reason the bill had never been reported out of committee in the Senate, although it had been passed in the House in 1948 and 1949 by substantial majorities. The oil industry, with the help of certain key senators, including Lyndon B. Johnson of Texas, set out to smear the record of Olds, accusing him of everything from incompetence to being a tool of the Communists. They succeeded in securing his defeat by a large majority in the Senate.[4] During the Senate debate, Senator Johnson argued that one of the major deficiencies of Olds was that "never once in his long career has Leland Olds experienced, first-hand, the industries' side of the regulatory picture."[5] The implication was that the best regulators are drawn from the ranks of the regulated. This gives private groups direct representation of their interests in government. In virtually all administrative agencies exercising regulatory functions, the most intense efforts are made by private groups to insure that appointees have a sympathetic understanding of their needs.

Influencing the Electoral Process

Just as interest groups seek to control the appointment process to key positions in government, they also make every effort to involve themselves in electoral campaigns to secure the defeat of candidates they consider unfavorable to their interests, as well as to the elections of proponents of their viewpoints. Contributions flow freely to candidates who are rated high on the list of supporters of particular groups. Groups such as the AFL-CIO and the Americans for Democratic Action communicate to all their members how legislators voted on issues of concern to the groups. The new public interest pressure group, Common Cause, is hoping to develop a citizens' lobby that will gain influence in government by supporting appropriate candidates. Although corporations and labor unions cannot legally make direct contributions from corporate and union funds to political candidates, they consistently violate this rule and provide financial support. All of the spending that interest groups undertake to publicize particular candidates can be considered as a financial contribution to their campaigns. The executives of business firms and labor unions often give substantial contributions to party candidates.

Rarely do corporations go so far as IT&T did in 1972, when the company's president promised $400,000 to underwrite the Republican National Convention in San Diego (the convention was later shifted to Miami). Although it seems to be a custom for hotel owners to raise substantial funds for conventions in their cities,

---

[4] For the story of Leland Olds see Joseph P. Harris, "The Senatorial Rejection of Leland Olds: A Case Study," *The American Political Science Review* 45 (1951): 674–92.

[5] Ibid.

the proposed gift by IT&T raised many eyebrows. This was particularly true because the sequence of events seemed to reveal that the contribution was made in return for a favorable Justice Department ruling on an IT&T merger case. After the contribution was promised by the company, the Justice Department terminated several important antitrust suits that it had filed against IT&T. The major evidence of improper company influence was an internal IT&T memo from Mrs. Dita Beard, an IT&T Washington lobbyist, to the Chief of the IT&T Washington office. In part the memo stated:

I just had a long talk with E.J.G. [E. J. Gerrity, IT&T's Public Relations Chief]. I'm sorry we got that call from the White House. I thought you and I had agreed very thoroughly that under no circumstance would anyone in this office discuss with anyone our participation in the convention, including me. Other than permitting John Mitchell, [California Lt. Gov.] Ed Reinecke, Bob Halderman and Nixon (besides Wilson of course) *no one* has known from whom the $400,000 commitment had come. . . . Now I understand from Ned that both he and you are upset about the decision to make it $400,000 in *services*. Believe me, this is not what Hal [Harold Geneen, IT&T President] said. Just after I talked with Ned, [Rep. Bob] Wilson called me, to report on his meeting with Hal. Hal at no time told Wilson that our donation would be in services *only*. In fact, quite the contrary. There would be very little cash involved, but certainly some. I am convinced, because of several conversations with Louie [former Kentucky Gov. Nunn] re Mitchell, that our noble commitment had gone a long way towards our negotiations on the mergers eventually coming out as Hal wants them. Certainly the president has told Mitchell to see that things are worked out fairly. It is still only [Antitrust Chief Richard] McLaren's Mickey-Mouse we are suffering. . . .

I hope, dear Bill, that all of this can be reconciled—between Hal and Wilson—if all of us in this office remain totally ignorant of any commitment IT&T has made to anyone. If it gets too much publicity, you can believe our negotiations with Justice will wind up shot down. Mitchell is definitely helping us, but cannot let it be known. Please destroy this, huh? [6]

In extensive hearings held on the propriety and legality of the action by the Justice Department as well as the contribution by

---

[6] *Congression Quarterly Weekly Report*, vol. 30, no. 11 (March 11, 1972), p. 524.

IT&T, only Jack Anderson, the syndicated Washington newspaper columnist who brought all of the details of the IT&T case to light originally, clearly stated the facts concerning the proposed IT&T contribution to the Republican Party. The immediate issue of the hearing was whether or not Richard Kleindienst, who was deputy attorney general at the time of the IT&T case, had the proper qualifications to become attorney general. He had been appointed to this post by President Nixon. In testimony before the Senate Judiciary Committee on the nomination of Kleindienst and the related matters concerning IT&T, Anderson pointed out that:

> . . . Mr. Kleindienst is a man who has trouble recognizing a crime when he sees one. Let us make no mistake about it. The contribution of $400,000 by a corporation to support a political convention is crime. It directly and clearly violates the Corrupt Practices Act, which specifies that it is "unlawful for . . . any corporation . . . to make a contribution or expenditure in connection with any . . . political convention." Yet when questioned about this, Mr. Kleindienst said he didn't have an opinion. He protested that it was "customary" for political conventions to receive such donations.[7]

The IT&T case illustrates that corporations have in the past become financially involved in one way or another in political campaigns, regardless of the provisions of the Corrupt Practices Act specifically prohibiting such contributions. Special prosecutor Archibald Cox, before being fired by President Nixon in 1973, revealed extensive contributions to CREEP (Committee to Reelect the President) by private corporations.

Controlling Campaign Financing

In part because of the ineffectiveness of the Corrupt Practices Act, and widespread circumvention of other legal restrictions on campaign financing, Congress passed a far stricter campaign finance law which went into effect in 1972. The main purpose of the new Federal Election Campaign Practices Act, as with its predecessors, was to reveal the sources of and place limitations on campaign contributions. The premise of such a law is that there is a direct correlation between campaign contributions and the ability to control the actions of candidates. This was certainly the implication in the IT&T case, where it was alleged that even the president of the United States could be influenced by a substantial contribution to

---

[7] Ibid., p. 567.

his political party. The effectiveness of such laws depends upon the machinery for enforcement. If an effective and highly motivated enforcement agency is established, it is likely that the provisions of the law will be upheld. This has been a problem in the enforcement of lobbying laws in the past. In the case of the Federal Election Campaign Practices Act, seven separate federal agencies and the Clerk of the House of Representatives were given responsibilities to enforce different provisions. Whether or not this disparate enforcement mechanism can succeed will be a matter for future determination.

Controlling Elected Government Officials The involvement of pressure groups in political campaigns again illustrates that these groups do not seek only to control policy from the outside, but attempt to determine who will be placed into positions of power in government. Elected as well as appointed officials are fair game. A common distinction that is usually made between political parties and interest groups is that the former are geared to supplying the personnel of government, whereas the latter seek only to influence political decision-makers from the outside. This distinction breaks down in those cases where pressure groups make definite commitments to one party or the other and to different party candidates. Interest group leaders know very well that the best way to guarantee control over the policy process is to determine who will have the final decision-making authority.

The fact that pressure groups are successful in their endeavors to control elected government officials is illustrated in a field such as oil policy where it has been stated that

. . . certainly it is difficult to find a congressman from an oil or gas state who will ever vote "wrong" on oil or gas legislation. The delegations from Kansas, Oklahoma, Arkansas, Texas, and Louisiana voted unanimously in favor of the Harris-Fulbright Bill to free gas producers from federal control. Many frankly refer to themselves as oil congressmen, in the same sense that others call themselves cotton or farm congressmen. They know what their attitudes on such matters as depletion ought to be. "We oil congressmen represent our people," explained Tom Steed of Oklahoma. "It is my duty to represent their views. I would be replaced otherwise and would deserve to be." [8]

---

[8] Robert Engler, *The Politics of Oil* (Chicago: University of Chicago Press, 1967), p. 397.

Where particular economic interests dominate the constituencies of congressmen or entire states (for example, oil interests in Oklahoma), they effectively control the electoral process, making it impossible for candidates to get elected without their support. It would be a rare congressman indeed who would not see the public interest in terms of the economic interests of his constituency. Similarly, administrators who wish to hold their jobs pay close attention to the demands of the most powerful groups within their constituencies. Administrative constituencies are different from the electoral constituencies of Congress, but nevertheless, in terms of the way our system operates, they function in the same way. Groups within administrative constituencies do not "elect" administrators, but they do influence administrators through the power that they exercise over the appointment process and their ability to harass bureaucrats through Congress and the presidency.

As one looks at all of the major domestic policy areas, it is clear that the primary shape of public policy is frequently determined by the interest groups concerned in conjunction with those parts of the government that are their "captives." No way has yet been devised to counterbalance the influence of dominant economic groups. However, these groups do not exercise significant power outside of their own economic sphere. That is, the Standard Oil Company of New Jersey, for example, cannot determine the government policy towards desegregation but only towards such matters as oil import quotas and policies concerning regulation of the oil industry that are of the most immediate concern to the company and its allies. The reason that economic groups dominate their own spheres is because of the lack of interest and understanding on the part of the general electorate and other pressure groups in the specialized concerns of particular industries.

When political awareness expands to what were once exclusive concerns of specialized interests then these interests no longer have the degree of control over the policy-making machinery that they possessed in the past. For example, there is tremendous public concern over problems of pollution, and this directly affects the operation of business firms throughout the country in virtually all industries. Clearly it is not in the interests of most firms to support strict pollution legislation. Nevertheless, in the atmosphere of acute public concern about environmental quality, it is a rare firm that wants to take a strong stand against any legislation to control the effects of pollution. It was not surprising, therefore, to see such firms as General Motors Corporation supporting minimum legislation to control air pollution. Legislation to strengthen air and water pollution controls was passed by Congress in 1969 and 1970. As is the case with general pronouncements of public policy, the effectiveness of legislation depends upon the actions taken by administrative agencies, such as the Department of the Interior and the Environmental Protection Agency (EPA) that have been given the responsibilities to carry out these laws. The EPA has demonstrated a reasonably zealous concern for the protection of the environment, but its effectiveness is reduced by enforcement machinery that is cumbersome.

Pressure Group Action on
Selected Policy Issues

To get some idea of the clusters of interest groups that are concerned with particular issues of public policy, in 1971, a recent typical year, Congress dealt with the following major policy areas: campaign spending, civil rights, consumer protection legislation, crime and law enforcement, defense, education, environment, foreign affairs, health, housing and urban development, labor and manpower, taxes and the economy, and welfare.[9]

Campaign Spending Legislation

Before the passage of the Federal Election Campaign Practices Act in 1972, intensive lobbying was undertaken by a variety of groups to shape the provisions of the bill to fit their interests. Representing "public interest" pressure groups were the National Committee for an Effective Congress (NCEC) and Common Cause. Both groups pushed vigorously to tighten restrictions on campaign spending, and to set up adequate enforcement machinery. The AFL-CIO also generally endorsed tighter restrictions on campaign spending. But a special labor group called the National Right to Work Committee vigorously opposed an amendment to the bill which would have prohibited the use of compulsory union dues for political purposes, a tighter restriction than had existed in the Corrupt Practices Act, which prevents direct payment to candidates from union funds. Labor groups finally succeeded in preventing a bill with tighter restrictions.

Another set of interest groups concerned with the campaign spending issue was the broadcasting industry. The National Asso-

---

[9] This and information concerning lobbying activities in 1971 is taken from *Congressional Quarterly Weekly Report*, vol. 30, no. 1 (January 1, 1972).

ciation of Broadcasters, along with ABC, NBC, and CBS succeeded in preventing the legislation from requiring that media advertising rates be reduced for candidates. However, they were not able to prevent continuation of the "equal time" provision of the original Communications Act, which requires broadcasting stations to give equal treatment to all legitimate political candidates. If they allow one candidate to appear on a television program, for example, they must give opposing candidates the same opportunity.

Proponents of strict campaign spending and practices legislation also attempted to require newspapers to give low-cost advertising rates, and equal access to advertising space. These provisions were analogous in the newspaper area to those in the broadcasting field, but did not become part of the final law.

The operation of private interest groups in the campaign spending policy area reveals that powerful groups were able to succeed in the protection of their special interests. Labor, broadcasting, and newspaper groups were able to veto proposed sections of the law that they felt adversely affected their interests. At the same time, the NCEC and Common Cause provided important inputs for the legislation that finally emerged. The final bill basically limits the amount of money that can be spent on various aspects of political campaigns, and requires full reporting of those who contributed and received money, as well as how the money is spent.

One might well ask why the law was passed in the first place, since it limits the discretion of congressmen and the president in their quest for re-election. Were the pressure groups favoring stricter legislation so strong that they were able to overcome the reluctance of legislators to control their own activities? Certainly the groups favoring such legislation, particularly the NCEC, let it be known to key congressmen that there was intense public interest in the issue. However, it is unlikely that the public had anything but the vaguest knowledge of the complex issues of campaign spending legislation. This is where the public interest pressure groups fill a gap seeking to act as spokesmen for the general public and pushing for programs that they consider to be in the interests of the nation. Congress responded to such pressure, probably fearing adverse publicity if no action was taken at all.

The final campaign spending legislation was passed by an overwhelming vote in the House, and by voice vote in the Senate. Once passed, many legislators hoped that its provisions would not be strictly enforced. By the time the law was to go into effect, there were indications that Congress was going to attempt to weaken its provisions. The House Clerk, charged with enforcing that part of the law pertaining to the receipts and expenditures of the primary and final election campaigns of House members, stated that "this law is going to scare the daylights out of these members, and I'm the one that is going to be getting the heat." [10] The chairman of the House Administration Committee, whose Subcommittee on Elections was responsible for the bill, proposed that this part of the enforcement be left up to a committee of members of the House. This would effectively guarantee protection to House members, and make the law meaningless.

The controversy that ensued after the passage of the 1972 election law, regarding the enforcement of its provisions, illustrates once again that key policy decisions are often made after the legislation has already been adopted. The final shape of public policy is given by those who enforce the law and write regulations on the basis of delegated legislative authority. Access to enforcement agencies may guarantee soft treatment to pressure groups. However, in the case of the 1972 Campaign Practices Act, such federal regulatory agencies as the FCC and the CAB drew up strict regulations concerning the extension of credit to political candidates. A common practice in the past, such credit extensions are forbidden, and bills must be paid within relatively short specified time periods. Also, the General Accounting Office wrote comprehensive regulations governing the reporting provisions of the act. It remains to be seen how these enforcement agencies carry out the provisions of the law in the future, and the extent to which candidates and other pressure groups are able to get around the intent of the law by pressuring those charged with enforcement. At least one of the public interest pressure groups, Common Cause, stated after the law was passed that it would set up a continuous monitoring system to reveal to the public any violations of the law's provisions.

Civil Rights Legislation In the field of civil rights, major pressure groups are the NAACP and the American Civil Liberties Union (ACLU), as well as such groups as the Southern Leadership Conference. These groups represent the liberal side of the civil rights and civil liberties field. Which groups oppose them depends upon the issues at stake. For example, in the

---

[10] *Congressional Quarterly Weekly Report*, vol. 30, no. 14 (April 1, 1972), p. 172.

case of desegregation, various southern states and local groups exert strong pressure for policies that are directly opposed to those favored by the NAACP. With regard to the rights of accused criminals, groups concerned with police enforcement—which include police organizations and other conservative groups that take a strong stand on the issue of law enforcement—oppose the liberal position of the ACLU.

In 1971, a major issue confronting Congress was aid to local school districts. The NAACP and the Southern Leadership Conference favored such aid, but opposed giving it to segregated districts. Court-ordered busing was strongly opposed in Congress, which eventually passed a bill declaring a moratorium on court orders forcing desegregation by busing. With the respect to the issue of federal aid, the American Federation of Teachers and the National Education Association supported increased aid to school districts. Anti-busing amendments were added to the bill to prevent the use of funds to carry out court-ordered busing plans. The same groups that lobby Congress concerning aid to education transfer their efforts to the Department of Health, Education and Welfare once legislation is passed. This is the agency through which Congress delegates the authority to carry out its aid to education legislation. HEW regulations give shape and substance to the provisions of the law.

The Supersonic Transport One of the most heavily lobbied issues in recent years concerned proposals to allocate government funds for the development of a supersonic transport plane (SST). A special coalition against the SST was formed in 1971, and included such environmental groups as Friends of the Earth, the Sierra Club, and Common Cause. Pitted against the environmental groups was an impressive array of political power, including the Nixon Administration, the AFL-CIO, and many private groups that would benefit from SST contracts, including aircraft manufacturers, steel workers, and airline pilots. Normally such a combination of interests in favor of a bill would guarantee its success. Environmentalists, however, succeeded in convincing Congress that grave environmental effects would flow from allowing the SST to fly. After the administration accepted this argument, and ruled out the possibility of SST flights over land, opponents of the aircraft suggested that it was still undesirable on economic grounds. The costs of producing and operating the SST would be excessive. A large number of prominent individuals balanced each other off on each side of the economic issue. The final vote in the Senate, too, reflected what was almost an even balance of power among the interest groups concerned. The supersonic aircraft was barely defeated by a 51–46 vote on March 24, 1971.

Foreign Policy   Pressure groups are not only instrumental in shaping domestic policy, but may affect foreign policy as well. The Vietnam policies of the administrations of Presidents Johnson and Nixon gave rise to a variety of new groups, as well as activating established groups. Most of these groups took a stand in opposition to the war. Although the activities of these pressure groups may have helped to persuade the government to withdraw gradually from Vietnam, the dramatic impact of the war upon a broad section of the public and the consequent public opposition to the war undoubtedly was also a persuader for a change in policy. The Vietnam war was one issue in which the public was intensely involved.

The constant pressure of various anti-war groups upon Congress undoubtedly helped to facilitate congressional anti-war sentiment. At the same time evidence suggests that both Presidents Johnson and Nixon believed that the public actually favored rather than opposed their Vietnam decisions. And although the public often registered discontent at the ballot box by defeating candidates supporting the administration and electing anti-war representatives, this was not always the case. The ambiguity of electoral behavior, and the existence of a few vocal pressure groups favoring military action, such as the American Legion, meant that clear-cut anti-war group pressure, causing both demonstrations and widespread anti-war publicity, may have been the deciding factor in de-escalation.

Pressure groups are deeply concerned with issues of foreign trade. Business firms and industries are always lined up on each side of the question of tariffs. Some groups, such as the textile and shoe industries, lobby vigorously in favor of increased protection for their products from foreign competition. Other groups, such as the multinational corporations, favor free trade because of their dependence upon foreign markets. In 1971 when President Nixon undertook to open trade and other relations with the People's Republic of China, he was supported by such diverse groups as the American Farm Bureau Federation, Xerox Corporation, several airline companies, and the Council on Foreign Relations. Whether or not corporations support free trade depends directly upon how their economic interests are affected.

Extent of Group Power
in Policy-making

No hard and fast rule can be given on the nature of private group influence in public policy-making. The diversity of groups makes it very difficult to pinpoint whether or not a "concurrent majority" system is in operation in particular areas. To determine this it would be necessary to find out for each policy field what are the dominant groups and whether or not they have a veto on legislation and administrative action affecting their interests. The rise of consumer groups in various areas, from those interested in automobile safety to those concerned with the protection of the environment, has injected an important new ingredient into the balance of pressure group power in relation to government. On the important issue of the SST, for example, in the absence of powerful environmental groups and fairly broad public awareness of the issues of environmental pollution, it would have been impossible to prevent the impressive line up of forces behind developing the supersonic transport from succeeding.

Until the passage of Medicare, in the health-care area, the American Medical Association (AMA) along with numerous private economic interests in the health field, were generally able to negate any government actions they felt were adverse to their interests. But various public interest pressure groups have become interested in this field, as well as older groups, such as the AFL-CIO, which have always been concerned with health policy. Together these groups are pushing vigorously for some form of comprehensive national health insurance, if not socialized medicine, and they are finding strong support among such powerful politicians as Senator Edward Kennedy. Once it might have been possible to say that the concurrent majority theory operated in practice in the health area, with the AMA having a veto over most health legislation proposals, but this is no longer the case.

Nevertheless, it is true that within most general policy spheres major pressure groups can be identified which often do control government policy-making through specialized access to decision-makers, particularly in administrative agencies. After legislation is passed the concept of concurrent majority is likely to have the most meaning. And, if pressure groups can control administrative decision-making they often can effectively control policy.

Pressure Group Use
of the Judiciary

In addition to having access to administrative agencies, private groups shape legislation through bringing cases before the judiciary. The courts cannot initiate cases and controversies because of the limitations placed upon them in Article III of the Constitution. They must wait for legitimate cases to be raised before they can act. The power of judicial review makes courts important to private groups in their attempts to control the policy process. This authority, not explicitly detailed in the Constitution, nevertheless gives the Supreme Court and lower courts the power to overturn acts of Congress if they are contrary to the terms of the Constitution. Even more important, executive decisions can be overturned if they are unconstitutional or beyond the intent of Congress. Most legislation delegating authority to the bureaucracy gives the courts the power to review administrative decisions within carefully defined boundaries. Within these limits, when private groups want to challenge an adverse administrative action, they will often go to the courts instead of to Congress or the president.

If administrative decisions are usually in favor of the powerful groups in their constituencies, why do such groups seek judicial review? Within most economic spheres, particular groups are in conflict with each other over how the largesse of government is to be divided among them. For example, when the Civil Aeronautics Board (CAB) grants an airline a lucrative route, those airlines that were in competition for the route may decide to challenge the agency's decision in court, provided they can find legal grounds for judicial review.

Judicial Response
to Group Inputs

In the past, powerful economic interests have, from time to time, dominated the judiciary. Although it is difficult to generalize, it can be suggested that over the last hundred years the courts have gone through two stages and now are in a third concerning their approach to reviewing the policy decisions of administrative agencies. In the latter part of the nineteenth and early twentieth centuries, the judiciary took a very conservative stance in relation to the bureaucracy, and frequently overturned any administrative decisions that were considered in the slightest way to be hostile to the interests of corporations. For example, the railroad interests were easily able to use the courts to stymie early efforts by the Interstate Commerce Commission (ICC) to exert control over them.

As the bureaucracy began to grow, particularly during the New Deal era, the courts were faced with both political and practical dilemmas in their quest for a meaningful doctrine of judicial review. Politically, strong demands were being made upon government from a wide range of interests, many of which were not highly organized, to expand the positive role of government in regulation and control of the economy. Any attempt to retreat into conservative doctrines would inevitably lead the courts into political controversy. Aside from political problems, the courts also faced a practical dilemma in attempting to deal with the tremendous number of cases that were beginning to arise before administrative agencies. Any attempt to exercise comprehensive judicial review could only cause a severe breakdown in judicial machinery. Clearly the best way to avoid both political questions and practical problems was to retreat into the doctrine of judicial self-restraint with respect to both areas.

In the political area, the courts developed a doctrine of restraint, suggesting that "political questions" were not appropriate for courts to handle. This meant, in reference to review of administrative action, that policy decisions of the agencies would be allowed to stand provided the proper procedural safeguards had been observed. The doctrine of judicial self-restraint in regard to political questions worked to reduce the practical workload of the judiciary, for by circumscribing their sphere of discretion the courts eliminated most of the policy decisions of administrative agencies from their jurisdiction.

In the second stage of judicial action, then, the courts became passive rather than active instruments of policy determination. There is evidence now that the judiciary is entering upon a third stage, characterized by a new activism that is responding to a broader range of inputs. Public interest law firms and pressure groups are succeeding in getting the courts to intervene more in the administrative process to force careful consideration of consumer interests and the interests of the broader public for formulating public policy. For example, environmental groups have succeeded in delaying administrative action licensing power plants in areas that they consider to be necessary to the preservation of the wilderness, and in delaying pipeline construction, and other actions detrimental to the environment. The trans-Alaskan pipeline was delayed for several years because of a judicial injunction that came after environmental groups sought to prevent entirely the construction of a pipeline which they felt would have highly adverse environmental effects. The courts are becoming the trustees of the public interest, at least as defined by public interest pressure groups.

GOVERNMENTAL PRESSURE GROUPS

Only in recent years has the concept of governmental pressure groups been widely recognized. These groups, at the national level, are essentially comprised of government agencies, including the presidency, which are constantly involved in lobbying Congress and other parts of the government, including other parts of the executive branch, to advance their objectives. Congressional committees may also be considered as public pressure groups. Different parts of government become pressure groups because they have separate goals. Although naive observers might feel that the government should work for only one, overriding "public interest," there are many public interests.

The diversity of governmental interest groups is fostered by the pluralism of government at the national, state, and local levels. At the national level, the existence of a separation of powers and checks and balances system means that there is no unified focus of power. In each branch of the government, and within the branches, separate groups vie for power among themselves. The greatest source of proliferation of public pressure groups comes from the pluralistic character of the executive branch. Each agency represents a separate constituency, and has organizational goals that differ from other parts of the bureaucracy. The goals of administrative agencies tend to tie in very closely with those of the private groups within their constituencies. Some idea of the importance of governmental interest groups can be gained from the fact that rarely is an important piece of legislation passed by Congress without clearance from the administrative agency that will be involved in its implementation. Expert bill drafting is often done by lawyers within administrative agencies, who supply their services to Congress. Private pressure groups also often offer drafts of proposed legislation to congressmen, but such inputs upon the congressional process are not considered to be quite as legitimate as those that come from the administrative branch. One reason for this is because the administrative branch is part of the government, and is supposed to reflect broad rather than narrow interests.

Administrative Agencies and the President as Pressure Groups

Administrative agencies are not supposed to be involved in lobbying activities, and indeed many administrators and legislators alike would not call the constant interaction between the bureaucracy and Congress "lobbying." The lack of congressional recognition that public lobbying poses a problem is reflected in the Federal Regulation of Lobbying Act of 1946, which circumscribes only the activities of private lobbyists. However, there are laws that specifically prohibit the use of public funds for the purposes of public relations activities on the part of administrative agencies. Regardless of such legislative proscriptions, many agencies engage in more extensive public relations campaigns than virtually any private group.

For example, the Defense Department for decades has undertaken skillful propaganda programs to aid in recruitment, and to indoctrinate the public on the importance of the military. Even the individual branches of the Defense Department—the Army, Air Force, and Navy—have their own full time public relations divisions involved in trying to convince Congress and the public, as well as the president, of the unique importance of their particular approach to warfare. Constant pressure is being exerted upon the legislature, for example, to embark upon new ship-building programs to support the Navy, or to supply funds for the development of new types of aircraft and missiles for the Air Force and the Army.

Although the Defense Department is probably more extensively involved in public relations activity than any other part of the bureaucracy, other agencies as well have undertaken important propaganda programs to advance their own goals. The Department of Agriculture puts out vast amounts of literature not only to inform its constituency of the nature and importance of the programs that it is involved in, but also to make constituents and legislators aware of the key role the Department plays in the maintenance and development of American agriculture. The Department lobbies vigorously to shape agricultural legislation before Congress, and is often the determining force in agricultural policy as it emanates from Congress.

When agencies embark upon legislative programs in Congress, they are supposed to go through the Office of Management and

Budget (OMB) which is within the Executive Office of the President. The clearance of all legislative proposals from the administrative branch is an important requirement that has been established by the OMB. A forceful presidency can be an extraordinarily powerful pressure group in relation to Congress, as well as to administrative agencies. But since the president does not have automatic control over the administrative branch, he is often placed in the same position as other groups in attempting to get administrative agencies to heed his requests. The president's power and influence are greatest where he has set forth a clear policy position. Under such circumstances he can exert strong influence upon the bureaucracy to fall into line behind his leadership and this gives him tremendous leverage with Congress. Where the president has not articulated a program, however, the process of clearance of proposals through the OMB does not enhance the power of the presidency, but merely gives the OMB the opportunity to coordinate different requests from within the administrative branch. If it is known that the president does not have a position on the proposals of administrative agencies, they are more likely to ignore the OMB and go directly to Congress, making their desires known informally. They may even go to the president in an attempt to secure his backing. All of this interaction among different parts of the government in the policy process should be considered as pressure group activity.

The superior position of the president and the bureaucracy as lobbyists before Congress is derived not only from the fact that they are legitimate parts of the government, but also from the delegation of specific legislative responsibility to the president in Article II, and to both the president and the administrative branch by Congress. The regulatory agencies are given the specific responsibility to recommend proposals to Congress. They are considered the agents of Congress, and in the regulatory field are supposed to be the primary inputs for legislative change. Congress will often wait for recommendations from these agencies before considering any new legislation dealing with regulatory matters. This is not to suggest that regulatory agencies are necessarily more powerful than other parts of the bureaucracy in lobbying Congress, but only that they are considered by Congress itself to be an integral part of the legislative process. This puts them in a better formal position to exert influence. However, informal factors often determine the power of the agencies. Such factors include the degree of constituency support for agency proposals, the level of expertise of the agencies as opposed to that of Congress, and whether an agency has the backing of OMB and the president. The same factors which shape the power of regulatory agencies in the legislative process also pertain to other parts of the bureaucracy which do not have the same relationship to Congress.

CONTROLLING PRESSURE GROUP ACTIVITY

The Federal Regulation of Lobbying Act requires a reporting of the receipts and expenditures of private pressure groups. Campaign practices legislation, following the tradition of the Federal Corrupt Practices Act of 1925, limits the political activities of unions and business corporations, and prohibits them from making direct financial contributions to candidates. Pressure groups can no longer extend unlimited credit to political candidates. Public pressure groups are controlled in part by laws preventing the expenditure of public funds for public relations purposes and lobbying activity. Laws aimed at private group activity seek to publicize expenditures and lobbying activities, while only controlling expenditures to political campaigns.

There are numerous difficulties associated with attempting to control pressure group activity through legal devices. Political power and influence depend upon money, access to decision-makers, expertise, and control over the channels of communication, among other things. These ingredients of power cannot be readily controlled by legislation. The laws regulating the activities of administrative agencies are so vague and nebulous that they are totally ignored even in the limited area—public relations—they are supposed to control.

Controlling Public Pressure Groups

Assuming that one could proscribe the public relations activities of administrative agencies, this would only partially reduce their influence in the policy process. They would continue to provide expert advice to Congress and to draft legislation pertaining to their area of responsibility, and they would also retain rule-making and adjudicative functions that are key ingredients in shaping public policy. All of the constitutional and statutory mechanisms designed to limit and control the authority of government relate to the control of public pressure groups. The constitutional separation of powers was nothing more than a device to control the "interest groups" of Congress, the presidency, and the judiciary. The doctrine of delegation of legislative authority is supposed to keep the discretion of administrative agencies within the boundaries of congressional intent, and thereby control administrative power. Insofar as these governmental arrangements work, the activities of public pressure groups are limited in accordance with constitutional and democratic criteria. The problem of controlling public pressure groups is one of political theory and practice.

As long as our system has no unified source of power, and does not operate on the basis of majority rule and party government, the activities of public pressure groups will continue to expand. Different administrative agencies will press for their own goals, just as Congress through congressional committees and the president will seek the realization of separate policy objectives, which may or may not be in accordance with those of the bureaucracy. The independence and powers of the federal judiciary guarantees that it will in the future be an important instrument of public policy, which it will often define separately from the other governmental branches.

The theory of the constitutional separation of powers supports the idea of conflict among the branches. Although the Constitution does not take into account the role of the bureaucracy, the way in which agencies function as pressure groups separately from the coordinate branches would fit into the concept of intragovernmental competition built into the constitutional system. Insofar as public pressure groups remain in competition, then, the criteria of the Constitution is being fulfilled. One of the major dilemmas posed by the operation of public pressure groups today to this competitive ethic of the Constitution is the frequent collusion that exists between administrative agencies and congressional committees. Since they often have the same outside constituency making demands and giving supports to them, committees and agencies take similar approaches to what public policies are in the "public interest." The separation of powers system was based upon the idea of contrasting constituencies among the branches of government, with a full recognition that similar constituencies would not produce sufficient motivation within the branches to oppose each other regardless of the fact that they would possess independent constitutional powers. It is this collusion of interests within different policy spheres between the legislature and administration that reduces the range of inputs to the policy process, and creates a condition whereby broader community concerns and interests more likely than not will be ignored.

Public-Private Collusion

Insofar as constitutional and statutory standards limit the operation of public pressure groups, they also to some extent place constraints upon private groups. To get what they want, private groups have to operate through the government. The purposes of the constitutional system were to limit the power of outside factions by making it impossible for them to gain unified control over the policy process. Public pressure groups never have interests that are entirely separate from the private sphere. If an agency such as the ICC, for example, is able to operate without significant constraints from other parts of the government, this means that those private groups having access to the agency are able to get what they want. Therefore, the first and most important consideration in approaches designed to limit the power of private groups in government is to recognize that government must first limit itself. However, this has generally not been recognized.

If the power and influence of the armaments industry is to be curtailed, then it is necessary to curb the Department of Defense and its close arrangements with the Armed Services and Appropriations Committee and the House and Senate. To control the power of pressure groups in regulated industries, such as airlines, railroads, broadcasting, telephone and telegraph, drug manufacturers, and agriculture, the administrative agencies and other parts of the government having jurisdiction over these industries must be limited. So far no way has been devised to prevent the collusion of private interests with government. The main idea behind the constitutional mechanism for controlling factions was that the different constituencies of the policy-making branches of the government would guarantee a balance of power. But, the specialization of the governmental process has made it impossible to implement such a system. Today the primary constituencies of government are composed of interests that have specialized policy concerns. Both the constituencies and those parts of the government formulating policy cut across the formal lines that are supposed to divide the branches of government.

Ineffectiveness of
Legislative Controls

Attempting to control pressure group activity through the enactment of legislation only touches the surface of the problems that arise in connection with interest group inputs of the policy process. Requiring the registration of the lobbyist, and reporting of receipts and expenditures for lobbying activities in connection with legislation pending before Congress at best deals with a tiny fragment of pressure group operation. It may provide information for such journalists as Jack Anderson, but even this is unlikely for those lobbying Congress are careful to keep up good appearances in public. Lobbying legislation does not touch upon the activities of pressure groups in connection with administrative agencies and the presidency. And with regard to Congress, groups have to register and report only if they are attempting to influence "directly" legislation pending before Congress. This is a matter of interpretation. There is no effective enforcement machinery for the lobbying law, and in recent years no one has been charged with a violation. Even if the law were rigidly enforced, it would not change in any way the nature of the demands made by groups in the policy process, or their impact.

There is little doubt that our system is very close to operating on the basis of concurrent majorities in many key areas of public policy. This means that in many cases minorities have vetoes over government actions, and are often able to shape the content of public policy. Whether or not one calls this system a democracy, it is a fact. The best advice for those who feel that they are being left out of important policy decisions is to encourage them to participate through groups in the policy process. But there is no way that those without influence can be given power unless they possess the tools of power. Simply becoming a member of a group does not guarantee anything in the way of exerting influence upon the political process. Most groups are managed by skillful elites who themselves possess the necessary skill to gain and retain positions of leadership within the group. Pressure group policy does not necessarily reflect the views of the membership, although insofar as the membership is made aware of what the groups leaders are doing, some control can be exerted, provided the group follows democratic selection procedures of its leaders. This is not always the case, and elections within groups can be as easily manipulated as within the political system. Moreover, in some groups, such as labor unions, where the leadership serves the economic interests of the membership, leaders are left relatively free to pursue political goals in other areas. Of course, all issues are interconnected, but some are seemingly of greater relevance to particular individuals than others. The AFL-CIO, for example, can and does take positions on a wide range of political issues which are not always clearly connected either favorably or adversely to the economic interests of its membership. For instance, in 1971, the AFL-CIO vigorously opposed the Supreme Court nomination of William H. Rehnquist to the Supreme Court. The nominee was allegedly a conservative and "strict constructionist." It is dubious that union members would care about such an issue one way or the other, and if they were knowledgeable they very well might support a more conservative justice on the Supreme Court. The AFL-CIO also opposed the admission of the People's Republic of China to the United Nations. This is certainly not an issue connected with the economic problems of workers. Admittedly, the AFL-CIO ranges more widely than most pressure groups in taking policy stands. But, there are other examples of groups whose leaders delve into policy areas that are not necessarily supported by or of concern to their memberships. The AMA, although primarily concerned with issues of medical care, occasionally will take a stand, usually conservative, on broader public policy issues. During the McCarthy era in the early 1950's, the AMA was vigorously involved in attempting to root out what it considered to be Communist influences in government. Of course, one could say that Communism and health care are intimately connected, in that socialized medicine is part of a Communist state. But, realistically speaking, the issue of Communism in the '50's should not have been related to the economic problems of medicine. The leadership of the AMA knew that there was no possibility of a Communist takeover.

The elites of pressure groups, both public and private, will continue to exercise pervasive influence in the policy process in the future. To some extent the rise of "public interest" pressure groups will modify the degree of control over public policy exercised by specialized interests. A trend in this direction has already been seen in such areas as environmental policy, and in legislation protecting the rights of consumers, including requirements for product safety. Without the pressure that has been exerted by public interest pressure groups, laws in these areas would not have been passed. Moreover, these public interest groups are putting continual pressure upon administrative agencies to adhere to the letter of the law. They are also beginning to use the courts as effective instruments to force administrative agencies to take effective action against private economic groups in these policy areas. Those who have organized public interest pressure groups recognize the legitimacy of our political system and its underlying pluralistic character.

Common Cause, for example, is attempting to change the character of the men who occupy the elected positions of government in those cases where John Gardner (the leader of Common Cause) does not feel that politicians are sufficiently taking into account the broader interests of the community. The hope of Common Cause is that by changing the character of the legislature major shifts in public policy emphasis can be made. Ralph Nader's Center For Study of Responsive Law lobbies Congress, and exerts pressure upon the other branches of the government to extract decisions that Nader considers to be favorable to the public interest. Although political philosophers for centuries have grappled with the difficult problem of how to define the public interest, Nader feels that it can be clearly articulated in some areas of public policy. In a letter sent in 1971 to a mass mailing list to raise funds to support his activities, he stated in part:

Let's suppose that a strong, citizen movement had begun in America, say, 25 years ago. A public interest movement which required industry and government to be responsive to the just needs and aspirations of all the people.

Think what might have been accomplished during these years of unprecedented national economic growth, if public-spirited values were applied to such aggregate influence:

—We would have "discovered" the hunger and poverty of the "other America" long before the '60's and reduced this massive suffering in a land of plenty.

—Our urban centers would not be choking with cars on concrete belts carving up polluted cities filled with slums, corruption, crime and public waste.

—Consumers would not be cheated by "planned obsolescence," price fixing, and goods and services which, according to Senator Philip Hart's studies, take at least 25 percent of every consumer dollar without returning any value.

—There would be far fewer inequities in our income and property tax laws. Why should a factory or office-worker pay 20 percent of his wages while men of great wealth are often assessed 40 percent—or less —of their income? Why should small businessmen and home-owners pay far more than their fair share of taxes because large corporate property owners of land, minerals and buildings pay far less than prevailing assessments require?

—Our rivers, lakes and oceans would still be safe for swimming, and would be producing untainted fish; the air would not be as filled with violent contamination and the land not abused with the ravages and spills of insensitive corporate and governmental forces.

—Thousands of Americans would not be dying or made sick each year from unsafe working conditions that too often prevail in factories, foundries and mines filled with toxic chemicals, gases and dust.

—Equal opportunity in education and employment and adequate medical care would have avoided the misery that cruelly affects many Americans.

—The power and expense of our military establishment and their civilian superiors might have been closely examined and modified long ago.

This is the public interest as Ralph Nader sees it. Nader's group alone has made progress towards the realization of many of these public interest goals. On many of his objectives there is intense disagreement among respectable and responsible individuals and groups. Is it sufficient to accept the argument that the public interest will properly emerge from the conflicting viewpoints in those areas where there is no common denominator of agreement?

One of the most important indictments of the group process of politics in recent years is that of Theodore J. Lowi.[11] In summing up his arguments against group theory, he stated first that the practice of the group process of politics runs against the grain of democratic theory and practice. It does not allow for majority rule, or for the establishment of a hierarchy of values within the political system. The values and demands of all interest groups are considered to be of equal merit. This means that "liberal leaders do not wield the authority of democratic government with the resoluteness of men certain of the legitimacy of their positions, the integrity of their institutions, or the justness of the programs they serve."[12] Government cannot plan on the basis of a scale of values different from those of dominant pressure groups. Congress, in the delegation of authority to administrative agencies, frequently gives up its responsibilities and asks the bureaucracy to make rules on the basis of vaguely worded statutory standards.

---

[11] Theodore J. Lowi, *The End of Liberalism* (New York: W. W. Norton, 1969).
[12] Ibid., p. 288.

The practice of delegation of legislative authority supports interest group liberalism because the legislature does not establish adequate standards to guide administrative action. The courts, because of vaguely worded statutes, find it difficult to intervene in the process of bureaucratic decision-making to force adherence to statutory principles. In Lowi's terms, most of the rules that guide the development of policy by the administrative branch should be developed by the legislature. The Constitution also establishes certain principles, but the reluctance of the judiciary to intervene in the administrative process makes even the Constitution an instrument of dubious value in controlling interest group determination of policy. Past doctrines of judicial review which are based upon the concept of judicial self-restraint have made it difficult for courts to establish principles to guide administrative action. As a result of the lack of formal rules and procedures, public policy is formulated on the basis of informal bargaining. Lowi suggests that: "there is inevitably a separation in the real world between the forms and the realities, and this kind of separation gives rise to cynicism, for informality means that some will escape their collective fate better than others." [13] The expectations of many people about how government should function, in contrast to the way in which it does, have caused grave discontent especially in the last decade, when higher levels of education for a broader segment of the public, in combination with an expanded mass media, have made it very difficult to hide the realities of politics.

Lowi indicts the theory as well as the practice of interest group politics. He points out that group theory has falsely propagated a faith that "a system built primarily upon groups and bargaining is perfectly self-corrected." [14] Supposed self-correcting mechanisms, such as overlapping membership, potential groups, countervailing power, and so on, do not in fact operate perfectly, if at all. Moreover, Lowi feels that we would be better off if we leaned toward Madison's concept of groups as expressed in *The Federalist, No. 10,* rather than towards the more sanguine view of the interest group theorists. Madison distrusted groups, and a "feeling of distrust towards interests and groups would not destroy pluralist theory but would only prevent its remaining a servant of a completely outmoded system of public endeavor. Once sentimentality toward the group is destroyed, it will be possible to see how group inter-

---

[13] Ibid., p. 291.
[14] Ibid., p. 294.

actions might fall short of creating that ideal equilibrium." In short, the notion that all is right in the political world as long as interest groups are allowed to function freely should be discarded.

Although Lowi's thesis is well argued and logical, the question of how to replace interest group theory and practice is not adequately solved. One can assert what we should be doing, but this is only a small step in helping to bring about those fundamental changes that are necessary to alter the way in which the system now operates. The central question is the extent to which some unity can be brought into our system of policy formulation that will reduce the pluralistic influences of groups. To what extent is it possible to develop more effective, disciplined political parties than exist at present? To what degree can the major institutions of government, the presidency, Congress, the courts and the bureaucracy be structured in such a way that their policy outputs will not be a simple reflection of pressure group inputs? We will treat these questions in the following chapters.

4

Political Parties and

Public Policy

The trend of most electoral studies in recent decades suggests that voting behavior is largely irrational, but somewhat predictable from a knowledge of key factors—such as occupation, education, religion, and national origin—in the background of the voter. However, V. O. Key, Jr., after analyzing a broad range of electoral studies, concluded that:

. . . [V]oters are not fools. To be sure, many individual voters act in odd ways indeed; yet in the large the electorate behaves about as rationally and responsibly as we should expect, given the clarity of the alternatives presented to it and the character of the information available to it. In American presidential campaigns of recent decades the portrait of the American electorate that develops from the data is not one of an electorate strait-jacketed by social determinants or moved by subconscious urges triggered by devilishly skillful propagandists. It is rather one of an electorate moved by concern about central and relevant questions of public policy, of governmental performance, and of executive personality. Propositions so uncompromisingly stated inevitably represent overstatements. Yet to the extent that they can be shown to resemble the reality, they are propositions of basic importance for both the theory and the practice of democracy.[1]

To the extent that voters believe electoral politics has a real impact in shaping the course of public policy, and vote accordingly, at least part of (parties may not be involved) the liberal democratic model of government is being followed. In that model a rational electorate participates in the determination of public policies by exercising the right to choose those who will occupy elected offices. The belief that electoral politics affects policy does not necessarily

---

[1] V. O. Key, Jr., *The Responsible Electorate* (Cambridge, Mass.: Harvard University Press, 1966), pp. 7–8.

include a dependence on political parties as the vehicles through which rational choices are made and finally put into effect. Political party identities have in recent decades been the most strong from the New Deal period until the mid-1960's. However, even during this time, in presidential elections the percentage of voters shifting their allegiance from one party to another ranged from 10 to 19 percent.[2] There is evidence of increased ticket-splitting at all levels of government.[3]

In recent years voters seem to be making their selections on the basis of the character, style, and personality of candidates rather than on their party affiliations. The cult of personality tends to have greatest impact at the national level, where the personal characterists of candidates are highlighted and emphasized to the public in the mass media. Often there seems to be little difference in the policy stance taken by Democratic and Republican presidential candidates on many key issues, resulting in an electoral choice based upon the personality projections the candidates make to the electorate.

PARTIES AS
POLICY INSTRUMENTS

In the party government policy model (liberal democratic model) the role of political parties is central to the formulation of issues of public policy and to the final policy choices that are made by government. At every stage in the political process parties are the key components, shaping issues in the first place for presentation to the electorate, and seeing to it that the electoral choice is given meaning through legislation and executive actions. The premise of this model of policy-making is that without disciplined parties, operating responsibly within a two-party system, it is impossible to give meaning to democracy. Parties are the necessary bridges between people and government, the channels through which the electorate transmits its will to government, and the mechanisms by which policy is made responsive once public choice has been made at the ballot box. In a two-party system, with single-member districts, the party that wins usually represents a majority of those who vote. Party government there-

---

[2] Ibid., p. 20.
[3] Walter Devries and V. Lance Tarrance, *The Ticket Splitter* (Grand Rapids, Mich.: William B. Eerdmans Publishing Co., 1972).

fore means rule of the majority, and in this respect it contrasts with the concept of concurrent majorities and interest group determination of policy, which implies minority control of the policy process.

Why are political parties so essential to the realization of majority rule? The assumption is that only political parties can give the necessary degree of definition, coherence, and unity to the process of formulation and implementation of policy based upon majority choice. Without parties the selection of candidates becomes haphazard, and although individual candidates may run their campaigns on the basis of policy issues, once elected they will be powerless within the maze of government to implement their promises to the electorate in the absence of party support. Therefore, although political campaigns may raise policy issues, where political parties are not functioning in any disciplined manner the public will be deceived if it feels that candidates can meaningfully connect policy preferences with government action.

In the American system, however, party backing is not necessary for elected politicians to exercise power. The president and senators and representatives who hold powerful committee chairmanships have the power to accomplish limited objectives within their spheres of influence. For example, when President Eisenhower promised the voters in 1952 that he would go to Korea and attempt to end the war, this was an important policy decision entirely within his control. Similarly, in 1968 when President Nixon announced that he would make every effort, if elected, to de-escalate the Vietnam war, there was little doubt that within very broad limits he had the power to do this.

The president can take many initiatives in foreign policy without first consulting Congress, and therefore without the need for the support of his party. But, in the domestic sphere, promises by presidential candidates usually cannot be carried out without the cooperation of Congress. For example, Senator George McGovern, as he was capturing one primary after another in the pre-convention campaign of 1972, was making very sweeping statements regarding the policies that he would put into effect if elected. This included an end to the Vietnam war, but also economic programs that would have provided a minimum income for a wide range of people, and tax redistribution programs. None of these latter programs could be put into effect without congressional assent. Voters choosing Senator McGovern on the basis of these kinds of promises could not help but be let down in the long run. When presidential candidates state that they will implement programs that are beyond the sphere of presidential power the public may falsely believe that the election of particular candidates will bring about changes in public policy.

THE CONTEXT OF
PARTY OPERATION

Many of the factors that affect interest group operation also influence, often in a contrasting way, the operation of political parties.

Effects of Constitutional
Fragmentation

The separation of powers and checks and balances system tends to augment the access of interest groups to the political process and increase their ability to negate legislative proposals, adding to their power. But the separation of powers diminishes the ability of political parties to unite the presidency and Congress, and thereby reduces the capacity of parties to operate in a disciplined fashion. Because the separate and contrasting constituencies of Congress and the president, and within Congress, the House and Senate, motivate these parts of the government in different ways, it is difficult for a superimposed party structure to unite them.

In *The Federalist, No. 10*, Madison conceived of faction as encompassing parties as well as interest groups. But whereas interest groups can function quite adequately within a fragmented system, the major purpose of parties is to unite diverse factions under the umbrella of the party ideology, and through the party machinery. Fragmentation of the apparatus of government does not aid efforts in this direction. In terms of public policy, this means that parties cannot implement at the governmental level party programs that have been presented to the electorate.

Federalism is another constitutional device that works differently upon the effectiveness of political parties and interest groups. The existence of multiple state and local governments increases the access points of interest groups and multiplies their number. But this same phenomenon fragments parties in a vertical fashion just as the separation of powers causes a horizontal division at the national level.

The existence of multiple state and local governments has given rise to numerous separate party organizations. This means that there are really no unified national parties, but loosely knit confederations of Democrats and Republicans who unite once every four years for the purpose of electing the president. As a policy force, then, it is impossible to speak of "the Democratic Party" or "the Republican Party." The reason that parties are organized in every state and many local units of government is not to put forth a general political philosophy that will be finally implemented in the form of public policy. It is rather to establish an organization that will be capable of gaining control of elected offices, which become the spoils of the winning party. Policy considerations become secondary to supplying the personnel of government.

Diversity of Interests

Constitutional factors alone do not account for the fact that our political party organizations are loosely knit and incapable of supplying a unified approach to public policy. The tremendous diversity of interests in the nation makes it difficult for parties to develop programs that will appeal to a sufficiently large coalition of groups to achieve a majority. The larger the constituency in which the party must function, the more difficult it is to put together winning coalitions.

At the national level, party leaders must appeal to an extraordinarily wide range of disparate interests. This diminishes their role in the policy process, because party programs must be constructed in the most general terms which more often than not have little more than symbolic meaning. Leaders attempting to take strong stands on particular issues will risk the possibility of alienating various party groups.

For example, the strong stands taken by presidential candidate George McGovern in 1972 on such issues as income redistribution and reduction of the defense budget alienated powerful Democratic politicians throughout the country, particularly in the South. The major appeal of Muskie to the professional Democratic politicians before the convention had been that he was a middle-of-the-road man, and avoided strong stands on key issues. Muskie, although unsuccessful, was the man who received the overwhelming support of professionals and of wealthy contributors within the Democratic Party.

The support for Muskie illustrated that the Democratic Party leadership did not attempt to take well-defined policy stands, but rather preferred the traditional brokerage operation of the past which was based upon the necessity to compromise if diverse party interests were to be held together. Generally, it is impossible for presidential candidates to emerge who do not reflect a middle-of-the-road stance. When they do, as in the case of Goldwater in 1964, and McGovern in 1972, they are overwhelmingly defeated because their firmly taken policy positions cannot entice a majority of the electorate to vote for them.

Role of Party Elites

It is the elites of the various interest groups, as well as of state and local party organizations, who are unwilling or unable to push for party programs that have a strong and well-defined policy orientation. It is the elites' perceptions of the voters that lead them to strike out in favor of ambiguity rather than definition. They believe that voters do not behave rationally in terms of their own interests, or even that they know their own interests.

One of the most prevailing themes of voting studies, emanating from such organizations as the Survey Research Center at the University of Michigan, is that voters are not issue-oriented, and rarely are aware of positions taken by political candidates. And, as V. O. Key, Jr., stated:

. . . Theories of how voters behave acquire importance not because of their effects on voters, who may proceed blithely unaware of them. They gain significance because of their effects, both potentially and in reality, on candidates and other political leaders. If leaders believe the route to victory is by projection of images and cultivation of styles rather than by advocacy of policies to cope with the problems of the country, they will project images and cultivate styles to the neglect of the substance of politics.[4]

Ignoring political issues, politicians tend to concentrate upon advertising their personalities in the hope that this will sway voters. They engage advertising firms to help them project favorable images. To a considerable extent political leaders control the flow of information to voters and the way in which the electorate perceives of the political process. They are responsible for deemphasizing issues of public policy in political campaigns. On the one hand, it can be argued that an important part of the context in which

---

[4] Key, *The Responsible Electorate*, p. 6.

parties and party leaders must function is the general disinterest and lack of concern on the part of the electorate. But, on the other hand, insofar as party leaders determine this condition, it is not an inevitable characteristic of the political environment.

Primaries vs. General Elections

The remarkable successes of Governor George Wallace and George McGovern in the 1972 primaries, due to a sharp definition of pressing issues of public policy by both men, ironically may actually support the arguments of political leaders and the research of political scientists that voters will not elect, at least at the presidential level, candidates who take extreme positions on major policy issues. The politics of primaries differs markedly from that of general elections. Turnout is low, limited to party regulars. Individuals may be quite willing to waste votes, or as George Wallace put it "send a message to Washington" by selecting extreme candidates in primaries with the knowledge that they will not be in a position as a result of the outcome of the primary election to implement their programs.

In the past, primary elections have generally not been significant in selecting the candidate who emerges from the convention, although in 1972 the increase in presidential preference primaries did allow George McGovern to garner enough votes to capture the Democratic nomination. The preceding argument suggests then that some who voted for Wallace or McGovern in the primaries would not do so in the final election. There is little doubt, however, that a very large segment of voters continue their loyalties beyond the primary to the general election. The cases of McGovern and Wallace emphasize that there are many voters who are deeply concerned with public issues and who want candidates and political parties to emphasize these issues. Of course, this depends upon the times in which elections occur. 1972 and the preceding years happened to be a time of major upheavals in American politics, due to the Vietnam war, unemployment, crime, difficulties in financing state and local governments, and increasing public awareness of air and water pollution. Events and circumstances almost automatically created an emphasis on issues by the public. Candidates simply couldn't ignore problems that were pressing in from all directions. This type of situation has occurred at certain periods in American history, but the more usual circumstances are periods of seeming stability where the public is lulled to sleep with regard to issues of public policy that seem remote to their lives.

Parties and Issue Identification

Suggesting that issues may from time to time be emphasized by candidates, and important to the electorate, does not reveal the role of parties in the formulation and presentation of such issues. To what extent do parties as a collective force develop issues and present them meaningfully? What does party identification mean in terms of issues? What does the election of a candidate of one party over another mean in terms of government action?

There are data that suggest that parties are a force in shaping the way in which issues are perceived by the electorate. Those who identify with the Democratic Party have different viewpoints with regard to many issues of public policy than Republicans. This does not mean that those who identify with one party or the other necessarily vote for the candidates of that party under all circumstances. Ticket-splitting is becoming a pervasive voting habit.[5]

The 1970's witnessed a trend towards less meaningful identification with political parties. Young voters do not identify with parties to the same degree as their elders. Strongly influenced by the media of television, these voters do not view policy issues along the traditional lines that have been established by the two major parties. It has always been the case that the public policy positions of the parties are established by the leaders, not by those who simply identify with the party. Indeed, there is a question whether, in the past, issue differences between the two parties constituted a primary motivation for individuals to identify with or vote for one party or the other. An extensive survey undertaken in 1957 and 1958 revealed that although there were sharp cleavages between the leaders of the two parties, the "followers" for the most part did not differ sharply on the way in which they viewed public issues.[6]

If the leaders of the parties practice their beliefs within government, then the cleavage between the parties is significant in formulating public policy. Of course, there are splits between conservatives and liberals among the leaders of both parties which tend to diminish the significance of the party label for the implementation of party programs that conform to an identifiable ideology. Nevertheless, Democratic leaders in general tend to favor more than

---

[5] Walter Devries and V. Lance Tarrance, *The Ticket Splitter.*
[6] Herbert McClosky, Paul J. Hoffmann and Rosemary O'Hara, "Issue Conflict and Consensus Among Party Leaders and Followers," *The American Political Science Review* 54 (June, 1960): 406–27.

their Republican counterparts positive government programs in such areas as regulation of business, civil rights, social security, and education, to mention a few. Republicans, reflecting their business identification, lean towards less government intervention in the economy and a greater reliance upon individualism. In the foreign policy area Democrats favor greater international involvement, including military and economic aid, than do Republicans.

On the domestic front the ideological cleavage between the two parties grew out of the crisis of the Depression and the response of the parties to it. Most of the group identifications and socialization of the older leaders of the parties occurred during that time. The programs of Franklin Roosevelt easily polarized political activists, and the impact was such that it lasted at least through one additional generation. With the exception of Presidents John F. Kennedy and Richard Nixon, all presidents since the New Deal were mature men during the 1930's. The policies of Franklin Roosevelt in the international field did not polarize private and public elites as much as did his domestic programs. However, there was at least initially a very sharp reaction against the policies that led to American entry into World War II. Conservative Republicans, particularly from rural areas, took a far more isolationist stance than did the Roosevelt Administration, and attempted to prevent many of Roosevelt's policies that committed the United States to aid foreign nations, especially Great Britain, that were under attack by the Germans.

Contemporary Party Ideologies

As the New Deal and World War II fade into history, and as a new generation of political leaders develops, polarization of political attitudes along traditional lines will inevitably vanish to be replaced by either a new dichotomy between the parties, or an overlapping and confusion of party ideologies. Although the Democratic Party still tends to play its New Deal theme "happy times are here again" at its national political conventions, and displays movies illustrating how the party brought the nation out of the Depression, reduced unemployment, and established economic prosperity, these themes do not touch many of the major issues of today. What will the party use to replace its classic theme?

Since the Republicans have been out of power far more often than the Democrats during the last forty years, they have not developed a positive ideological emphasis at the national level, but rather have concentrated upon criticism of the party in power. Their philosophy has been primarily laissez-faire and individualist in theory, if not in practice. Until very recently, just as the Democrats have based their party platforms upon New Deal issues, the Republicans have reacted by emphasizing an anti-New Deal philosophy.

President Nixon's Administration, although not developing any coherent philosophy for the Republican Party, has extended in the foreign policy field those policies of the liberal wing of the party begun during the Eisenhower era. Instead of retreating into isolationism, supported by conservative Republicans during the New Deal and thereafter, President Nixon has boldly involved the United States throughout the world in new arms limitation treaties, mutual cooperation agreements, and the establishment of relations with Communist China. The Republican platforms of the 1960's would never have dared to predict such far-reaching international involvements coming from a Republican presidential victory. On the domestic front, President Nixon has adhered to the traditional Republican line which has generally been conservative. He has attempted to stack the regulatory commissions with pro-industry members, and has made operational the Republican doctrine of individualism and states' rights by substituting revenue sharing for the categorical grant programs of the Democratic Party.

Clearly the major issue of the presidential election in 1976 will be Watergate. However, this is not entirely a party issue, but rather reflects upon the capabilities of President Nixon, and those components of the party that have consistently supported him. Many Republicans have rushed to disassociate themselves from Nixon, recognizing the disastrous impact that Watergate will undoubtedly have at the polls upon any who were involved. After President Nixon fired special Watergate prosecutor, Archibald Cox, 47 percent of a nationwide sample favored impeachment, and 54 percent favored resignation of the president.[7] In the Harris and Gallup polls of October, 1973, President Nixon's job rating dipped to a record low of slightly above and below 30 percent respectively. But Watergate is not an issue upon which to build meaningful ideological differences between the parties. The place of other critical issues—such as the energy crisis, environmental problems and control, law enforcement, and civil rights—in future party programs remains to be seen. In 1976 the issues of inflation and

---

[7] *U.S. News and World Report* (November 19, 1973): 23.

unemployment will undoubtedly be critical; however, whether the parties will develop significantly different programs in these areas is doubtful. Both parties favor programs to control inflation, foster prosperity and economic security, control pollution, and eliminate crime. In the area of civil rights the Democrats and Republicans differ somewhat, in that the Democrats are more in favor of governmental action to protect the rights of individuals, whereas the Republicans want to leave far more discretion to state and local governments. However, even this attempt to distinguish between the parties has to be modified since a significant part of the Democratic Party consists of southern representatives, who are more conservative on civil rights than most Republicans. Also, on an issue such as busing, politicians of both parties have been responsive to what they believe to be a national sentiment against busing to achieve integration. Even northern liberals in the Democratic Party have voted in favor of anti-busing proposals in Congress, once federal court orders have threatened their urban and suburban constituents.

To the extent that issue formulation by the parties is sporadic and responsive only to temporary concerns of the public, party identification means little if anything in the electoral or governmental process. Under such conditions the electorate might as well vote on the basis of the individual who is running rather than his party.

Party Discipline and Policy

Under certain circumstances parties can be cohesive units without having policy positions. Before the introduction of a civil service system at the national, state, and local levels, parties in power could provide patronage for a large number of supporters. Many people would work for and vote for political parties in the hopes of obtaining government employment. Perhaps even more important, at the local level constituents received important services from parties. Party bosses would act as a buffer between constituents and the harsh realities of living in urban communities. They would help constituents when they were in trouble with the "authorities," whether public or private. Under such circumstances parties were not performing policy functions in the sense of defining programs that were offered to the electorate for consideration and choice. Machine politics usually involves the domination of one party over the other, which negates the possibility of choice except in primary elections. Even in primaries machines dominate the selection of candidates. Where machine politics exists so do disciplined political parties. However, these parties do not meaningfully connect people with policy formulation in government.

The "policies" that machine politics developed were very sporadic, and were designed to serve the interests of the members of the parties and their supporters. No national, cohesive party organization could be developed in the same way, primarily because of the tremendous diversity of interests throughout the nation with which the party would have to deal. National parties cannot provide those intimate services to individuals that lead to mass support at the polls. Although national politicians are always involved in granting political favors in return for support, party control is not sustained on this basis. The major political tradeoffs are not favors, but programs that promise to benefit the interests of the divergent groups within the coalition supporting each party. Franklin Roosevelt did not build the Democratic Party on the basis of individual favors, but on the basis of comprehensive programs that responded to the pressing concerns of various parts of the nation.

Diversity Within Party System

The differences between national parties on the one hand, and state and local party organizations on the other, illustrate the diversity within the American party system. This makes it very difficult to characterize parties in general terms. Party ideologies may or may not exist, depending upon the times and the level of party organization. In some electoral constituencies there is a meaningful two-party system, in which each party expresses contrasting viewpoints on a number of issues of public policy, offering choice to the electorate. But parts of the nation even today are characterized by one-party government, such as has traditionally existed in the South, where competition if it exists at all takes place during primary elections within the dominant party.

As one looks at the entire spectrum of party politics in the United States, it is difficult to identify comprehensive policy programs with one party or the other. In the vast realm of state and local politics, the programs of individual candidates as well as their personalities count in the electoral process. Policy programs may be presented to the electorate by candidates, for example, in gubernatorial and mayorality elections, but these are not as distinguishable along party lines as the platforms and programs of national presidential candidates. Certainly, taking the nation as a whole, it would be impossible to predict the kinds of programs which would be advanced by the candidates in state and local elections of one party or the other. A Democratic governor in the South will not have the same kinds of programs as one in the North or the West. Some states have more highly developed party systems than others, and more effective and meaningful two-party competition. California could be cited as an example in this respect at the gubernatorial level. But even in California in state and local elections one often finds "non-partisanship," and party lines are obscured if not totally invisible.

PARTIES IN OPERATION

As one observes the parties in operation at the national level, is there reason to suspect that in the future they will more sharply define their role as policy-making instruments? First of all, how do they formulate the issues of public policy that are presented to the electorate? Except for what one might term the "presidential party," which is defined as the party organization that comes together once every four years to select a candidate and place him in the White House, every national political candidate has discretion to shape issues as he sees fit on the basis of inputs from his particular constituency. At state and local levels, party organizations often help to shape the issues on which national candidates will run.

Platforms and Policy

Generally speaking, party platforms not only state the policy positions of the party on various matters, but also attack the opposition party and contain a certain amount of rhetoric designed to provide a rallying point for the party members. Powerful politicians in the parties often have a very strong voice in the planks which will be included in the platform. The president is always able to guide the platform for his own party if he is running for a second term. A party platform that does not have the support of its own presidential candidate would be of little meaning, for only if the president supports the positions of the platform will he strive to implement them once elected.

The "out-party," that is, the party which does not have an incumbent in the White House, has far more difficulty than the party of the president in focusing its platform issues, unless there is a clear balance of party power in favor of a potential presidential candidate. In 1972, for example, the Democratic platform reflected the views of Senator George McGovern who had virtually won the nomination through a series of primary victories at the time that the platform committee was meeting. The committee itself, in the case of the Democratic Party in 1972, a 150 member body, is representative of all segments of the party. This is also true in the Republican Party. Hopefully this brings about a representative platform. But, in order to secure an agreement among all sections of the party it usually is necessary not only to compromise on specific platform planks, but also to state them in such vague terms that they often lack any meaningful content.

Some of the more specific parts of the Democratic platform of 1972 were the following:

1. We urge abolition of the Draft.

2. Reduce United States troop levels in Europe in close consultation with our allies, as part of a program to adjust the North Atlantic Treaty Organization.

3. To those who for reasons of conscience refuse to serve in this war [Vietnam], and were prosecuted or sought refuge abroad, we state our firm intention to declare an amnesty, on an appropriate basis when the fighting has ceased and our troops and prisoners have returned.

4. American support for the repressive Greek military government must cease.

5. The Democratic Party commits itself to make the Social Security tax progressive by raising substantially the ceiling on earned income. To permit needed increases in Social Security benefits we will use general revenues as necessary to supplement payroll tax receipts.

6. To reduce the local property tax for all American families, we support equalization of school spending and substantial increases in the federal share of education costs and general revenue sharing.

7. The Nixon policy of intimidation of the media and administration efforts to use government power to block access to media by dissenters must end if free speech is to be preserved.

8. Public service employment must be examined to make the government the employer of last resort and to guarantee a job for all.[8]

---

[8] *Congressional Quarterly Weekly Report*, vol. 30, no. 29 (July 15, 1972), pp. 1726–49.

Other parts of the Democratic platform dealt with the need for tax reform, proposals for cuts in military spending, and reform of the welfare system.

The platforms of both parties always contain statements pledging that the party will work for peace and prosperity. Both parties are firmly against inflation. Often the platforms will contain specific planks aimed at gaining the support of important blocs of voters. These are aimed at such groups as labor, veterans, farmers, the elderly, and youth. The 1968 Republican platform contained a plank aimed at Indians and Eskimos, which stated:

The plight of American Indians and Eskimos is a national disgrace. Contradictory government policies have led to intolerable deprivation for these citizens. We dedicate ourselves to the promotion of policies responsive to their needs and desires and will seek the full participation of these people and their leaders in the formulation of such policies.

Inequality of jobs, of education, of housing and of health blight their lives today. We believe the Indian and Eskimo must have an equal opportunity to participate fully in American society. Moreover, the uniqueness and beauty of these native cultures must be recognized and allowed to flourish.[9]

Whether or not Indians and Eskimos would be encouraged to vote for the Republican Party on the basis of a plank such as this is difficult to say. The rhetoric is basically meaningless, but designed to tell these minority groups that the Republican Party knows of their existence and the difficulties which they face, and will hopefully do something about it in the future. President Nixon did in fact make some efforts to revamp and reorganize the Bureau of Indian Affairs to deal more adequately with the problems of the American Indian. The actions that were taken, however, have little to do with the plank in the party platform, which offered no concrete guidance or suggestion as to the specific proposals of the Republican Party.

Party platforms are the result rather than the cause of the lack of party government. Presidential and congressional candidates know that they cannot be held to account for the general policy positions taken by the parties in presidential elections. However,

---

[9] *The Presidential Nominating Conventions*, 1968 (Washington, D.C.: Congressional Quarterly Service, 1968), p. 49.

they are aware that the voters may look at various sections of the platform, and any extreme positions taken will certainly be publicized to the disadvantage of the candidates. Therefore, from the standpoint of those running for office the best platform is one which maximizes the promises it makes to various groups of the electorate, without at the same time taking positions which might alienate anyone. As the Democrats fought over their 1972 platform, they rejected suggestions that the party take a strong stand in favor of legalized abortion, fearing that large numbers of Catholic voters would be alienated from the party. Interest group leaders take very seriously what the parties include in their platforms, which is evidenced by the intense pressure they exert to secure favorable planks. Any platform statements that are contrary to their interests will be immediately noted and may result in attempts to persuade the membership of the group not to vote for the party. Regardless of the reality that party platforms have little meaning and do not bind candidates, symbolic importance is attached to the rhetoric of the platforms.

Both before and after general elections, the inputs upon candidates and office-holders are different from the forces that shape the development of party platforms. The platform is basically geared to the election of the president, and is therefore designed to represent a broad cross-section of the nation. Congressmen, however, have far more narrow constituencies than the president, and the inputs upon them will come from more specialized interests. In order to get elected in Mississippi, a Democratic congressman cannot run on a national platform that pledges the use of federal funds for the desegregation of schools and local facilities, or supports busing to achieve integration. He must base his political pitch upon the interests of his own constituency, which is at odds with the position of the national party organization that is often dominated by forces that are far more liberal than those of the Democratic Party of the South.

In the initial 1972 Democratic platform draft, for example, the forces of Governor George Wallace of Alabama filed minority reports to a large number of planks that did not conform to the interests of southern voters as they were perceived by Wallace. The Wallace forces opposed the Democratic stand favoring busing as a means of achieving integration. They did not agree with the position of the party which supported effective legislation to control the sale of hand-guns. Wallace members filed a minority report that upheld the constitutional right of citizens to bear arms. Moreover, they took a strong position in support of capital punishment, which was not mentioned in the Democratic platform.

Minority reports are also filed by other individuals who feel that the interests of their particular constituencies are not reflected in the party platform. It must be remembered that these minority reports and attempts to change the platform take place during the formative stages of platform development, in the hope of molding it to meet the concerns of particular groups. The final platform does not contain minority or dissenting views.

Just as those running on the Democratic ticket seek to mold the platform to be more responsive to the needs of their particular constituencies, Republican candidates also may be faced with a wide divergence between the platform and the prevailing opinion of the particular constituency they represent. Regardless of party, whether in presidential election years or off-years, each individual political candidate will shape his campaign to be responsive to the constituency he represents, rather than to adhere to the national party line.

In the preelection stage, voters cannot help but be confused about what party labels may or may not mean in terms of ultimate effect on policy formulation. This is one reason that ticket splitting, a process whereby voters ignore party labels and simply vote for the individual that they feel best reflects their concerns, is becoming very widespread. In particular constituencies the same electorate may select individuals who are entirely different in their political outlook and party affiliation, which suggests that the voters may indeed be selecting individuals on the basis of personality rather than policy positions.

In 1970 the Californian voters elected Republican Ronald Reagan as governor, but at the same time selected a liberal Democrat, John Tunney, as their United States Senator. In the same year in Pennsylvania, a Democratic governor was elected while a Nixon supporter, Hugh Scott, was reelected to the Senate. Also in 1970, the voters of Ohio selected a Democrat as governor while electing conservative Republican Robert Taft as United States Senator. In state after state, voters elect governors of one party, while placing another party into one or more of the branches of the state legislature. At the national level during Republican presidential administrations, voters generally elect Democratic Congresses. And, in the 1972 primary campaigns many of the same kinds of voters, who wanted to register a dissent, were attracted to Wallace and Mc-

Govern, who in fact reflected diametrically opposed points of view on major issues of public policy.

The increasing amount of ticket splitting is not just an indication that party policy positions in no way unite the electorate into opposing coalitions. It also reveals that party identification itself, whether on a policy basis or for other reasons, is on the decline. It is quite possible and indeed probable to have straight ticket voting, which means that voters are closely identified with one party or the other, for reasons other than policy preferences. Before the era of the 1960's straight ticket voting was the rule rather than the exception in most elections.[10] By 1968 George Gallup estimated that 57 percent of the American voters did not vote a straight party ticket. During the 1950's, 60 to 70 percent of the electorate voted a straight ticket.[11]

Public Policy, Public Relations, and Political Candidates

Just as political parties obscure the formulation of issues of public policy for presentation to the voters, politicians often avoid taking stands on public issues during campaigns for election. Political public relations men act as intermediaries between the voters and the candidates. They have convinced the latter that the best way to win an election is to project a favorable personal image, rather than to concentrate upon debating policy. The watershed national election that emphasized this approach was the presidential contest in 1952. Eisenhower's advisers highlighted his personality and war-hero attributes and obscured issues—not that Eisenhower's personality needed artificial boosting. More often than not candidates who take a stand on a broad range of public policy issues face difficulty in the electoral process, because they always risk the possibility of alienating blocs of voters.

The wide use of television in political campaigns emphasizes the need to project favorable images to the voters, rather than to appeal to them on the basis of a rational consideration of the issues. This is not to suggest that in the past, when political candidates relied upon person-to-person contact and printed media, primarily newspapers, to reach voters, that they necessarily paid any greater atten-

---

[10] Walter Devries and V. Lance Tarrance, *The Ticket Splitter*, p. 22.
[11] Ibid.

tion than now to the presentation of policy issues. However, it can be argued that appealing to voters through printed media at least requires that, from time to time, issues be stated, for the projection of personal images in this way is far more difficult than it is through television.

The attention span of television audiences has been geared to very short time intervals, which both encourages and often necessitates that political candidates make their television presentations as short as possible. The use of the political "spot," which is a very brief advertisement, is a commonly used device for political as well as for commercial advertising. Television not only encourages brevity, but also contrived staging. The use of television tapes enables politicians to produce any type of program and to project any image they want. It encourages politicians to become actors, their performance being based upon what pleases the audience. Just as the television networks find that they often cannot get commercial sponsorship for public affairs programs, politicians, too, shy away from "heavy" presentations in favor of light entertainment.

The presentation of public issues on network television is also made more difficult because of its national coverage. Candidates cannot say one thing in one part of the country and not be seen and heard in another. They can attempt to do this in packaging their own political advertising for local use, presenting different kinds of images to take into account the different composition of the electorate from one area of the country to another. However, the national news media acts independently of the candidates and any formulation of issues will be immediately seen and heard from coast to coast or, in the case of state elections, throughout the state. This necessitates compromising positions on the part of political candidates, and encourages equivocation and vague generalities in the presentation of issues of public policy.

In the ideal democratic model of party government, campaigns form a very important part of the process of "government by discussion." It is through campaigns that the electorate is supposed to be presented with meaningful choice between the two major political parties. This not only requires the presentation of a series of contrasting stands on issues of public policy between the two parties, but also debate between rival party candidates which will help to sharpen the issues in the minds of the electorate. Political campaigning in America does not, to say the least, encourage this type of presentation.

Although debates do take place from time to time between candidates, they occur in the contrived atmosphere of television, in which makeup may be more important than intelligence and moral fiber. Candidates who engage in debates are not concerned with refuting the arguments of opponents on a rational basis, but rather with projecting the proper image to the electorate, just as in the case of spot political advertising. The debates hardly follow formal debating rules, and do not resemble the Lincoln-Douglas debates of the nineteenth century. There are no formal, skilled judges who award points to one side or the other. Victory is determined on the basis of the impressions made upon the electorate.

Debating among the parties does not have to occur on television, but also takes place in the printed media. But the entire emphasis of political campaigning is away from the sharpening and debating of issues. At the presidential level, for example, no incumbent agrees to debate his opponent simply because he knows that giving national television coverage to the opposition can only increase its relative strength. There are no rules of the political game that require debates between party candidates, so that each candidate decides for himself whether or not it would be advantageous to enter into an issue-oriented debate with his opponent.

The net result of political campaigning is more confusion on the part of the electorate regarding the policy positions of the various candidates. Moreover, there is no way for voters to know or be assured that candidates will support whatever positions they take during elections once they are in office. The kind of continuity of the political process which results from unified parties that are capable of dominating the governmental process, if elected, is absent. Issues are raised sporadically by individual candidates, who may or may not have the power once elected to affect the course of public policy.

PARTY INPUTS
TO POLICY-MAKERS

Are political parties any more effective as collective forces in the policy process after elections than before? To what extent are the public policy outputs of government influenced by "party" inputs to the branches of the government, all of which have power to shape public policy in various ways? Does it make any difference in terms of public policy which party has a majority in Congress or occupies the White House?

Certainly if one looks at the policy outputs of government in the very broadest terms, the impression is gained that Democrats and Republicans do have a different outlook on many critical issues. Observing the presidential administrations since the New Deal period, it is possible to observe that during Democratic administrations the government became far more involved in regulation of the economy, welfare programs, and international involvements, including three major wars. Even though the president has to depend upon Congress for the approval of most of his policy decisions in the domestic field, he has enough discretion and influence so that he alone can have a profound impact on the course of public policy. It does make a difference who occupies the White House, and party identification is often able to predict the president's general approach to various issues of public policy. Because the president relies upon the collective force of the party to get elected in the first place, insofar as he can identify a common denominator of agreement among party factions on policy issues he will strive to advance these positions within the limits of his powers and responsibilities. Often the president will lead rather than follow the party in shaping policy positions.

Presidential vs. Congressional Parties

There is a difference between what is called the "presidential party" and the "congressional party." The former refers to those components of the party that are instrumental in getting the president elected. In both the Democratic and Republican parties the more liberal elements are usually essential in securing the election of the president. The policy inputs upon the president from his own party will tend to reflect these party factions.

Because of the electoral college system, and the weight that it gives to the more populous states, it is the party machines and bosses in these areas that presidential candidates must rely upon in order to win. Examining this proposition in closer detail, if one were to list all of the states with their electoral votes, it is clear that the candidate who can secure the votes from the large industrial states—California, Illinois, Michigan, New York, Ohio, and Pennsylvania—can easily win the election. This is based on the assumption that the electoral votes from the remaining states will split roughly equally between the two parties. The electoral vote of these large states collectively equals 185, which although far from the 270 votes needed in the electoral college to win, nevertheless would give any candidate a sufficient boost even if he fell far short of splitting the votes from the other states.

These key "swing" states form the most important part of the president's constituency, and in terms of his party, the state organizations in the larger states must unite to deliver a state plurality for their candidate. In the past the politicians from the key states have dominated the national party organization, and have been able to dictate who would be the nominees of the parties. This is why big city mayors, provided they have effective party machines, as in the case of Mayor Daley of Chicago, wielded such power within the Democratic Party: both they and the city electorate were predominately Democratic.

The 1972 Democratic Convention marked a departure from the traditional nominating process. The reform rules instigated under the guidance of Senator McGovern were designed to give the grass-roots electorate far more power in the nominating process and prevent the hand picking of delegates to the convention by powerful Democratic politicians. Ironically, even though the authority of party bosses was reduced (Mayor Daley's delegation to the convention was not seated because its membership and the way in which it had been selected did not conform to the convention guidelines) in the *nominating* process, the support of such people was necessary to secure the *election* of the Democratic candidate. In states such as Illinois, without the massive delivery of votes by the Chicago machine, the Republicans, on the basis of their support in the more rural areas of the state, would win the electoral votes. This is exactly what happened in 1972, and was one factor in accounting for the defeat of Senator McGovern.

While the presidential wing of the Democratic Party has traditionally been oriented in the large cities of the North, it is not so easy to pinpoint the focal point of power within the Republican presidential party. The Republicans must concentrate upon the rural areas of the country, particularly within the large industrial states, in order to counterbalance the city based support of the Democrats. In states such as New York, California, and Illinois, while the Democrats control the major urban areas, the Republicans have widespread backing in the rural sections. Rural electorates are more conservative than their city counterparts, which means that the Republican presidential wing has a decidedly conservative cast relative to the Democrats. In the past this distinction was clearer. It was based upon the existence of large numbers of blue-collar workers in the cities, in contrast to independent farmers, and upper-middle class management types in the suburbs. The distinctions between the presidential wings of the parties were based upon economic differences and consequently differing political attitudes. Today, these economic distinctions are breaking down and are being overshadowed by less class-oriented issues, such as the energy crisis, pollution, crime control, race, and the spiraling cost of living.

Although the working class base of the Democratic Party still exists, it is not as much intact as in the past. President Nixon was able to appeal very effectively to many urban dwellers with his emphasis upon the need to curb crime and stop busing, even if it meant a diminution of civil rights. By the time of the 1968 elections, both presidential candidates were running on the basis of party platforms that had very similar approaches to many problems. Although there were echoes of the individualism versus positive government contrasts between the two parties as in the past, in 1968 this distinction was not as sharply drawn, and by the time the parties entered the 1970's the old New Deal–anti-New Deal debates were even less pronounced.

Each presidential candidate in 1972 was seeking to form a new coalition of interests that could endure and support the presidential party in the future. On the one hand, Senator McGovern, with his programs for redistribution of wealth, reduction of defense expenditures, and welfare reform was attempting to form a coalition of the disenchanted and alienated voters of all ages. President Nixon, on the other hand, stuck to a middle-of-the-road position on all issues. Citing the achievements of his administration, he proposed no radical new programs.

In the Democratic Party, 1972 witnessed a remarkable change in the process of selecting the presidential candidate. On the basis of the "McGovern reforms," a set of guidelines issued to the party to shape the way in which delegates were chosen to the National Convention, the composition of that convention no longer represented, as in the past, powerful party politicians—governors, mayors, party bosses, and wealthy and influential individuals—but rather opened up the process of delegate selection to a far broader range of party members. Quotas were assigned to the delegations to guarantee a fair representation of groups that had been virtually excluded in the past, such as blacks, women, and young people. In 1973, a special Democratic delegate selection commission voted to rescind the quota system, and in its place voted to encourage minorities, women, and young people to participate in party affairs "as indicated by their presence in the Democratic electorate." [12] Other changes that were made restored power to state and local political machines, enabling them to present slates of delegates under their control to party members in the primaries, and, if elected, to control them at the convention. The 1976 Democratic Convention will restore a great deal of power to old line politicians who were virtually excluded from the Democratic Convention of 1972.

The drastic effects of the McGovern reforms were revealed by a *New York Times* computer analysis of the 3,085 delegates to the 1972 convention:

1. Only 290 are members of the unions (fewer than 10 percent), and a substantial number of those are from unions not affiliated with the AFL-CIO.

2. Only 997 hold offices of even the most obscure sort, either in government at any level, or in the party. Almost exactly two-thirds have no such affiliation—that is, they come from the ranks of ordinary citizenry.

3. At least 830 of the 3,085—almost 27 percent—are under 30 years of age. No precise figures for four years ago are available, but there were probably no more than 100 delegates under 30. Several states have no young people.

4. At least 1,163 of the 3,085—almost 38 percent—are women. They constituted only about 13 percent of the group in 1968, 13 percent in 1964, and 11 percent in 1960.

5. At least 454 of the 3,085—almost 15 percent—are black, compared with only 5.5 percent four years ago. At least 95 are Chicanos, 34 Puerto Ricans and 22 American Indians, setting new records in all of the minority categories.

6. Only 344, or slightly more than 11 percent, of the delegates were at the 1968 Convention in Chicago.[13]

As *New York Times* reporter, R. W. Apple, Jr. stated, this composition of delegates reflected the "agonizing period of realignment through which the Democratic Party is passing." [14]

---

[12] *Congressional Quarterly Weekly Report* (November 3, 1973), p. 2913.
[13] *The New York Times* (July 9, 1972), p. 33.
[14] Ibid.

1972 also marked a major departure from past practices in the Democratic Party because the presidential candidate was selected on the basis of victories in the expanded number of presidential primaries used by the party to select delegates. Delegate selection by primaries has existed in both parties since the early part of the twentieth century. However, never before in the Democratic Party has a candidate been able to win nomination solely on the basis of victories in the primary campaigns. In fact, running in primaries has always been a risky business, because candidates always lose some primaries which makes them vulnerable to the charge that they do not have the necessary vote-getting ability to win the general election. In the 1950's Senator Kefauver won a number of primaries, only to lose the nomination to Adlai Stevenson who was the personal choice of President Truman in 1952, and the favorite of party leaders in 1956. In 1968, Senator Eugene Mc-Carthy conducted a strenuous primary campaign, and Robert F. Kennedy was killed in the process of primary campaigning, while Vice-President Hubert Humphrey walked off with the Democratic nomination because he had the support of party leaders throughout the country.

The 1976 Democratic Convention process will restore in large part the power that party leaders lost in the nominating convention of 1972. The nominating constituency of the president will in both parties reflect more the inner core of party leaders than widespread grassroots party opinion. And, whatever occurs at the nominating conventions, legislators are going to go their separate ways in garnering votes unless they feel that the candidate of their party has strong support in their electoral constituency.

PARTIES IN GOVERNMENT

The effects that political parties have upon the policy process differ in the pre–election and post–election stages. The party in the electoral stage shapes appeals to the electorate, which may or may not be based upon policy issues, in order to gain public support. At this stage party candidates try to keep closely in tune with public sentiment within their particular constituencies. After the election is over party campaigning becomes dormant, as victorious candidates begin to concentrate their attention upon the multiplicity of tasks confronting them as elected officials.

What kinds of "parties" exist after the heat of the election campaign is over? At the national level, within Congress, the members of each party associate loosely within their "legislative parties," which consist of the members of the legislature of their own party. The legislative parties perform a variety of functions, perhaps the most important of which is to determine the allocation of committee seats among party members.[15] In a disciplined party system, the job of the legislator depends upon his acquiescence to the dictates of party leaders. This is because the leadership determines who will be permitted to run on the party label, and candidates must have a party affiliation in order to compete effectively in election campaigns. In Great Britain, for example, the Conservative and Labour parties have complete control over who they will allow to join the parties and run in local districts. They provide financial backing for candidates of their own party. Once elected to Parliament, party members must conform to the dictates of the leaders of the "Parliamentary party," composed of those members of a party in Parliament, led by the Cabinet in the case of a majority party, and by the shadow Cabinet in the opposition party.

In the United States legislators have their own party organizations within states and congressional districts that provide them with the necessary support to remain in Congress. Legislators form and control their own party organizations, although in some instances they are selected by powerful local politicians who have control over a party machine. In either case, members of Congress are not responsible to the leadership of the congressional party, or to the president. They are representatives of their state and local constituencies, not of a national party constituency. They can defy the wishes of national leaders as much as they want so long as they keep the support of their primary party organization within the constituency they represent. This means that in terms of public policy, legislators attempt to represent the interests of their constituency, which may or may not be entirely separate from those of the legislative party.

Legislative Parties

The concept of legislative parties, however, is not entirely irrelevant to the interests of members of Congress. In considering the makeup of legislative parties, both the formal and informal aspects of congressional party organization

---

[15] For a fuller discussion of legislative parties see Chapter 6.

should be considered. The formal leadership of the parties in both the House and Senate is determined initially through selection by caucuses of the members. The majority and minority leaders are elected along with party whips. Deputy and assistant whips are appointed by these elected leaders.

In both the House and the Senate each party has a committee that assigns members of the party to the various legislative committees. In the House, in the Democratic Party, this is done by the Democratic members of the Ways and Means Committee. The Republicans have a special Committee on Committees for this purpose in the House. In the Senate, the Democratic committee assignments are made by the Steering Committee, which is appointed by the leader of the Senate Democrats. Senate Republicans have a special Committee on Committees to make assignments. In addition to these organizational components, the legislative parties have various other committees to advise the leadership on policy, to aid legislators in their attempts to seek reelection, to advise the leadership on patronage positions that exist within the House and Senate, and various other ad hoc committees that may be assigned special tasks from time to time by either party. In this latter category, for example, the House Republicans have a Research Committee that is supposed to consider major issues of public policy from a long-range viewpoint with the purpose of informing members of the House of its findings.

Apart from the formal positions of party leadership, informal power within the parties in both branches of Congress is exerted by key members who have seniority, and who are the chairmen of the most influential committees. The chairman of the Rules Committee in the House, for example, does not hold a formal position of party leadership, but is nevertheless a key individual within the majority party in determining the course of legislative action. Wilbur Mills, chairman of the House Ways and Means Committee, has tremendous informal influence in addition to his formal position as chairman of the committee that makes Democratic committee assignments. His control over tax legislation affects vital interests in the constituencies of every congressman, and for this reason alone his power within the legislative party is enormous.

In the Senate, power was exerted by the "Establishment." This consisted of an inner club of powerful and usually senior senators of each party. They had access to key power points, and adhered to a common ethic based upon reverence for the Senate as an institution and respect for its procedures. Regardless of the formal leadership of the Senate parties, it was the Establishment that determined the composition of particular committees, and the fate of most legislative proposals. The Establishment no longer exists.

Party leadership in both the House and Senate reflects the fragmentation and specialization of the legislative process, rather than a coordinated and consistent policy-oriented position. Insofar as legislative parties operate as a collectivity, it is through their majority leadership. But, even here it is very difficult for majority leaders themselves to develop any kinds of consistent programs, and their actions often reflect the disparate fiefdoms within the legislative parties. The degree to which party members in Congress can operate in a cohesive fashion depends to a considerable extent upon whether or not the party has an incumbent in the White House. Under such circumstances, the president gives leadership to Congress, which may or may not respond to presidential initiatives depending upon what can be gained in terms of political power. The basic orientation of both Republican and Democratic congressional parties is towards the conservative end of the political spectrum, because of the seniority system and the power that conservative congressmen are able to exercise over the committee system and therefore the legislative process.

Effective party government requires the merging of presidential and congressional parties, but we seem to be as far away from this now as ever. The events of 1972, the nomination of McGovern and the shift of the presidential nominating constituency from regular party leaders to a grassroots base, caused a vast chasm between the presidential and congressional wings of the party. Very few congressmen or senators were even delegates to the Miami Beach Convention of the Democratic Party in 1972. Carl Albert, the Speaker of the House, was present but not a delegate. He was unrecognized by many of the "people's delegates" to the convention. Such a situation can only help to solidify four-party politics in America, as described by James MacGregor Burns.[16]

The Burns thesis is that although we have formally a two-party system, in reality each party is composed of two distinct branches, one reflecting the constituency of the president, and the other that of Congress. The congressional parties, largely because of the seniority rule and the domination of the legislative process by senior members, are more conservatively oriented than the presi-

---

[16] James MacGregor Burns, *The Deadlock of Democracy* (Englewood Cliffs, N.J.: Prentice-Hall, 1963).

dential parties. If the "deadlock of democracy" is to be broken, somehow the gap between presidential and congressional parties must be bridged. Under the present circumstances, this seems highly unlikely, because the only way in which this could occur would be to abolish the seniority rule and establish close coopera- tion between the majority party leadership in Congress and the president. Since there is no guarantee that the majority of Congress will be of the same party as the president, regardless of what changes might be made in legislative procedures, as long as the separation of powers remains, a party bridge between Congress and the president is unlikely to be built.

One of the important components of the party model of govern- ment is the existence of an opposition party which constantly criticizes the policy positions of the majority party where the opposition leadership feels this to be appropriate. Moreover, it is the task of the opposition to keep the public continuously informed about major issues of public policy being debated in the legislature and considered by the executive, and through criticism to point out to the electorate viewpoints in contrast to the government party. If government can formulate public policy without opposition or publicity, the capacity for arbitrary action will be virtually un- limited during its term in office. The concept of an effective opposi- tion party implies that public policy is controlled by the majority party, rather than by the bureaucracy, the courts, or pressure groups. Moreover, the government party must be forced to expose itself to criticism from the opposition.

The fragmentation of the American party system, as well as of government, makes it virtually impossible for an opposition party to function meaningfully. What is the opposition party? If the president is of one party and the majority of both branches of the legislature of another, is the presidential wing of the party the opposition or is the party that controls Congress? Because the presidency is the focal point of power in the political system, the opposition must be considered that party which is opposed to the president's policy. Generally, this implies the congressional wing of the out party. From time to time, the leadership of the opposition party in Congress will criticize certain policies of the president, but he may be attacked by members of his own congressional party. The neat symmetry of government party versus opposition party simply does not exist.

In a responsible parliamentary system, such as Great Britain, when the opposition leaders criticize the government they know that they may be called upon to face the electorate and to take over the reins of government. This tempers their criticism and directs it responsibly in relation to the policies of the prime minister. In the American system, the leadership of congressional parties know that they will not be running for the presidency in a collective capacity, and probably not as individuals. Their criticism of the president can therefore be self-serving, designed to appeal to their congressional constituency. Moreover, under the separation of powers, the president may choose not to debate in any way major decisions with members of Congress, although administration witnesses usually do appear in a nondebating capacity to testify before congressional committees and to inform Congress of the reasons for presidential actions. But in exercising foreign policy prerogatives the president can operate without prior congressional consultation, calling in members of Congress for support if he feels this is appropriate after decisions have been made. The natural opposition between Congress as a whole and the president forecloses any meaningful policy debates along party lines. Charges and counter-charges are constantly made both within and between members of the two parties, but consistent and continually coordinated and effective debate is nonexistent.

CONCLUSION

Whether or not more effective party government will be developed in the future is an open question. At the present time, and for the foreseeable future, parties as a collective force do not significantly shape the content of public policy. Given the tremendous diversity of the nation, the parties have done the best that anyone could expect in helping to bring together opposing groups. If the nation ever divides itself into two clearly contrasting camps, these will undoubtedly be reflected in two fairly disciplined political parties. But the innate individualism of the American character, in combination with the almost inevitable continuation of diversity of interests, will most likely prevent political parties in the future from becoming organizations with distinctive and contrasting policy orientations. The extent to which this situation diminishes the democratic process depends upon the responsiveness of the major conversion mechanisms of government, the presidency, the Congress, the bureaucracy, and the courts to public needs and aspirations. In the policy process, parties, per se, are largely rhetorical, symbolically attempting to express the feelings, often deeply held, of party supporters with regard to broad issues of public policy. The rhetoric of parties at least offers some guidelines to government decision-makers about the broad feelings of the electorate.

5

The President

as a Policy Force

Even more than parties and interest groups, the presidency is thought to be the focal point of policy-making by most citizens. Witness the tremendous interest in presidential election campaigns, and the relatively large voter turnout compared to that in state and local elections or in elections for congressmen and senators. In our folklore, the president is at the same time king and prime minister. Although the *office* is held in higher repute than the incumbent, the occupant of the White House usually gains from the stature of his position; people tend to forget that the president is always involved in the realities of exercising political power, meaning compromise and deals undertaken in the capacity of a politician, not king.

The belief that the president shapes most public policy is immediately shattered by the statistics on the success of his recommendations to Congress. Over the years Congress rarely enacts more than 50 percent of the legislative proposals sent to it by the White House. In recent years President Lyndon Johnson, with a box score of over 60 percent during several years of his administration, was by far the most successful president in dealing with the legislative branch. Even the most charismatic presidents, such as John F. Kennedy, have an exceedingly difficult time in getting the legislative branch to support recommendations from the White House.

Regardless of the separation of powers and the tendency of Congress to frustrate presidential wishes, the electorate is often convinced that the election of one presidential candidate or another may bring about profound changes in the course of public policy. For example, in 1972, Senator George McGovern promised wide-ranging changes in public policy, from tax reform to massive cuts in defense expenditures. Had he been elected he would not have been able single-handedly to enact these public policy proposals, which lie within the jurisdiction of Congress. And, within Congress, matters of taxation and appropriations are under the control of the House Ways and Means Committee, the Senate Finance Committee, and the Appropriations Committees in each branch.

Before the Democratic National Convention in 1972, Senator McGovern wrote a letter to a New York businessman hoping to reassure him that he was not in fact a radical. He went so far as to state that if he were elected his more "radical" proposals could not be enacted by him without congressional assent, and he assured the businessman that congressional assent would be unlikely. The letter was published in a full-page ad in the *Wall Street Journal,* among other papers. In effect, McGovern said that regardless of what he proposed, it was really up to Congress in such important areas as taxation to determine the public policies that would be finally enacted. Therefore, he said, "fear not what I say, because the power reality is that the president is but one actor in determining public policy." Without the support of Congressman Wilbur Mills, chairman of the House Ways and Means Committee, and Senator Russell Long, chairman of the Senate Finance Committee, no president can hope to enact tax reform legislation. Clinton Rossiter, in *The American Presidency,* called the president "chief legislator." In reality, he initiates legislative proposals, but rarely does Congress enact even a majority of presidential recommendations.

Of course, the formulation of public policy involves far more than the passage of legislation. Examples of the "imperial presidency," to use the phrase of Arthur Schlesinger, are commonplace in American history.[1] The actions of Lincoln, FDR, Truman, and Johnson in exercising the war power without always consulting Congress are good examples of independent presidential policy-making of far-reaching consequences. It has been primarily in the foreign and military policy spheres that the president has been able to operate without being significantly checked.

THE CONTEXT
OF THE PRESIDENCY

Effects of the
Separation of Powers

The imperial presidency has developed because of the separation of the executive from Congress, and the establishment of independent prerogative powers in the

---

[1] Arthur M. Schlesinger, Jr., *The Imperial Presidency* (Boston: Houghton Mifflin, 1973).

presidency under the Constitution. An executive dependent upon the legislature is weakened unless he can consistently control a majority of legislators. Such executive control can only result from a disciplined two-party system such as in Great Britain. The multiplicity of interests and the lack of a disciplined two-party system in the United States mean that dependency of the executive upon the legislature decreases presidential power.

The independent powers and separate constituency given to the office of the president in Article II of the Constitution have formed the basis for a vast expansion in presidential prerogatives as the responsibilities of the office have increased. Without having to rely upon legislative ratification, presidents from Washington to Nixon have taken bold initiatives in both foreign and domestic policy. Like the courts and parts of the bureaucracy, the White House is capable of making decisions without going through the tedious deliberations of the legislative process. Under the Constitution, the presidency is the only political office under the domination of one man.

Clerk or King?

One should not overemphasize the powers given to the presidency in the Constitution, however, because without the necessary political support and acquiescence on the part of other branches of the government, vigorous presidential action can be and has been nullified. Richard Neustadt claims that the Constitution makes the president more of a "clerk" than a king. He is a clerk not in a sense that he is powerless, but rather because the Constitution establishes no clear hierarchical lines of power and responsibility in government; therefore, all other parts of the governmental process look to the president for leadership, guidance, and for help in performing the tasks that they themselves are incapable of carrying out because of the fragmentation of the system. As Neustadt states:

In form all presidents are leaders, nowadays. In fact this guarantees no more than that they will be clerks. Everybody now expects the man inside the White House to do something about everything. Laws and customs now reflect acceptance of him as a great initiator, an acceptance quite as widespread at the Capitol as at his end of Pennsylvania Avenue. But such acceptance does not signify that all the rest of the government is at his feet. It merely signifies that other men have found it practically impossible to do *their* jobs without assurance of initiatives from him.

Service for themselves, not power for the president, has brought them to accept his leadership in form. They find his actions useful in their business. But transformation of his routine obligations testifies to their dependence on an active White House. A president, these days, is an invaluable clerk. His services are in demand all over Washington. His influence, however, is a very different matter. Laws and customs tell us little about leadership in fact.[2]

Just as in many areas the other branches of government need the president in order to take effective action, the president in turn relies upon his governmental "constituents" to carry out his orders.

The history of the presidency reveals numerous examples of recalcitrance to heed presidential demands not only on the part of the coordinate legislative and judicial branches, but even in the case of those parts of the bureaucracy that are supposed to be directly under his supervision. Even in foreign and military policy areas the president cannot automatically control policies that he initiates. For example, he can begin "police actions," which is in reality the same as a declaration of war, but he cannot necessarily control the actions of the military commanders in the field. President Truman had to fire General MacArthur for insubordination, because MacArthur was taking actions that threatened to widen the Korean war far beyond what the president wanted. In recent years, examples of independent military action in Vietnam without presidential knowledge have been brought to light, particularly in regard to the selection of bombing targets in North Vietnam during 1972. Air Force General John D. Lavelle had ordered his pilots to undertake twenty-eight missions to strike unauthorized targets in North Vietnam. In testimony before Congress, after he had been demoted and retired from the Air Force, General Lavelle pointed out that:

The rules of engagement [in the air war], although being fairly specific, also require some interpretation or judgment factor added. . . . I chose to make a very liberal interpretation of these rules of engagement. In certain instances, against high priority military targets, I made interpretations that were probably beyond the liberal intention of the rules. I did this since the crews were operating in an environment of optimum enemy defense. It was isolated instances reported as protective reaction strikes that resulted in General Ryan recalling me and questioning me on what we were doing. From his viewpoint in Washington, I had exceeded my authority. I can sit here now and understand his position,

---

[2] Richard E. Neustadt, *Presidential Power* (New York: John Wiley & Sons, 1960), p. 6.

but at that time as the Commander on the spot concerned with the safety of the crews, and, at the same time, trying to stop the buildup that was going on, I felt that these were justifiable actions.[3]

This incident illustrates that even where there is a tight chain of command, the president cannot foresee and control all of the events which occur on the basis of general policy decisions which he makes.

Policy-making Powers of the President

The constitutional context in which the presidency operates provides for policy-making responsibilities in several ways. The president is given the charge in Article II to recommend legislation to Congress, and the president's legislative program forms an important starting point for congressional action. The president can veto congressional legislation, and although Congress has the authority to pass legislation over the veto by a two-thirds vote, it does so rarely because of internal divisions within the legislature itself.

Another important way in which the president affects policy under the Constitution is through his appointments to the Supreme Court. Although he cannot control the actions of men once they are appointed—sometimes presidents are surprised to find that their Supreme Court appointments do not act in a predictable way —nevertheless a determined president can go a long way towards giving a liberal or conservative cast to the Court. President Nixon set out to appoint "strict constructionists," by which he meant conservatives, to the Court and he succeeded in shifting the balance of power on the Court in a conservative direction. Since the Court is one of the most important policy-making instruments in government, the presidential appointment power is a strong policy force. Constitutional appointments made by the president to the Supreme Court must be approved by the Senate. Sometimes there is strong opposition to presidential decisions on particular appointments, such as occurred during the Nixon Administration with respect to his first two appointees to fill a vacancy on the Supreme Court. Historically, however, rarely does the Senate interfere significantly with the presidential appointment process. The initiative clearly lies with the Chief Executive.

---

[3] *Congressional Quarterly Weekly Report*, vol. 30, no. 25 (June 17, 1972), p. 1494.

It is commonly assumed that one of the most important constitutional powers of the president is that of "Chief Executive." Article II states that the president is to see that the laws are faithfully executed. He is given the power to appoint "public ministers," and "officers of the United States," by and with the advice and consent of the Senate. He also may "require the opinion in writing of the principal officer in each of the executive departments, upon any subject relating to the duties of their respective offices." These legal powers are hardly sufficient to enable the president to control the policy-making activities of the bureaucracy. The key to potential presidential control over the administrative branch lies with Congress, for the Constitution delegates to the legislature the most significant authority over the bureaucracy. Administrative agencies cannot be set up in the first place without congressional approval, and Congress outlines what the agencies are to do. Whether or not an agency is placed under the legal control of the president is entirely at the discretion of the legislature.

The Policy Constituency
of the President

Congress, the bureaucracy, and the Supreme Court all become independent forces in the president's constituency because of the way in which the Constitution has structured the system. The positions that these branches of the government take with regard to various issues of public policy cannot help but influence the policy stance of the White House. Legislation cannot be enacted without the consent of Congress; this is complicated because the legislature is a bicameral body, split internally with different constituencies for the House and the Senate. Assuming that the president is able to get one of his legislative proposals passed, he next must deal with the bureaucracy, which is delegated responsibility to implement congressional laws. Whether or not the bureaucracy follows presidential wishes will depend upon the relative power of the presidency within the constituencies of administrative agencies. Finally, legislation and executive actions may come under the scrutiny of the Supreme Court, which will not hesitate to overrule the president if it feels that he has acted *ultra vires* (beyond authority) in terms of constitutional or statutory law.

Just as presidential policy outputs are shaped by a variety of governmental institutions, the policy inputs to the White House are often complex and conflicting. These inputs include demands from Congress, the bureaucracy, party and pressure group leaders, public opinion, and leaders of other nations. Clear mandates for presidential action rarely exist. The president must balance a variety of demands from many sources before he makes a policy decision. Public opinion may constrain presidential actions; however, the president usually leads rather than follows public opinion on most policy issues. Although he must depend upon broad public support at election time to remain in office, the public is far too fragmented itself to be able to speak with one voice to the White House.

As one observes the variety and contrasting nature of the inputs upon the presidency, it becomes difficult to make generalizations about how particular presidents arrive at policy decisions. This will depend to a considerable extent upon the nature of the man who occupies the office, and the way in which he assesses the different forces affecting him. The character of the man who occupies the White House is largely determined by the selection processes of the national parties. Rarely do either the Democratic or Republican parties nominate an "extremist" to run for the office, because the general preference of the electorate is for a middle-of-the-road candidate, a man who can take compromising positions on the broad issues facing the nation. The nominating and election processes usually guarantee that the occupant of the White House will be a skillful politician, because with the rare exceptions of charismatic leaders such as General Eisenhower, it is difficult for any other type of person to win both the nomination and the election. When presidents combine both charisma and political skill, as in the case of Franklin D. Roosevelt, a particularly forceful presidency results.

Limits Upon Presidential
Policy-making Discretion

An important part of the constitutional and legal context within which the president formulates policy arises from the legal definition of his constitutional prerogatives based upon Article II, and on the extent to which Congress by statute can delegate him discretionary authority. There is little doubt that if both the Supreme Court and Congress want to control the president, his legal discretion will be severely limited. Rarely, however, is there such agreement between the legislative and judicial bodies. The Supreme Court has not placed strict limits upon the legal authority of the president either in the domestic or in the international spheres. It has stated that there is a greater presumption of the validity of discretionary presidential decisions in foreign than in domestic policy. That is, the president has a great deal more leeway to act without consulting Congress when he is engaged in foreign policy-making. This is the formal context within which the president operates. Informal forces may expand or curtail his policy-making discretion.

It is an unusual president, especially in modern times, who will embark upon bold foreign policy actions without attempting to secure a base of political support in the legislature, even though this may even not be strictly needed under the terms of the Constitution. President Johnson was proud of the fact that he was able to attain overwhelming congressional approval of the Gulf of Tonkin Resolution, which he cited as authorizing his initiatives in the Vietnam war. Historic foreign policy decisions have more often than not been presented to Congress. The League of Nations Treaty had to be approved by the Senate, which failed to ratify President Woodrow Wilson's dream. It would have been unthinkable at that time, even if it had been possible in terms of international politics, to bypass the Senate by negotiating some form of executive agreement that would have involved the United States in the League of Nations. Of course, where appropriations are necessary to carry out a foreign policy, congressional assent is required, as in the case of the Marshall Plan after World War II.

The Curtiss-Wright Case Where Congress delegates authority to the president to act as its agent in foreign policy-making, it does not need to place the same kinds of boundaries upon presidential discretion as when it delegates authority for domestic policy-making. The key case here is *United States* v. *Curtiss-Wright Export Corp.* (1936), in which congressional law was challenged on the basis that it delegated to the president power to "legislate" which should properly have been retained by Congress. Under the doctrine of delegation of legislative power, Congress cannot transfer to the executive its lawmaking function. It cannot, presumably, say to the president "go forth and make policy," when this is constitutionally reserved to the legislature itself.

In the *Curtiss-Wright* case, Congress had transferred to the president the authority to establish an embargo on the sale of arms and ammunitions by American companies to countries that were at war in Paraguay and Bolivia. By granting the authority to put an embargo into effect, Congress was really giving the president a legislative function. This is constitutionally proper, provided that Congress retains control over the policy that is finally implemented by the agent (the president in this case) to which it delegates authority. Theoretically this is done by establishing strict legislative "standards" to guide the agent in decision-making. The agent cannot go beyond the boundaries set by Congress, which means that the "primary" authority still resides in Congress even though power to shape and implement the policy has been delegated.

In fact, it is virtually impossible for Congress to establish definite enough standards to control the authority which it delegates. In the *Curtiss-Wright* case, the president could proclaim an embargo if he found that such action "may contribute to the reestablishment of peace between those countries." This was to be the guiding standard that would assure that control would remain in the hands of Congress. But in reality its vagueness left complete discretion in the hands of the president. The Court recognized this, but nevertheless held that since foreign policy-making was involved, it was constitutionally proper for the president to be able to exercise such discretion.

In its opinion, the Court cited favorably a report of the Senate Committee on Foreign Relations issued in 1816, which stated in part:

The president is the constitutional representative of the United States with regard to foreign nations. He manages our concerns with foreign nations and must necessarily be most competent to determine when, how, and upon what subjects negotiation may be urged with the greatest prospect of success. For his conduct he is responsible to the Constitution. The Committee considers this responsibility the surest pledge for the faithful discharge of his duty. They think the interference of the Senate in the direction of foreign negotiations is calculated to diminish that responsibility and thereby to impair the best security for the national safety. The nature of transactions with foreign nations, moreover, requires caution and unity of design and their success frequently depends on secrecy and dispatch.

In upholding the broad grant of authority to the president in the *Curtiss-Wright* case, the Court held that congressional legislation "must often accord to the president a degree of discretion and freedom from statutory restriction which would not be admissible where domestic affairs alone are involved."

Interestingly enough, the same Court held that in domestic affairs, strict standards should be established by the legislature to assure that the president would not be able to act in an arbitrary fashion, and beyond the intent of Congress. This Court held key New Deal legislation unconstitutional on this basis, the only time in our history that legislative delegations of authority have been declared unconstitutional. This was done in the cases of *Panama Refining Company* v. *Ryan*, and *Schechter Poultry Corp.* v. *United States*, decided by the Supreme Court in 1935.

The Panama and Schechter Cases

At issue in both cases was the National Industrial Recovery Act of 1933, which contained sections granting broad authority to the president and subordinate administrative officials appointed by him to establish codes of fair competition within industries. The Act contained very few standards to guide the president in the formulation of codes, and the plaintiffs claimed that this constituted too broad a delegation of legislative power. In the *Panama* decision the Court held one section of the Act unconstitutional for its overly broad delegation of legislative authority. In the *Schechter* case the Court finally declared the entire Act unconstitutional, not only on the basis of unwarranted delegation of legislative authority, but also because Congress did not have the power to enact such legislation under the provisions of Article I of the Constitution.

In that portion of the *Schechter* decision concerning the delegation of power, the Court noted:

. . . Section III of the Recovery Act is without precedent. . . . Instead of prescribing rules of conduct, it authorizes the making of codes to prescribe them. For that legislative undertaking, Section III sets up no standards, aside from the statement of the general aims of rehabilitation, correction, and expansion described in Section I. In view of the scope of that broad declaration, and of the nature of the few restrictions that are imposed, the discretion of the president in approving or prescribing codes, and thus, enacting laws for the government of trade and industry throughout the country, is virtually unfettered. We think that the code-making authority thus conferred is an unconstitutional delegation of power. . . .

Although *Schechter* established the principle that the president is limited by the Constitution in his capacity to exercise the law-making function, which is properly reserved to Congress, the fact that neither before nor after that decision did the Court ever hold another delegation of presidential power to be unconstitutional because of vague standards makes the issue seem academic. During

World War II in particular the president was granted extraordinary discretion to "legislate" in the domestic arena to meet emergency conditions.

The Steel Seizure Case   Just as the president is theoretically limited by congressional laws where these have granted jurisdiction to him, where no such statutory delegations exist he is bound by the Constitution. To what extent does Article II limit his prerogatives? The key case here is the *Steel Seizure* case of 1952.[4] During the Korean war, President Truman, threatened with a crippling strike on the part of steel workers that had not been settled by the Federal Wage Stabilization Board to which the dispute had been referred, issued an executive order directing Secretary of Commerce Sawyer to seize most of the steel mills and operate them. As authority for doing this, President Truman cited his Article II powers as Commander-in-Chief and Chief Executive.

Although Congress had previously passed the Taft-Hartley Act which established procedures for such emergencies, the president did not invoke its provisions. At that time the Taft-Hartley Act was the major *bête noire* of the Democratic Party, and repeal of it was a key plank in the platforms of the party during the Truman and Eisenhower administrations. While ignoring the Taft-Hartley Act, President Truman, after seizing the mills, did send a message to Congress telling them what he had done, and requested supporting legislation or some other proposal to settle the dispute.

After the seizure order was issued, the companies involved immediately sought an injunction in the district court of the District of Columbia. The court issued a preliminary injunction, which, however, was stayed on the same day by the Court of Appeals. On May 3 the Supreme Court, bypassing the Court of Appeals, granted a *writ of certiorari* (a writ to review the record of the lower court), heard oral argument on May 12, and decided the case on June 2. All of this constituted an incredibly fast time period for a case to be decided by the Supreme Court. In brief, the Court had to decide whether or not the president was acting within his constitutional power when he seized the steel mills. Since the president did not act on the basis of a statute, the question before the Court was whether or not such authority could be implied from the Commander-in-Chief and Chief Executive clauses of Article II. The majority

---

[4] *Youngstown Sheet and Tube Company, v. Sawyer*, 343 U.S. 579 (1952).

of the Court found no such inherent authority in the Constitution, and declared the presidential action to be *ultra vires*. It found that the order to seize the mills was essentially legislative in character and therefore within the jurisdiction of Congress. The Court implied that if a real emergency had existed, perhaps presidential prerogatives would have extended to taking possession of private property if necessary for national defense. But the Court could find no such emergency at the time President Truman took over the steel mills.

Is the Court's decision in the *Steel Seizure* case an isolated example of curtailment of presidential policy-making discretion in the domestic arena, or has it created an important precedent? The four dissenting Justices, led by Chief Justice Vinson, pointed out that the decision was not based upon precedent. The dissenters noted that numerous actions similar in implications to the *Steel Seizure* case were taken by Presidents Lincoln, Wilson, and Franklin D. Roosevelt. For example, in referring to Lincoln, the dissenting opinion stated:

Without declaration of war, President Lincoln took energetic action with the outbreak of the war between the States. He summoned troops and paid them out of the Treasury without appropriation therefor. He proclaimed a naval blockade of the Confederacy and seized the ships violating that blockade. Congress, far from denying the validity of these acts, gave them express approval. The most striking action of President Lincoln was the Emancipation Proclamation, issued in aid of the successful prosecution of the war between the States, but wholly without statutory authority.

. . . President Lincoln without statutory authority directed the seizure of rail and telegraph lines leading to Washington.

Although later affirmed by Congress, these actions of President Lincoln, as well as other actions in later years of Presidents Wilson and Roosevelt, were *faits accomplis* in every case. Presidential actions before the *Steel Seizure* case suggest that there is no constitutional impediment to the exercise of arbitrary presidential power during times of recognized crisis.

It has been argued that presidential actions in times of emergency require public and congressional approval to be upheld. John P. Roche, writing shortly after the *Steel Seizure* case, sanguinely stated that:

The danger of unconstitutional presidential dictatorship, based on vigorous exercise of domestic prerogative, seems virtually nonexistent. In real terms, Congress and the public must agree with presidential emergency actions if they are to be effective. The silences of American constitutional history lend strong support to this proposition for, with the exception of the seizure of the steel industry, there has not been one single instance of the president actually taking prerogative action in a domestic crisis against the wishes of Congress.[5]

Endorsement by Congress does not necessarily mean that the wishes of the legislature are being followed, but only that a majority of legislators recognize the impracticality and undesirability of overruling the president once he has made his decision in a crisis situation. An entirely different legislative action might occur if the president sought congressional approval in advance. Presidential decisions carry their own momentum, difficult to overcome once put into motion.

Political Checks on the President

If Congress and the electorate are stirred up enough to oppose the president in an important decision-making area, then ultimately they may act together as a check upon the course of presidential decisions. The difficulties of obtaining congressional majorities and marshalling meaningful public opinion make it very unlikely that such a check would be invoked except under the most extreme circumstances. For example, the adverse public reaction to U.S. involvement in Vietnam, once the true import of the war was brought home to the American people, played an important role in President Johnson's decision to step down in 1968. Ultimately, public opinion forced the decision of President Nixon to withdraw our armed forces from Vietnam.

But adverse reaction did not occur in the early stages of escalation, when President Johnson was left with a virtually free hand to embark upon what turned out to be a disastrous policy. The Gulf of Tonkin Resolution, passed by an overwhelming vote in Congress in 1964 after North Vietnamese had attacked American destroyers off the coast of North Vietnam, reflected congressional

---

[5] John P. Roche, "Executive Power in Domestic Emergency: The Quest for Prerogative," *Western Political Science Quarterly* 5 (December, 1952): 592–618.

acquiescence in at least retaliatory strikes against the North Vietnamese. At that time Congress and the people were fully behind President Johnson, not realizing that major plans for escalation were being laid. Nor was Congress aware that its Gulf of Tonkin Resolution would be used later as a justification for a full-scale war.

The President as Constitutional Dictator

Every political system must have a mechanism that provides for rapid policy-making to meet crisis situations. The presidency is the best vehicle for this in our system, although both the bureaucracy and the Supreme Court as well as Congress have been known in extreme situations to act with dispatch to meet crises. It took Congress only a few hours to declare war upon the recommendation of the president in 1941 after the attack on Pearl Harbor. But such situations are rare for Congress, which is bogged down in cumbersome parliamentary maneuvers and a disjointed committee system.

Administrative agencies often play it safe rather than take decisive action, rendering the bureaucracy less efficient than the president in providing for the necessary decisions in emergencies. The president might also wish to avoid difficult situations arising from bold crisis decisions, but as President Harry S. Truman remarked: "The buck stops here." The president has no alternative but to face up to the responsibilities that inevitably are placed upon his shoulders. Every other branch of the government can more readily avoid responsibility for immediate action.

In a constitutional democracy the necessity for strong executive leadership at times poses dilemmas for the maintenance of the principles of the constitutional system. Our government is supposed to be limited, and based upon popular representation in the policy-making process. Insofar as the president is able to take independent action, without consultation of Congress and outside of the jurisdiction of the Supreme Court, limited and democratic government is diminished. Clinton Rossiter pointed out in 1948:

That constitutional dictatorship does have a future in the United States is hardly a matter for discussion. Dismal and distressing as the prospect may be, it seems probable that in the years to come, the American people will be faced with more rather than fewer national emergencies. . . . [T]he continuing tensions of a world of sovereign nations and the irrepressible economic convulsions of the twentieth century . . . have made it plain that the Second World War was not to be the last but only the latest of the American Republic's great national crises. . . .

That this nation's present-day institutions and procedures of emergency government present considerable room for improvement seems equally beyond dispute.[6]

Rossiter felt that the instruments of "constitutional dictatorship," particularly the broad delegation of powers from Congress to the presidency and administrative agencies, should be constructed to render the system politically responsible. Dates should be set in advance for the termination of delegated power. Moreover, every possible measure should be taken to make certain that the legislature and not the president determines the extent of authority to be exercised during the crisis. Rossiter particularly emphasized that: "the decision to institute a constitutional dictatorship should never be in the hands of the man or men who will constitute the dictator."[7]

The difficulty in the American constitutional system is that although presidents can be checked after they exercise their independent constitutional prerogatives under Article II, the prerogative decisions that they make initially can set the course of future events. Virtual automatic approval by Congress and the Supreme Court for prerogative actions is often assured. When Rossiter speaks of constitutional dictatorships he is referring to relatively long time spans, during which governmental authority is centralized in the hands of the Chief Executive and the bureaucracy. But single presidential prerogative actions can have drastic consequences for the political system, particularly when they lead to involvement in a major war. The residual powers of the constitutional dictatorship reside in many important areas in the hands of the president, and at any given time he can make an independent decision having far-reaching consequences. The political checks upon the president under such circumstances are not sufficient to curb his constitutional powers.

Although the president may sometimes become for a while a "constitutional dictator," there is little possibility that such a condition will last for long, or that the political system in itself could

---

[6] Clinton Rossiter, *Constitutional Dictatorship* (New York: Harcourt Brace Jovanovich, 1963), pp. 306–307. This book was first published by the Princeton University Press in 1948.
[7] Ibid., p. 299.

ever become a dictatorship. This would require the elimination of all other bases of independent political power, which is clearly an impossibility. The diverse forces within the nation, the structured conflict designed by the Framers of the Constitution among the branches of the government, and the limitation of the president's term, all work together to prevent any permanent coalescence of power in the hands of the president. Ironically, these factors make it all the more imperative to have a presidency capable of taking vigorous and direct action in crisis situations.

Some of the most disturbing aspects of political power within our system do not stem from the constitutional prerogatives of the president, but from coalitions of administrative agencies, congressional committees and other parts of the government with private interest groups which form closed policy subsystems. The "military-industrial complex" is one example of such a policy sphere. President Eisenhower warned against the domination of military and industrial elites in the policy process, and during his administration he stood firmly against overzealous impingement of military leaders in the formulation of public policy.

There are many policy subsystems apart from the military-industrial complex. In such areas as agriculture, the spheres of regulatory policy, and health, policy is outside of the purview of the president and within the hands of a relatively narrow set of interests, both governmental and private. A strong presidency is a countervailing force to these interest group clusters. The president is anything but a "constitutional dictator" when he confronts the almost impossible task of curbing the power of the groups within these specialized subsystems. There are those who, far from decrying the arbitrary powers of the president, feel that the office should be strengthened to bring some unity and overall planning to the amorphous forces of policy-making. President Nixon has made a major effort to concentrate power in the White House and to avoid bureaucratic duplication of effort.[8]

Statutory Limits
on the President

Just as the Constitution grants and limits powers to the president, Congress by statute may grant broad delegations of authority to the president, or it may decide to limit him strictly. One of the major limitations upon the legal

---

[8] For a discussion of this facet of the Nixon presidency see Chapter 8.

authority of the president comes from congressional restrictions in statutory law. Frequently Congress grants independent authority to administrative agencies to formulate policy, and at the same time limits presidential supervision over the agencies. In some cases Congress establishes agencies on an independent basis, outside of the president's jurisdiction. These independent agencies have limited accountability to the White House. The independent regulatory commissions, for example, are not accountable to the president for their day to day operations, or for their decisions. One exception is the awarding of international air routes by the Civil Aeronautics Board which, because of the international implications, is subject by statute to presidential veto. Although the president appoints the commissioners of the independent regulatory agencies, by and with the advice and consent of the Senate, it is difficult for him to remove them during their fixed term of office. Conditions of removal are established by statute, and generally require a demonstration of malfeasance in office before removal can be upheld. The president's appointment power to these agencies, however, is significant in that he can stack them with men favoring his point of view. Moreover, he does have the power to appoint the chairmen of all regulatory agencies except the Interstate Commerce Commission.

Outside of the area of independent regulatory agencies, Congress frequently grants independent powers to parts of the executive departments, which in the conduct of their broader activities are under presidential supervision. Those who feel that a strong presidency is vital to the preservation of the Republic seek to eliminate such congressional undermining of presidential authority within the bureaucracy. The President's Committee on Administrative Management in 1937, and the Hoover Commission of 1949 strongly recommended that Congress remove the numerous legal limits upon the president's authority over the administrative branch.

Whether the president is the recipient of broad congressional and constitutional delegations of authority, or whether his powers are legally curtailed, his real power does not depend solely upon these formal definitions of the office. It is determined by a number of informal factors that affect his power of persuasion over others. For instance, the president has complete legal authority over the Army Corps of Engineers, but traditionally because of the independent political constituency of the Corps, and its power base in Congress, the president has not been able to turn his legal authority into political power.

The president can get others to move for him when he holds the balance of political power within the constituency of the persons involved. His party in Congress will heed his requests if the disparate membership of the legislative party considers it to be in their collective interest to support the White House. Bureaucrats will heed the president if he is important to them for present or future trade-offs.

Theodore C. Sorensen has pointed out that the president is free to make a decision only:

1. Within the limits of permissibility; 2. Within the limits of available resources; 3. Within the limits of available time; 4. Within the limits of previous commitments; and 5. Within the limits of available information.[9]

The "limits of permissibility" refer to legal and constitutional restraints upon the president, and in the foreign area upon the acceptance of other nations where that is required to put a presidential decision into effect. A president, for example, cannot order other nations into war to support the United States unless they agree to become part of a collective effort, as was the case in the Korean war after United Nations involvement.

Although the context of the presidency points up the limitations upon the policy-making powers of the office, these powers pertain to the ability of the president to make effective decisions, what might loosely be called "good" decisions in terms of political realities, rather than the capacity of the office to make decisions at all. That is, the president is perfectly free to make whatever decisions he wants, but he may not see them implemented or, if they are put into effect, achieving the result that he originally intended. President Johnson was perfectly capable of escalating the Vietnam war, since the military went along with him, and he received the initial backing of Congress. He had all the constitutional and statutory authority he needed to wage the war. However, he was unable to control the series of events that occurred as a result of his decision. He could not control the government of South Vietnam, nor did his military policy eliminate the Viet Cong or bring North Vietnam to heel. His policy failed, not for lack of authority, but because he attempted to extend his power beyond his reach.

In the domestic sphere, presidents can and have ordered admin-

9 Theodore C. Sorensen, *Decision Making in the White House* (New York: Columbia University Press, 1963), p. 23.

istrative agencies to implement policies only to see their orders vanish in the bureaucratic maze. The limits upon the presidency pertain not to decision-making per se, but to effective and responsible decision-making. The responsibilities that have been placed upon the office demand that the president not waste his time tilting at windmills, but that he use whatever resources are at his command to perform adequately.

Growth of Presidential Responsibilities

What is "adequate performance" in the White House? An important part of the context within which the president must function is the expectations that people have concerning the responsibilities of the office. Virtually every group that is within the constituency of the president looks to the White House at one time or another for positive action, but this has not always been true. In the early days of the Republic, many people viewed the potential power of the presidency with caution, and men such as Thomas Jefferson (before he became president) viewed with alarm the possibility of an overly vigorous executive. Although the Constitution emerged as a Hamiltonian document, during the Constitutional Convention serious consideration was given to making the presidency a potentially weaker branch of the government. This would have resulted, for example, from proposals to make the executive dependent upon the election of the legislature.

Originally, the narrow electoral constituency of the president reduced popular expectations concerning the office, and gave to the president far less of a political base upon which to operate. Broadening the base of popular involvement in presidential elections did not immediately increase the prestige of the office; election statistics indicate that voter turnout in early presidential elections was less than half of that in congressional and gubernatorial elections. But the democratization of the office provided an important base for the expansion of presidential prerogatives, as well as inputs for an expanded policy-making role for the White House.

The modern presidency resulted from the culmination of many factors that made it evident that a strong presidency is necessary in order for the political system to survive. Repeated crises, and vigorous presidential responses to them established precedents for a strong executive. Time and time again it became evident that in certain kinds of crisis situations no other branch of the government was capable of providing the necessary political response. The present day responsibilities of the presidency have grown out of the inadequacies of other parts of the government in certain areas of public policy-making. In particular, the dominant role of the president in foreign and military affairs is based on a general recognition that the dispatch and secrecy necessary for the proper conduct of policy-making in these areas reside only in the president.

The most elaborate list of responsibilities assigned to the presidency is that enumerated by Clinton Rossiter in *The American Presidency*.[10] The jobs that Rossiter attributed to the presidency are truly imposing, and certainly could not possibly be carried out by one man acting alone. Under the Constitution, the president is Chief of State; that is, he must exercise the ceremonial functions of the government. Article II makes the president Chief Legislator and Chief Executive. Also stemming in part from Article II, the president is Chief Diplomat. He is Commander-in-Chief, a provision put into Article II to ensure civilian supremacy over the military.

Apart from these constitutional roles, the presidency has assumed a number of other responsibilities that have developed as events have unfolded. For example, he is considered to be responsible for the state of the economy, making him "manager of prosperity." He is the head of his political party, reflecting the deep involvement of the presidency in politics. His party role requires that he hold together the national party organization, and do everything that he can to ensure the election of party members. As a result of the cold war that ensued after World War II, the president has become the leader of the free nations of the world, because of the predominant position of the United States among non-Communist countries. The president is expected to be the voice of the people, to express the feelings of the nation at appropriate times. For example, President Franklin D. Roosevelt voiced the anger of the American people after the attack on Pearl Harbor in 1941. After natural disasters, people look to the president to aid them by declaring a state of emergency and releasing federal funds for reconstruction.

Although people expect the president to perform these various policy-making roles, he does not necessarily have the power to carry them out. There is often a gap between expectations and reality, which may cause disillusionment with the president and with government itself. The president can perform virtually none

---

10 Clinton Rossiter, *The American Presidency*, 2nd ed. (New York: Harcourt Brace Jovanovich, 1960).

of these roles without the cooperation of coordinate branches of the government, particularly the bureaucracy.

Need for Presidential Leadership

Because of the multiple responsibilities of the presidency, the modern conception of the office is that effectiveness requires strength, vigor, and a positive approach on the part of the incumbent. People expect leadership in their president. Good presidents use the office to its fullest capacity and capabilities. They employ the authority of the office in combination with its political power to initiate and advance important legislation, to attempt to control the bureaucracy, and to take necessary action to deal with foreign and domestic problems. People agree now more than at the time it was written with Alexander Hamilton's statement in *The Federalist, No. 70*:

Energy in the executive is a leading character in the definition of good government. It is essential to the protection of the community against foreign attacks; it is not less essential to the study of administration of the laws, to the protection of property against those irregular and high-handed combinations, which sometimes interrupt the ordinary course of justice, to the security of liberty against the enterprises and assaults of ambition, of faction, and of anarchy.

. . . A feeble executive implies a feeble execution of government. A feeble execution is but another phrase for a bad execution; and a government ill-executed, whatever it may be in theory, must be in practice a bad government.

Energy in the executive must be directed for "good," not "bad" ends. A major dilemma of the modern presidency is how to balance the need for independent action with the maintenance of responsible presidential decision-making. Perhaps too many policy-making responsibilities have been placed on the shoulders of the president. The great visibility of the White House makes it impossible for presidents to shift the burden of decision-making to others, as Congress does when it delegates authority to the White House or the bureaucracy.

Presidents tend to be blamed for those things that go wrong during their administrations. But many of the most important policy decisions that are made in those areas commonly attributed to the presidency are made by parts of the government outside of the White House. Realistic expectations concerning the policy role of the president would not expect him to be able to single-handedly bring about significant shifts in the course of public policy. The limits upon the office are too great. The expectations of most people are too high concerning what the president is able to accomplish. A reevaluation of what constitutes "proper" performance in the White House should put less emphasis upon the policy roles of the president and more upon his general leadership posture and usefulness to those other parts of the government that are deeply involved in the formulation of policy, particularly the bureaucracy. And where the president is capable of policy leadership, as in foreign and military affairs, the possibility of personal decision-making should be avoided at all costs, because this will mean that the nature of the decision will depend upon the character, particularly the emotional makeup, of the man who occupies the office. A rational decision-making process should be used, where various viewpoints are weighed.

The confusing and complex context of the presidency cannot help but befuddle new occupants of the office. The president finds that upon his shoulders have been placed numerous and often conflicting responsibilities, but he does not necessarily have the power to meet his obligations successfully. Each man brings with him his own personal equipment, which may or may not make a strong imprint upon the office.

Effects of the Political Culture upon Presidential Policy-making

Although the presidency is an institution, composed of numerous staff aides in the Executive Office of the President, including the White House staff and the Office of Management and Budget, there is little doubt that presidential character has a considerable impact upon the performance of the office.[11] Presidential character may not only have a profound effect upon the policies, but also upon the responsibilities of the White House that do not directly pertain to policy-making. Presidential style, the way the president appears to the people, and moral leadership are deeply affected by presidential character. These attributes of the presidency have an important indirect effect on policy-making.

---

[11] See James D. Barber, *The Presidential Character* (Englewood Cliffs, N.J.: Prentice-Hall, 1972).

James Barber has listed recurrent themes in American political culture that set the stage for presidential action and deeply influence the way in which presidents perceive their responsibilities.

Americans vastly over-rate the president's power—and they are likely to continue to do so. The logic of that feeling is clear enough: the president is at the top and therefore he must be able to dominate those below him. The psychology is even more complicated. The whole popular ethic of struggle, the onward and upward, fight–today–to–win–to–morrow spirit gets played out vicariously as people watch their president. The president should be working, trying, striving forward—living out of his life what makes life meaningful for the citizen at work. Life is tough, life is earnest. A tough, earnest president symbolizes and represents that theme, shows by the thrust of his deeds that the fight is worth it after all. Will he stand up to his—and our—enemies, or will he collapse? Has he the guts to endure the heat in the kitchen? Will he (will he please) play out for us the drama that leads through suffering to salvation?

To a character attuned to power, this popular theme then can convey a heavy message . . . for Wilson, Hoover, Johnson and Nixon and for active–negative presidents in the future, the temptation to stand and fight receives wide support from the culture.[12]

Barber defines "active–negative" presidents as those who bring a Protestant Ethic attitude to the office, devote a great deal of energy to their tasks, but because of inner struggles demanding perfection a great deal of the energy is misdirected. To these kinds of men the tasks of the presidency are painful, not enjoyable. This belief in the need to do what is right, regardless of how painful it is, is reflected in the following passage from President Johnson's memoirs:

Every president must act on problems as they come to him. He must search out the best information available. He can seek the counsel of men whose wisdom and experience and judgment he values. But in the end, the president must decide, and he must do so on the basis of his judgment of what is best—for his nation and for the world. Throughout these years of crucial decisions I was sustained by the memory of my predecessors who had also borne the most painful duty of a president— to lead our country in a time of war. I recalled often the words of one of these men, Woodrow Wilson, who in the dark days of 1917 said: "it

---

[12] Ibid., p. 446.

is a fearful thing to lead this great peaceful people into war . . . but the right is more precious than peace."[13]

Another attribute of the political culture that Barber suggests is important is people's need for affection, and their focus upon politicians and particularly the president as a charismatic and affectionate leader. This constant stroking of the president can bolster his self-image and may lead either to striving for greater and greater power, or simply to passive and pleasant acceptance. The fact that people seek in the presidency both a friend and a charismatic leader affects the style of presidents, who therefore seek to strike the right pose to fulfill the image that the public has of them and they of themselves. This part of the political culture, by concentrating upon presidential style, tends to deemphasize the policy role of the president.

Another important factor in the political culture, according to Barber, is that "in our culture the religious-monarchical focus of the presidency—a tendency to see the office as sort of divine-right kingship—gets emphasized . . . in a quest for legitimacy."[14] To operate in a legitimate fashion, presidents must not go too far in attempting to change the rules of the game of the political system. Legitimacy can also be sullied by any demeaning of the "image of the president as dignified, episcopal, plain and clean in character. Part of the public mind always realizes that the president is only a man, with all man's normal ability to moral error; part wants to deny that, to foist on the president a priestliness setting him above the congregation."[15]

After the Democratic Convention of 1972, when vice-presidential candidate Thomas Eagleton of Missouri revealed that between 1960 and 1966 he had been hospitalized three times for nervous exhaustion and fatigue, pressure was immediately put upon him by politicians and influential newspapers to step down because of what they felt would inevitably be an adverse public reaction. Actually, public opinion polls revealed a great deal of sympathy for Senator Eagleton, and although a certain amount of voter-switching because of the relevation of his "mental illness" was indicated, there was no immediate strong indication of a large-scale desertion of the party because he was on the ticket. Nevertheless, the reaction of

---

[13] Lyndon B. Johnson, *The Vantage Point* (New York: Holt, Rinehart and Winston, 1971), p. 531.
[14] Barber, *The Presidential Character*, pp. 450–51.
[15] Ibid., p. 451.

Democratic leaders and influential newspapers reflected the idea that the presidency might be "demeaned" by such a man, and that any person with such a past history might not be capable of fulfilling the responsibilities of the office. The real reason that Senator Eagleton was asked to step down was that he did not fit the classical image of the president as a man invulnerable to ordinary afflictions. The "legitimacy" of the office might be reduced if he were to occupy it.

When in office, presidential policy-making is affected when presidents are highly aware of the need to maintain the image of the office as a legitimate, almost nonpolitical institution. Examples of presidents straying from this rule occurred during the New Deal Administration, when Franklin Roosevelt attempted to "pack" the Supreme Court by pressing Congress to pass a law that would have given him the authority to appoint a new justice for every justice over seventy years of age. This was widely attacked in the press as being an "unconstitutional" plan, entirely inappropriate for the president. President Truman's seizure of the steel mills in 1952 invoked a similar, if not so intense, response. And, as the Vietnam war pressed on, increasing criticism was directed at Presidents Johnson and Nixon for abusing the authority of the president as Commander-in-Chief by directing our military forces into inappropriate foreign engagements.

The image of the president as High Priest of the political system raises support for the White House among many elements of the population, because of reverence for the institution and the man who occupies it. A king is criticized if he behaves in an un-kingly way, but at the same time, being king, he has greater latitude of behavior than ordinary individuals. One possible result of the Watergate scandals may be to destroy in large part the reverence that Americans have traditionally held for the presidency. Clearly the priestly character of the office did not rub off on President Nixon, when, after firing special Watergate prosecutor Archibald Cox, approximately 50 percent of the electorate favored impeaching him. It may take many years for the sullied image that Watergate has given to the White House to wear off.

THE PRESIDENCY
IN OPERATION

What should be the role of the president in policy-making? Clearly the office cannot be expected single-handedly to meet all of the responsibilities that have been given to it. As long as the political system remains highly fragmented, the presidency is going to stand out symbolically as the focal point of action. There seems to be little question of whether or not the president should be powerful, at least in the domestic realm. From the President's Committee on Administrative Management in 1937 to the present, presidential commissions and task forces have recommended that the White House be given vastly increased staff assistance to meet presidential responsibilities. "The president needs help," has been the repeated theme of these commissions.

Presidential Staff and the Executive Office

On the basis of recommendations of the President's Committee on Administrative Management, the Executive Office of the President was created in 1939 to assist the president in developing policy, and in dealing with his multiple administrative responsibilities. The Office of Management and Budget (OMB), originally the Bureau of the Budget, is the key component in the Executive Office. It is responsible for sifting the numerous legislative and budgetary proposals that come from administrative agencies before they go to Congress.

Before the Bureau of the Budget was originally given this responsibility, it was common practice for administrative agencies to go directly to Congress to recommend legislation and budgets dealing with matters under their jurisdiction. Today, OMB not only carefully reviews the legislative proposals coming from the bureaucracy, but also holds tight reins on the budgetary proposals of the agencies. No agency can legally submit a budget proposal to the legislature without first going through OMB.

It is difficult to say to what extent OMB really dominates the bureaucracy. Administrative agencies are often more capable of dominating the president and OMB than vice-versa, due to the agencies' political power and expertise in the policy-making areas with which they deal. Specialization and political power are characteristics of administrative agencies. To deal with the bureaucracy, the president and his staff must be able to counterbalance these forces by developing independent political power and expert knowledge. This is a very difficult task, because expert knowledge in many policy-making areas is virtually monopolized by specialists in the bureaucracy and outside interest groups. To get advice that is "independent" of experts in the field is impossible by definition.

Regardless of the existence of procedural formalities requiring the channeling of legislative and budgetary proposals through OMB, the major source of OMB inputs remains the bureaucracy. OMB is often able to do nothing more than coordinate the many complex proposals coming to it. Where the president knows his own mind, and has a definite policy that he wishes to see carried out, OMB can be his agent; but in the absence of clear presidential viewpoints, OMB is left alone in its confrontations with the bureaucracy.

It is vitally important for the president to be able to exercise some measure of control over the bureaucracy if he is to have any effect upon public policy, because it is within administrative agencies that policies are formulated and carried out. Merely coordinating the policy-making activities of agencies does not put the president in an ascendant position. In practice, the president is only one part of the governmental system, and must enter what is often unequal combat in attempting to persuade other branches, including the bureaucracy, to follow his wishes.

The staff of the president contains several other agencies besides OMB. The White House office consists of the personal staff of the president. The president can rely upon his personal staff to any degree that he sees fit, just as he can utilize any components of the Executive Office as he wishes. Presidents from Eisenhower to Nixon have relied a great deal upon their personal staff, in some cases to the exclusion of other parts of the Executive Office as well as the Cabinet. President Nixon not only relied upon his personal staff, but delegated substantial decision-making powers to them. Former White House aides John Ehrlichman and H. R. Haldeman ruthlessly wielded power in the name of the president. Watergate was partially a result of the president's failure to oversee his personal staff operation.

In the foreign policy area, Henry Kissinger totally dominated foreign policy-making in his capacity as advisor to the president. Again, President Nixon was using Kissinger not solely as an advisor but as a person to whom he delegated considerable policy-making responsibilities. After Kissinger became secretary of state he continued to be foreign policy advisor to the president, resulting in a great deal more coordination between State and the White House than had previously existed.

Kissinger operated in conjunction with the National Security Council, created by the National Security Act of 1947. This Council, consisting of the president, the vice-president, secretary of state, secretary of defense, and director of the Office of Emergency Preparedness is convened by the president when he feels that it can give him useful advice concerning foreign and military policy matters. In fact, during critical foreign policy crises the president convenes whatever group of advisors he feels most appropriate, which may or may not include all of the members of the National Security Council. In other words, he does not rely upon the formal mechanism of the National Security Council for foreign policy advice.

The Council of Economic Advisors was established in 1946 to aid the president in planning economic policy. This three-member Council issues a yearly economic report to the president and the Congress assessing the state of the economy. The Office of Emergency Preparedness is a little-known component of the Executive Office, and is involved in planning for possible emergencies. For example, it coordinates federal activities assisting states that have been hit by major disasters. In addition, it plans for the eventuality of military attacks, listing bomb shelters and evacuation routes from cities.

President Nixon, in 1970, reorganized the Executive Office of the President and created the Domestic Council. The Domestic Council includes the members of the Cabinet with the exceptions of the secretaries of state and defense. The Council is supposed to plan and to coordinate domestic policy recommendations to the president. Ehrlichman, before his demise, was executive director of the Council, which met on a fairly regular basis. However, like the Cabinet, it is not an effective planning body and after the exit of Ehrlichman its importance within the Executive Office declined.

President Nixon's seemingly endless passion to create bureaucratic staff agencies led also to the establishment of the Office of Consumer Affairs in 1971. About all that this office does is issue a newsletter advising consumers of developments in industry and government that presumably affect their interests. President Nixon even created a Council on International Economic Policy in 1971 and added it to the Executive Office. This council consists of Cabinet members concerned with international economic policy, the director of OMB and the chairman of the Council of Economic Advisors, and, of course, Henry Kissinger. It goes without saying that the Council is to advise the president on international economic policy. However, in reality, this Council, like the Domestic Council, is far too large and unwieldly to be an effective policy instrument. Less significant components of the Executive Office include the

Council on Environmental Quality created by the National Environmental Policy Act of 1969, and the Office of Intergovernmental Relations established by the president in 1969 to give Spiro Agnew something to do (he was the director of the Office). Minor parts of the Executive Office also include the Office of Science and Technology, and the Office of the Special Representative for Trade Negotiations, both created in 1962. The Office of Science and Technology is supposed to advise the president on science policy and to conduct various programs which evaluate major science policies, and to help coordinate federal activities in science and technology. The Office of the Special Representative for Trade Negotiations advises the president concerning trade agreements and supervises trade negotiations with foreign countries.

Although the Executive Office of the President is theoretically an extension of the man who occupies the White House, in fact it has grown into a bureaucracy that is often independent of the man it is supposed to serve. This is particularly true under President Nixon, who tends to delegate most of his responsibilities to staff assistants. A remarkable instance of this was during the October 1973 confrontation between the United States and the Soviet Union over the Arab-Israeli war. At that time President Nixon essentially delegated his foreign and military policy responsibilities to Henry Kissinger.[16] And, as noted above, preceding the Watergate fiasco Ehrlichman and Haldeman had a free hand to develop and coordinate domestic policy in the name of the president. Unless the president keeps tight reins on his staff, it can act irresponsibly. The staff is not politically accountable to the electorate, as is the president. It can become in effect an invisible and irresponsible presidency, and can control in many areas what the president sees and hears, thereby controlling his actions. The president's staff certainly greatly affects his perception of the world around him.

The Presidency as an
Instrument of Policy Innovation

In most areas of public policy the president cannot significantly innovate unless there is substantial support both within and without the government for such action. Broadly based forces of change focus upon the presidency. This is what caused the election of President Roosevelt in 1932. It is when

---

[16] See the *New York Times*, November 21, 1973, p. 1.

the presidency is riding the crest of a wave of change, such as occurs after critical elections in which major shifts take place in voter alignments from one party to the other, that the White House can be the catalyst for new directions in public policy. Critical elections do not occur because large parts of the public have specific ideas of policies they want to see put into effect. They occur because voters feel that something has to be done which is different from the policies the party in power has supported.

The electorate was discontented, to say the least, in 1932 because of the Depression, and naturally blamed the inaction of President Hoover. A variety of proposals were made to Hoover by experts within and without government as to how he might meet the crisis of the Depression, but those who were unemployed and marching in the streets did not know of these nor did they have specific policy recommendations of their own. They only wanted to see Hoover out, and someone, anyone, in to replace him. At such times the president must offer leadership to shape new programs, although this is no guarantee that they will be accepted by Congress, the Supreme Court, or the bureaucracy.

President Franklin Roosevelt was the major force behind the New Deal, but it took a long time before New Deal legislation was acceptable to Congress and not declared unconstitutional by the Supreme Court. Once Roosevelt's "honeymoon" with Congress was over in 1933, he met increasing resistance to his proposals in the legislature. Although a large majority of the voters supported the president, as revealed in his landslide election in 1936, they were supporting the man more than the specific content of his policy proposals. Regardless of Roosevelt's continuing frustrations on the domestic front in policy innovation, there is little doubt that it was his tenacity in the pursuit of his goals that brought the New Deal from the realm of ideas to reality.

The Nixon presidency attempted to innovate in domestic policy through revenue sharing, and in his first term through the establishment of a guaranteed national income. The former will most likely be disbanded and the latter never passed Congress. In foreign policy the establishment of relations with Communist China constituted a major change. However, the innovations of the Nixon administration seem very transient because there is not the necessary underlying support for the kinds of changes Nixon sought, which is the reason for disbandment of some of his programs and outright failure of others. The era of FDR has been labeled "the Roosevelt Revolution." [17] No such appellation can be given to any president since.

The Exercise of
Presidential Prerogatives

Today the president, while continuing to be frustrated in much of his domestic pursuits, nevertheless possesses the power of life and death over the nation. This is a true paradox, because with relative ease a president can involve the United States in a major war that might mean the destruction not only of this country, but of all mankind; however, he cannot secure the passage in Congress of the most trivial legislation, nor necessarily receive the support of the bureaucracy for the implementation of his own policy initiatives.

These far-reaching prerogative life and death decisions reflect a distinctly personal attribute of presidential power, for they are often dependent solely on the man, his perceptions of the world and his character.[18] Perhaps the most important issue of today in relation to presidential power and policy-making pertains to this area where the president acts in a personal capacity to shape the course of the nation.

Presidential discretion in the military and foreign policy spheres is generally accepted. However, this general compliance has been punctuated from time to time with criticisms that the president has too much power. During the twentieth century the actions of all presidents that have involved the United States in wars have been severely criticized by various groups. Woodrow Wilson was subject to criticism for leading the country into World War I, and the initiatives taken by Franklin D. Roosevelt to aid our allies against Germany before World War II were criticized by various isolationist groups as inappropriate and exceeding the constitutional authority of the office. One of the main campaign issues in 1952 was the Korean war; the Republicans implied that once again the Democratic "war party" had improperly led the United States into a foreign involvement.

---

[17] Mario Einandi, *The Roosevelt Revolution* (New York: Harcourt Brace Jovanovich, 1959).

[18] For a brilliant analysis of the way in which presidential character affects decisions see Barber, *The Presidential Character*.

The Korean Decision   President Truman's decision to send troops to Korea without consulting the U.N. or Congress was at first generally accepted by congressional leaders. But as the war dragged on, and American commitments in Asia began to mount, along with casualties, so did criticism of the president's discretionary authority. On January 5, 1951, Senator Robert Taft in a major Senate speech accused the administration of formulating defense policy since the end of World War II without consulting either Congress or the people. Taft asserted that without authority the president had "involved us in the Korean war and without authority he apparently has now adopted a similar policy in Europe." A few days after Taft's speech, Senator Wherry introduced, with the support of his fellow Republicans in the Senate, a resolution that expressed the sense of the Senate that American ground forces should not be sent to Europe in the absence of a congressional policy relating to the issue.

In characteristic style, President Truman contended that he could and would send troops wherever he wanted without consultation with the legislature. During 1951, hearings were held by Senate committees on alleged plans of the secretary of defense to send more troops to Europe. Resolutions were reported out of these committees asking that the president not take action on troop deployments abroad without first consulting the Senate and House Foreign Relations, Affairs and Armed Services Committees. Intensive debate ensued and attempts were made by Republicans to amend the resolutions to increase congressional control over the president. The Senate finally passed a resolution which stated that no more than four divisions could be sent to Europe without Senate approval. President Truman hailed the action as an endorsement of his troop plans, and skillfully avoided the question of Senate approval. The controversy over the scope of presidential authority and discretion in military and foreign policy-making was a precursor to Vietnam. President Johnson's decisions were based on clear historical precedents as was the political feedback.

The Vietnam Decision   The Vietnam war once again gave rise to extensive discussion within Congress about the proper role of the legislature in the exercise of the war power. Quick to give President Johnson his Gulf of Tonkin Resolution, many congressmen later regretted their vote, for it was widely interpreted as giving Johnson blanket authority to pursue whatever military action he wished in Southeast Asia. The president himself used the Resolution as a reminder to legislative critics that he was pursuing the war with the consent of Congress.

The mounting congressional criticism of President Johnson's Vietnam policies continued into the Nixon administration. President Nixon's decisions to invade Cambodia in 1970 and Laos in 1971 provoked particularly heated congressional opposition. After the United States assisted the South Vietnamese invasion of Laos, Senator Edmund S. Muskie of Maine expressed the views of many of his colleagues when he stated: "I think that the use of combat air support . . . goes beyond the spirit of any policies that Congress has endorsed. . . . And, I think before we get involved in that kind of activity in Cambodia and Laos, the president ought to come to Congress to ask for its support, define his proposals, so that we can consider it on its merits." [19]

Prior to President Nixon's unilateral actions in Cambodia and Laos, various resolutions had passed Congress attempting to limit the president's war-making discretion. In June of 1969, the Senate passed a resolution much like that passed during the Korean war, declaring it to be the sense of the Senate that no further military commitments overseas should be undertaken without the consent of Congress. By a vote of 288–38 the House on November 16, 1970, passed a joint resolution stating that, "whenever feasible" the president should consult with Congress before involving the country in an armed conflict. If it is not feasible for him to do so, then the resolution stated that he should at least promptly report his actions to Congress, which presumably would give legislators a small, if belated, role in the decision-making process.

During 1971, the Senate considered additional ways to curb presidential war-making authority. Characteristic of the various proposals made was a resolution introduced by Senator John C. Stennis (D. Miss., chairman of Senate Armed Services Committee). The Stennis Resolution would prevent the president from involving United States forces overseas except: (1) to repel an armed attack on the country or on American troops; (2) to prevent or defend against a nuclear attack if the president had clear and convincing evidence that such an attack was imminent; (3) finally, to evacuate

---

[19] *Congressional Quarterly Weekly Report*, vol. 29, no. 7 (February 12, 1971), p. 363.

United States citizens from a foreign country if the government of that country would no longer protect them.

In these categories where the president would be authorized to use troops without consulting Congress first, he would under the terms of the Resolution have been required to give a "detailed account of the reasons of so using the Armed Forces" to Congress, which in turn would be given thirty days to decide whether or not to extend or terminate the president's authority. Therefore, specific congressional authorization would be required for the continuation of any war beyond thirty days. The introduction of this Resolution by Senator Stennis prompted Senator Jacob Javits (R., N.Y.) to remark, "I say we are witnessing a miracle. . . . it is both a miracle of the human personality and a miracle of this Chamber." [20] For his part, Senator Stennis noted that the Resolution did not reflect his views on the Vietnam conflict for it expressly did not apply to that war. But, he said, "the war power should be reasserted by Congress, for . . . the decision to make wars is too big a decision for one mind to make and too awesome a responsibility for one man to bear. There must be a collective judgment given and collective responsibility shared." [21]

Responding to the Stennis Resolution and other similar proposals, Secretary of State William P. Rogers testified before the Senate Foreign Relations Committee in 1971 that the proposals went too far in limiting the discretion of the president to deploy armed forces. The president, Rogers stated, should be able to take immediate action without consulting Congress, and without necessarily having to report to Congress afterwards. Early attempts to curb presidential authority were unsuccessful, as had been their predecessors; however, in 1972 the Senate finally passed by a margin of only two votes (49–47) a resolution calling for the withdrawal of all troops from Vietnam within four months, provided the North Vietnamese released American prisoners. If the House of Representatives had gone along with the Senate (which it did not do) in this resolution, great pressure would have been exerted upon President Nixon to conform to congressional wishes; however, it is doubtful if Nixon would have changed his course of action in Vietnam, claiming presidential prerogatives as Commander-

---

[20] *Congressional Quarterly Weekly Report*, vol. 29, no. 21 (May 21, 1971), p. 1103.
[21] Ibid.

in-Chief for ignoring congressional legislation in this area. In 1973 Nixon was forced to stop bombing Cambodia on August 15, a deadline set by both Houses of Congress, but only after Congress threatened to cut off appropriations for the entire federal government if the president continued the bombing.

The most serious congressional incursion upon the war-making authority of the president occurred on November 7, 1973 when Congress overrode a Nixon veto of the War Powers Resolution of 1973, first passed by Congress in October of that year. Under the terms of this resolution the president "in every possible instance" must consult with Congress before involving the armed forces in hostilities. The resolution requires regular presidential consultation with Congress during war to keep the legislature informed of presidential actions. Where the president orders troops into the war without a declaration of war from Congress, he must submit to the Speaker of the House and to the president pro tem of the Senate a report within forty-eight hours setting forth:

1. The circumstances necessitating the introduction of United States armed forces;

2. The constitutional and legislative authority under which such introduction took place;

3. The estimated scope and duration of the hostilities or involvement.

After this report is submitted to Congress, the president must terminate within 60 days the use of United States armed forces unless Congress has declared war or given other specific authorization for the use of the armed forces, or has extended by law the 60-day period or is physically unable to meet as the result of an armed attack upon the country. The initial 60-day period during which the president can take independent action cannot be extended by Congress under the resolution for more than thirty additional days. President Nixon's veto of the bill was overridden by a vote of 284–135 in the House, and 75–18 in the Senate, indicating strong congressional sentiment to limit the president's war-making powers. The 1973 resolution would have prevented President Truman's unilateral action in sending troops to Korea. However, it can be argued that the Gulf of Tonkin Resolution met the conditions of the War Powers Resolution. Certainly President Johnson would have interpreted it in that way. However, had the War Powers Resolution been in existence Congress might have been far more careful in its terminology, recognizing that there was a possibility that a resolution such as the Gulf of Tonkin could and undoubtedly would be used by the president as a blanket authorization to engage in war in Southeast Asia.

Presidential Policy-making and Public Opinion

History reveals that presidents are least influenced by the public in military and foreign policy-making. This is partially because of the amorphous and ambiguous nature of public attitudes concerning policy issues in this area. Presidents may completely ignore public opinion polls that clearly demonstrate opposition to a particular foreign or military policy, in the belief that under certain circumstances it is the responsibility of the president to do what is "right" regardless of political opposition. President Johnson quoted fondly the words of Woodrow Wilson: "It is a fearful thing to lead this great peaceful people into war. . . . but the right is more precious than peace." President Johnson did not waver, until the very last days of his first full term of office, in his Vietnam policies, and even then there was very little evidence that substantial changes were taking place in his mind regarding what should be done in Vietnam.

Until recently, presidents didn't have the advantage of public opinion polls to tell them what the majority might support in the way of foreign or military actions, making it far easier to justify virtually any policies. When President Lincoln made those critical decisions which provided a spark igniting the Civil War, he was not listening to national public opinion, or even to strong northern opinion opposing the war. Woodrow Wilson knew that much of his popularity would vanish if he led the country into World War I, and he even promised during the election campaign of 1916 to stay out of foreign involvements. Nevertheless, as soon as the election was over he made the necessary decisions causing American entry into the war.

Major decisions made by Franklin D. Roosevelt in the 1930's to draw the country away from its isolationist stance and into a posture that would inevitably involve it in World War II were not made on the basis of electoral opinion, nor were they in any way geared to the electoral process. Roosevelt, like Wilson before him, promised in the campaign of 1940 that Americans would not be involved in foreign wars, but he knew that such involvement was inevitable, and the "right" course of action.

President Truman, like his predecessors, made major decisions on military aid and involvement in Greece, Turkey, and Korea. All of these decisions were made on the basis of his own judgment, fortified by inputs of foreign governments, the bureaucracy, and from advisors within the presidency itself. President Truman told President Johnson that "his confrontation of those international challenges—particularly in Korea—had been horrors for him politically, bringing his popularity down from a high of 87 percent to a low of 23 percent." [22]

The Johnson presidency received a wide range of inputs in the domestic arena, from both governmental and private sources. President Johnson never lost sight, however, of his leadership role. He noted in his memoirs that "I saw my primary task as building the consensus throughout the country, so that we could stop bickering and quarreling and get on with the job at hand. Unfortunately, the word consensus came to be profoundly misunderstood." [23] He continued that to him obtaining a consensus did not mean reaching for the lowest common denominator of public opinion by simply attempting to support programs acceptable to the majority of the people. Rather, consensus meant:

. . . First, deciding what needed to be done regardless of the political implications and second, convincing a majority of the Congress and the American people of the necessity of doing those things. I was president of the United States at a crucial point in its history, and if a president does not lead he is abandoning the prime and indispensible obligation of the presidency.[24]

The President and Congress

Johnson applied his general philosophy of leadership in both the domestic and international arenas. "Deciding what needed to be done" involved essentially internal presidential decision-making processes, and inputs from the executive branch. After the exhaustion of this procedure, the next step was to convince Congress of the correctness of the course of action decided upon or already taken. Although there were extensive

---

[22] Lyndon B. Johnson, *The Vantage Point*, p. 31.
[23] Ibid., p. 27.
[24] Ibid., p. 28.

congressional inputs upon the formulation of many of Johnson's programs, he looked upon Congress not as a partner, but as a necessary ally because of its authority over legislation. If congressional inputs had to be taken into account in order to get a law passed, then they shaped the drafting of the legislation by the executive branch. However, in no case did Johnson allow potentially strong congressional opposition to deter him in a course that he considered to be essential and right for the nation. For example, he noted in his memoirs:

Under our system of government, with its clearly defined separation of powers, the greatest threat to the Chief Executive's right to 'govern' comes traditionally from the Congress. Congress is jealous of its prerogatives. All too often jealousy turns into a stubborn refusal to cooperate in any way with the Chief Executive.

The Congress had been in such a mood from the first day that John Kennedy took office in 1961. . . . An entire program of social legislation proposed by President Kennedy—from aid to education to food stamps to civil rights—remain bottled up in committee while the Congress defiantly refused to budge or act in any way. . . .

We were, in my opinion, facing a real crisis, and it was more than a crisis of unfulfilled needs throughout the nation. There was also a crisis of confidence in our system of government. There was a clear reason for moving forward, and moving with dispatch and energy; for acting while the sobering influence of national tragedy caused men in all walks of life to think of the country's interest rather than their own.[25]

Johnson pressed a recalcitrant Congress for a wide range of legislation that he felt was in the national interest.

While President Johnson could not afford to ignore Congress in the domestic field, in the international arena he had far greater initiative. Although he proclaimed an interest in gaining congressional support for his foreign policy actions, he did not really consider such support a necessary precursor to the implementation of his decisions.

The history of the Gulf of Tonkin Resolution, passed by Congress in August 1964, reveals the true relationship between president and Congress in the foreign policy area. At 11 a.m. on August 4, 1964, a message was received by the Pentagon that two United States destroyers were being attacked by North Vietnamese tor-

---

[25] Ibid., pp. 33–34.

pedo boats. Immediately the Joint Chiefs selected target options for reprisal air strikes, drawn from a list that had been prepared as a contingency plan in May of 1964. A National Security Council meeting had been previously scheduled for 12 o'clock on August 4. The Tonkin Gulf crisis was discussed briefly at that meeting, and according to Johnson's memoirs, after the meeting his principal advisors unanimously recommended retaliation for what had been a second strike against the United States naval vessels off the coast of Vietnam. President Johnson agreed with his advisors, and "we decided on air strikes against North Vietnamese P. T. boats and their bases plus a strike on one oil depot." [26] According to *The Pentagon Papers*, while President Johnson was at lunch with his advisors (Rusk, McNamara, Vance, McCone, and Bundy) the director of the Joint Chiefs of Staff telephoned McNamara reporting that the Joint Chiefs had unanimously agreed on the nature of the retaliatory action that should be taken. The recommendation of the Joint Chiefs was in fact the decision that was unanimously endorsed by the president's advisors and supported by the president himself.[27]

President Johnson officially ordered the reprisals at a second National Security Council meeting early in the afternoon. After a short delay, due to uncertainties regarding whether or not an attack on the destroyers had actually occurred, the formal execution orders for retaliation were sent to Honolulu at 4:49 p.m., specifying that within approximately two-and-one-half hours United States aircraft carriers were to launch their planes for the attack.[28] At the second National Security Council meeting on August 4, it was decided that a congressional resolution of support should be immediately sought, and with this in mind the president met with sixteen congressional leaders from both parties at approximately 6:45 p.m. By this time, of course, the decision to launch a retaliatory strike had already been made on the basis of plans drawn up months earlier. According to Johnson's memoirs, at this meeting with congressional leaders:

I told them that I believed a congressional resolution of support for our entire position in Southeast Asia was necessary and would strengthen

---

[26] Ibid., p. 114.
[27] See Neil Sheehan, "The Covert War in Tonkin Gulf: February–August, 1964," in *The Pentagon Papers* (New York: Bantam Books, 1971), p. 262.
[28] Ibid., pp. 262–63.

our hand. I said that we might be forced into further action, and that I did not "want to go in unless Congress goes in with me." At this meeting "McNamara described in detail what had happened in the Gulf of Tonkin and what we proposed to do." I then read a statement that I planned to deliver to the American people later in the evening.[29]

Whether or not the congressmen present were fully aware that the formal order had been issued for the attack, and that the planes were in fact to be airborne while the meeting was taking place, is not fully clear although it can be inferred that they were apprised that the decision had been made. This is confirmed by *The Pentagon Papers*, which reported that the president "told them that because of the second unprovoked attack on the American destroyers, he had decided to launch reprisal air strikes against the North and to ask for a congressional resolution. . . ."[30] Presented with this *fait accompli*, the congressional leaders had no alternative but to support the president. As President Johnson noted, at the conclusion of the meeting:

I went around the table asking each Senator and Representative for his frank opinion. Each expressed his whole-hearted endorsement of our course of action and of the proposed resolution.
   "I think it will be passed overwhelmingly," said Congressman Charles Halleck.
   "I will support it," said Senator Fulbright.
   At the close of the meeting I felt encouraged by the show of solidarity and support. As Speaker McCormack said near the end of our discussion, we were presenting a "united front to the world."[31]

During the Cuban Missile Crisis, President Kennedy also consulted with congressional leaders after the internal executive decision-making processes had come to the conclusion that a blockade of Cuba was the suitable response to the Soviet Union. At no time during the deliberations leading to this decision did President Kennedy or his staff feel that it was appropriate to extend the discussions to include congressional leaders. The decision was made on the basis of inputs from presidential advisors, the Joint Chiefs of Staff, several members of the Cabinet, and a few other selected

---

29 Johnson, *The Vantage Point*, pp. 115–116.
30 *The Pentagon Papers*, p. 263.
31 Johnson, *The Vantage Point*, p. 117.

individuals from the executive branch, and Vice-President Johnson.[32] This group reflected the spectrum of views on what action should be taken, from those few who felt no action was required to those who wanted to take the most drastic military reprisals against Cuba.

After settling upon the decision to carry out the blockade, President Kennedy informed those members of the Cabinet not present during the deliberations of the crisis and the decision that had been made. After this, and shortly before he was to announce his decision in a nationwide address, the president called in congressional leaders and informed them for the first time of the crisis and what action he was going to take. They reacted sharply, as Robert Kennedy describes:

Many congressional leaders were sharp in their criticism. They felt that the president should take more forceful action, a military attack or an invasion, and that the blockade was far too weak a response. Senator Richard B. Russell of Georgia said that he could not live with himself if he did not say in the strongest possible terms how important it was that we act with greater strength than the president was contemplating.

Senator J. William Fulbright of Arkansas also strongly advised military action rather than such a weak step as the blockade. Others said that they were skeptical but would remain publicly silent, only because it was such a dangerous hour for the country.[33]

The president carefully explained to the congressional leaders that military action might produce devastating consequences, and therefore he was not willing to take such a gamble until he had exhausted all other possible courses of action. The initial militant reaction of most of the congressional leaders was, according to Robert Kennedy, similar to the first reactions of the executive group upon hearing of the missiles. It is quite possible that if the congressmen had been consulted over a longer period of time, and put into a position where they would have had to bear part of the collective responsibility for the decision that was ultimately made, they would have taken a more judicious approach and weighed the various alternatives carefully. Nevertheless, it is interesting to observe that at the time the response of the congressional leadership, including Senator Fulbright (who was later to lead the doves in an attack on

---

[32] Robert F. Kennedy, *Thirteen Days* (New York: W. W. Norton, 1969), p. 8.
[33] Ibid., pp. 31–32.

President Johnson's Vietnam policies), was in favor of direct military intervention. Consultation with the leaders of Congress inevitably means consultation with the most conservative parts of the legislature and at the time of the Cuban Missile Crisis these key legislative leaders leaned towards strong military intervention where they felt United States interests were at stake. Many of these same individuals by the latter stages of the Vietnam war were far more cautious in their attitudes towards military involvement, and led congressional efforts to curb the discretionary authority of the president to make war.

CONCLUSION

Our system of government was originally constructed with a negative orientation, designed to prevent the effective exercise of governmental authority. The intricate intermeshing of the various branches of the government that was required before a policy output could be produced was to limit potentially "evil" influences upon government, emanating from factions and demagogic individuals who were more concerned with their own interests than with the national interest. However, a government primarily designed to work inefficiently, if at all, obviously could not meet the wide range of responsibilities that inevitably were placed upon it, nor could it produce effective government during times of crisis. The bureaucracy developed to take over expanded governmental responsibilities and the powers of the presidency grew to provide leadership and effective decision-making in times of crisis.

In the foreign and military affairs areas, the presidency does not conform to traditional constitutional restraints. Although the Constitution did foresee in part that the president would have to have wider discretionary powers in the foreign than in the domestic sphere, nevertheless, the authority to declare war clearly resided with Congress, and the Senate was to advise and consent on treaties and ambassadorial appointments. A major question for the future of the presidency is how to balance the need for power with constitutional requirements of responsibility and constraints. In the domestic arena, without the development of stronger parties which will bring about closer linkage between the White House and Congress, the president will be severely curtailed in his legislative activities. Moreover, the bureaucracy inevitably will place constraints on the ability of the president to shape and implement public policy. Even in parliamentary governments with a strong two-party system, such as Britain, the administrative branch exercises wide discretion in policy-making.

Although the presidency is usually called an institution, the fact remains that the White House is more a reflection of the man who holds the office than of its bureaucratic components. It is an extension of the president's preferences and inclinations in most critical areas of decision-making. Each president shapes the institution more than it shapes him, particularly in the way in which it deals with foreign policy.

It is inevitable that many changes will be made in the institution of the presidency in the future. The Watergate affair will make future presidents more cautious about relying on staff. Watergate has also led to a partial restoration of the balance of powers between Congress and the president. The president himself will remain the focal point of political responsibility in our system, regardless of whether or not he has the power to carry out this role effectively. Real power will continue to be exercised in most domestic policy spheres in other parts of the government, whose responsibilities are to far narrower constituencies than that of the president. It can be argued that insofar as presidents have been able to exercise arbitrary power, it has been because coordinate branches of government have looked the other way. Perhaps the answer to achieving true responsibility in the White House does not stem from restructuring the institution of the presidency, but from buttressing and changing the attitudes of other branches, particularly Congress, so that unwise presidential decisions will be promptly subjected to intense debate and possible reversal.

6

Congress

as a Policy Force

Every two years, after elections are held for the House of Representatives and the Senate, those who have been elected to Congress for the first time often take with them a high sense of mission. They hope to influence new directions in public policy. Not only do they hold the institution of Congress in high regard, and consider it to be the primary influence upon public policy in government, but they also feel that their individual roles can be significant within the framework of the legislature. After all, doesn't the Constitution designate Congress to be the primary legislative body? And doesn't legislation mean public policy? No other branch of the government is given direct legislative authority by the Constitution.

At least one "public interest" pressure group, Common Cause, feels that if new directions are to be made in public policy the electoral process should be the primary channel through which demands for change are made. In the early 1970's John Gardner, the head of Common Cause, mounted an extensive effort to elect congressmen that he considered to be sympathetic to the policy interests of his organization. A central premise of this effort was that changes in the makeup of Congress could have a major impact upon public policy.

At times during the Johnson and Nixon administrations, groups of students traveled to Washington hoping to convince their congressmen to vote against the Vietnam war. In some cases, classes were recessed at election time so that students could work for peace candidates. Nationwide appeals were made to support senatorial doves threatened with the possibility of defeat in 1968. And, in many districts and states, representatives and senators were elected primarily on the basis of their stand against the war. The primary effect of these efforts was not reflected in legislative proposals opposing the war, but in making the White House aware of national sentiment on the war issue. It was not until 1973 that

Congress was able to agree on policies to limit the president's war-making prerogatives, by establishing the August 15 deadline for stopping the bombing of Cambodia and in the War Powers Resolution (see Chapter 5).

Characteristics of Congress

The most important characteristic of Congress is that it is an amorphous body. It is not a collective force. "The Congress" simply does not exist in reality. Congress is composed of numerous subgroups, particularly committees, which exert power in the policy process. If the legislature were dominated by one party, then Congress would cease to be amorphous and would become identified with a majority party. In Britain, Parliament speaks with one voice through the majority party, and although there are a few powerful standing committees, they do not control the flow of legislation as is the case in the Congress.

While delegating legislative business to committees diminishes the meaning of Congress as a collective force, the combined legislative power of the committees makes Congress anything but a rubber stamp. In his dealings with Congress, the president cannot count on a majority of his own party to enact proposals that he submits. Relative to most other democratic legislatures in the world, Congress is a powerful countervailing force to the executive.

The fragmentation of the legislative process makes it difficult for Congress to be responsive to broad forces for change in the community. It usually acts on a specialized basis, with its individual committees being responsive to narrow sets of interests that are concerned with particular policy spheres. The narrow and localized constituencies of Congress are in sharp contrast to the national constituency of the presidency. This is not to suggest that the president always takes into account "the national interest" while Congress represents something else. It is merely to point out that congressional committees tend to be more specialized and to reflect narrower interests than does the presidency. President Nixon, for example, feels that he has a national mandate to cut costs and eliminate a wide range of government programs. Congressional committees, on the other hand, dominated by Democrats and responsive to specialized bureaucratic and private interests, have been consistently challenging the president's authority to impound funds and cut back upon government programs. Various congressional committees and their chairmen have fought against President

Nixon's attempts to disband OEO, eliminate many public service hospitals, and replace categorical grant programs in a variety of fields with general revenue-sharing funds. Presidents, both Democratic and Republican, who have attempted to reduce defense expenditures have generally run into very strong opposition from the Armed Services and Defense Appropriations Committees of Congress. These committees have often supported the Defense Department when the president has attempted to cut defense expenditures.

Legislation and Public Policy

The distinction between legislation and public policy is important to bear in mind. The mere passage of legislation does not always produce public policy. In areas of intense group conflict Congress frequently resorts to the passage of "skeleton" legislation in order to avoid directly confronting difficult political questions. That is, it purposely passes vague legislation, with statutory language couched in very general terms, requiring interpretation by the president or the administrative agency to which the legislature delegates authority to carry out its intent.

Ambiguous statutory provisions are not only the result of congressmen attempting to avoid taking political stands, but also of the complexity of the problems before the legislature. It is difficult for Congress to write comprehensive laws. Legislative reliance upon the technical expertise of the bureaucracy is common. The technological problems that must be taken into account in most areas of public policy also change rapidly from year to year. Even if a legislative committee has the expertise to deal with such matters, it is cumbersome to pass new legislation as frequently as conditions change. Legislation must be kept flexible, delegating a large amount of discretionary authority to the administrative agencies charged with implementation. Legislative committees may oversee agencies on a fairly continuous basis (although this is rare) and in this way affect the nature of the policy that is being formulated and carried out by the administrative branch. However, this is not the same thing as legislating. The policy outputs of government, then, are often not to be found in the language of statutes, but in interpretations made by legislative committees, administrative agencies, and sometimes the presidency and the courts, after legislation has been passed.

Except where the president and the Supreme Court are exercising independent constitutional prerogatives, all public policy decisions have a statutory basis, however vague. Through legislation, Congress determines the general areas in which government agencies will have policy-making authority, the boundaries of their authority, and the amount of money needed for particular programs. Complementing statutory law is administrative law, that is, the rules and regulations formulated by administrative agencies. These fill in the details of congressional legislation, and are supposed to follow the intent of Congress. Ambiguity of congressional intent often leads to challenges of administrative actions in the courts, which may overrule agencies if they find that they are acting beyond the authority (*ultra vires*) granted to them by Congress, as interpreted by the judges.

Adjudication is a very important ingredient in the policy process, both as carried out by courts and administrative agencies. It is often through the settlement of individual cases and controversies that policy is clarified and given concrete meaning for individuals. Outside of the areas of constitutional law-making by judges and the exercise of independent constitutional powers of the presidency, the policy process goes through three fairly identifiable formal stages: (1) the passage of a statute; (2) the promulgation of regulations based upon that statute by administrative agencies; (3) the the adjudication of disputes that arise under statutory and administrative law by administrative agencies, initially, and under certain circumstances by the courts where they exercise their authority to review the decisions of the agencies.

Congressmen as Policy-makers

Individual congressmen and congressional committees are involved in all three stages of the policy process. They initially shape and vote upon legislation. They may informally influence the administrative agencies before the promulgation of regulations. And, they may become involved indirectly in the adjudication of disputes by the agencies. Neither congressmen nor anyone else are supposed to make *ex parte* (for one party only) representations in formal adjudicative decisions, whether in the administrative or the judicial processes. However, most administrative adjudication is informal, in which there are far less restrictions and in most instances congressional intervention is perfectly proper.

The complexities of the policy process, and the numerous access points to those who have power to shape it, means that many congressional activities besides legislating may affect the course of public policy. This poses an interesting dilemma for constituents: if they are interested in public policy, some judgment must be made about the effectiveness of congressional candidates within government. If the candidate is an incumbent, judgment can be made as to his position in Congress, what committees he is on, and what rank he holds. This in turn will have an important effect upon his influence in government generally. If a candidate is running for the first time, there is virtually no way to predict his performance within Congress in opening avenues to power.

The general policy statements of congressmen on broad issues may in reality be of little importance to his constituents. But if he holds a powerful committee chairmanship, he may be able to serve his constituents very well in shaping the impact of policy to meet their needs. In the election campaigns of 1968 and 1970, a great deal of effort was directed by the anti-war movement to remove congressmen who supported President Johnson and who did not oppose the war. In one district in Massachusetts, Congressman Philbin, a ranking member of the House Armed Services Committee with twenty-six years tenure in the House, was defeated by Father Robert Drinan, a liberal Democrat who took a strong stand against the Vietnam war. Presumably a majority of the people voting for Drinan thought that they could better influence public policy, at least a particular policy concerning the war, by electing the new congressman than by retaining the incumbent. They valued Drinan's anti-war stance more than Philbin's seniority and clout. The senior congressman had a very powerful position within the legislature, and his capacity to influence policy favorable to his district was considerable. He was clearly a more influential person than any new freshman congressman could be. Assuming that senior congressmen want to be of service to their districts, constituents lose a powerful voice by turning them out over one issue.

THE CONTEXT OF CONGRESSIONAL POLICY-MAKING

Formal Structure of Congress

The formal constitutional provisions governing the operation of Congress shape its approaches to policy tasks. The bicameral nature of the legislature inevitably causes internal conflict between the House and the Senate. Bicameralism is fortified by differing constituencies for the two legislative branches, by contrasting powers, and by different terms of office. These internal legislative differences make it impossible to develop a unified legislative policy. It also is a partial cause for the fragmentation of legislative power in the hands of diverse committees.

Originally, the major reason for the bicameral legislature was to secure the representation of differing interests—the states in the Senate, and the people in the House. It was not until 1913, with the adoption of the seventeenth amendment, that the Senate was elected directly by the people; previously, senators were selected by state legislatures. The indirect selection of the Senate, in combination with longer tenure and a slightly older age qualification (senators have to be 30 years of age, representatives, 25), was to give the Senate a more conservative cast than the House.

In *The Federalist* Hamilton and Madison argued that the House and the Senate were to have different policy orientations and responsibilities. Direct election and a two-year term of office rendered the House continuously dependent upon the interests of local constituents. The Senate, on the other hand, was capable of acting in a more deliberative fashion; it could give greater thought to important issues of public policy, particularly in foreign affairs, and where necessary check rash actions by the House. The most important objects of federal legislation within the purview of the House were to be the regulation of commerce, taxation, and regulation of the militia (*The Federalist, No. 56*).

Constitutional Division of Power
All bills for raising revenue must originate in the House under the terms of the Constitution; the House thus has powerful initiative that often determines the course of tax policy. The exalted status of Congressman Wilbur Mills, Chairman of the House Ways and Means Committee, is rooted in part in this constitutional provision. Although the Senate, usually acting through the Senate Finance Committee, can amend or reject any revenue raising proposals of the House, traditionally major tax policy is shaped more by the House Ways and Means Committee than by the Senate Finance Committee. The latter cannot originate its own proposals but can only reject or amend those coming from the House.

The Senate, within the legislature, is predominate in foreign policy because of its constitutional powers. It must approve ambassadoral appointments and treaties. But because the initiative in foreign policy lies largely within the sphere of presidential power today, the role of the Senate has been greatly diminished. It has never been possible for any president to secure the passage of domestic legislation within the authority of Congress without the concurrence of the legislature, while it has been possible for presidents to ignore the legislature by resorting to the use of prerogative powers in foreign affairs.

Judicial Interpretation of Policy-making Authority under Article I

The Constitution can be interpreted both as a negative and as a positive document. That is, powers enumerated for the national government can be conceived of as limiting or extending its authority. With but few exceptions, the course of American constitutional interpretation by the Supreme Court was set by Chief Justice John Marshall in the early nineteenth century. In such famous cases as *McCulloch* v. *Maryland* (1819) and *Gibbons* v. *Ogden* (1824), a "loose" rather than "strict" constructionist view was taken of the Constitution, and particularly of the Implied Powers clause which gives the legislature all authority that is "necessary and proper" to implement its enumerated powers. Although from time to time in American history the Supreme Court has limited the authority of Congress, the major trend of judicial decisions has been toward permitting Congress to do whatever it wishes, provided that there is not a clear violation of the Bill of Rights.

It was during the New Deal era that the most serious challenge to congressional authority occurred, when the Supreme Court ruled several important pieces of New Deal legislation unconstitutional for exceeding the enumerated powers of Congress. The era of the New Deal was not the only time when the Supreme Court struck down congressional legislation because it was *ultra vires*, but it was the most serious judicial threat to the actions of the political arms in government—Congress and the presidency—based upon the idea of constitutional restraints.

After the elections of 1936, and the attempt by Roosevelt to change the composition of the Supreme Court, the more liberal Court interpreted the Constitution more loosely, thus upholding New Deal legislation. What is or is not unconstitutional is a matter of subjective opinion on the part of the Court, and proponents of the New Deal had argued vigorously that their standards of constitutionality were as valid as those of the justices. The latter, they held, were rewriting the Constitution in line with their conservative orientation.

During the early New Deal, such important legislation as the Agriculture Adjustment Act of 1933, and the National Industrial Recovery Act of 1933 were invalidated as beyond the authority of Congress. However, in the historic case of *NLRB* v. *Jones and Laughlin Steel* (1937), Chief Justice Charles Evans Hughes, and Justice Owen J. Roberts switched to the liberal side of the Court, thus giving the New Deal a victory.[1] At issue in the case was the Wagner Act (National Labor Relations Act) of 1935, which on the basis of the Commerce Clause extended federal regulatory power to deal with labor disputes that burdened or obstructed interstate commerce. The National Labor Relations Board (NLRB) was created with the authority to issue cease and desist orders that would be enforced through the courts, against business firms that were found guilty of engaging in "unfair labor practices." The terms of the Act did not extend merely to businesses involved in transporting goods across state lines, but included manufacturing firms that were antecedent and separate from the process of transportation of goods.

In cases previous to *NLRB* v. *Jones and Laughlin Steel*, the Court had held that such extensions of federal regulatory power were beyond the authority of Congress under the Commerce Clause. After upholding the extension of regulatory power in labor relations, the Court went on to support New Deal legislation in agriculture on the basis of the Commerce Clause. Early New Deal legislation in this field had been declared unconstitutional because Congress had attempted to base it upon its authority to tax and to provide for the general welfare.

The New Deal settled once and for all the controversy over whether the boundaries of congressional authority in domestic legislation were to be narrow or broad. It also revealed that in reality this is a political, not a constitutional, question, decided not by the Supreme Court operating in a vacuum, but by the ebb and flow of political forces. Roosevelt's unrelenting pressure upon the Supreme Court caused it to reverse its position, with the full knowledge that behind Roosevelt stood enormous popular support.

A month before the *Jones and Laughlin* decision, the Court had indicated a more liberal stance in *West Coast Co.* v. *Parrish*. Harold L. Ickes noted the case in his diary:

---

[1] For an extensive discussion of this case, see Chapter 7, pp. 224–226.

The Supreme Court yesterday did a complete somersault on the question of minimum wages for women. It reversed itself on the Adkins Case decided in 1923, in which the Court declared unconstitutional a law establishing minimum wages for women. . . .

. . . I do not know just what the effect on public opinion will be, or on the Court fight, but it seems to me that it is an admission on the part of the Supreme Court of charges that we have made to the effect that it hasn't been following the Constitution, but has been establishing as the law of the land, through Supreme Court decisions, the economic and social beliefs of the judges of the Court. It seems to me that on the whole, the effect will be to weaken the prestige of the Court in public estimation because when it was under fire, the Court ran to cover. For my part, I would have had more respect for the Court if it had gone down fighting and smiling after the manner of Justice McReynolds [who wrote a vigorous dissenting opinion]. Hughes and Roberts ought to realize that the mob is always ready to tear and rend at any sign of weakness.[2]

Policy-making Based Upon Treaties Another, and rather esoteric, area in which the authority of Congress has been challenged is in relation to its powers to implement treaty provisions. Congress, in addition to having the authority to carry out its enumerated powers, may "make all laws which shall be necessary and proper for carrying into execution . . . all other powers vested by the Constitution in the government of the United States, or in any department or office thereof." The treaty-making power is an example of a power vested by the Constitution "in the government of the United States, or in any department or office thereof," on the basis of which Congress can enact laws. Article VI of the Constitution provides in part:

This Constitution and the laws of the United States which shall be made in pursuance thereof; and all treaties made, or which shall be made, under the authority of the United States, shall be the supreme law of the land. . . .

Since treaties and the Constitution are equally legitimate sources of authority, can Congress in pursuance of the treaty pass laws that would be unconstitutional solely on the basis of its enumerated powers?

---

[2] Harold L. Ickes, *The Inside Struggle* (New York: Simon and Schuster, 1954), pp. 106–107.

In *Missouri* v. *Holland* (1920), the Supreme Court held that Congress can make a law to put into effect the provisions of a treaty that would be unconstitutional in the absence of the treaty, because it could not be implied simply from its enumerated powers. However, the law in the *Missouri* case did not violate a specific provision of the Constitution. The Court has held that Congress cannot use a treaty or an executive agreement (treated as a treaty by the Supreme Court) as authority to pass a law that violates an explicit provision of the Constitution.

In *Reid* v. *Covert* (1957) the Court, after citing the language of Article VI making treaties the supreme law of the land along with the Constitution, pointed out that:

There is nothing in this language which intimates that treaties and laws enacted pursuant to them do not have to comply with the provisions of the Constitution. Nor is there anything in the debates which accompanied the drafting and ratifications of the Constitution which even suggests such a result. . . . It would be manifestly contrary to the objective of those who created the Constitution, as well as those who are responsible for the Bill of Rights—let alone alien to our own entire constitutional history and tradition—to construe Article VI as permitting the United States to exercise power under an international agreement without observing constitutional prohibitions. In effect, such construction would permit amendment of that document in a manner not sanctioned by Article V. The prohibitions of the Constitution were designed to apply to all branches of the national government and they cannot be nullified by the Executive or by the Executive and the Senate combined. . . .

The *Reid* case involved an executive agreement between the United States and Great Britain which provided that United States military courts would have exclusive jurisdiction over criminal offenses committed in Great Britain by American servicemen and their dependents. Violations of British laws by Americans would be tried by court martial. The case involved a court martial trial that had convicted the wife of a serviceman of murdering her husband. Court martial trials do not provide the full protections of the Bill of Rights, and on this basis the Supreme Court upheld a lower district court judgment that Mrs. Covert (the wife) should be released from custody. Provisions for court martial trials, established by Congress, cannot be extended to civilians on the basis of executive agreements because such action would violate the Bill of Rights.

Effects of Judicial Interpretation of Article I Today, the issue of constitutional limitations upon Congress is dormant. In the past, such limitations have always resulted from political rather than legal factors, that is, from the conservative orientation of the Court which led to a desire to curb what it considered too liberal policies of Congress. Certainly from the standpoint of the Constitution itself it is difficult to visualize how Congress might be limited in the future. Except for clear violations of the Bill of Rights, constitutional restraints upon the legislature are largely irrelevant. Congress has been able to use the war power, the power to tax and to provide for the general welfare, and the Commerce Clause to justify virtually any legislation expanding the role of the federal government.

Congressional Structure and Policy-making

Although judicial interpretation of Article I does not place significant boundaries upon the authority of Congress, constitutional provisions fragmenting the legislature continue to render it less potent as a policy instrument. Legislative committees are extraordinarily powerful. But the legislature as a whole would be a more powerful policy instrument if a majority of its members consistently acted together on major policy issues. The Constitution, however, was designed to ensure that no "faction" or political party would be capable of controlling the legislative process.

Two-Year vs. Four-Year Term Part of the way in which the Constitution prevents majority party control of the legislature is to give to each branch differing terms of office as well as contrasting constituencies. From time to time the two-year term of office for representatives is attacked by legislators and political scientists for being too short. Various proposals have been made, including recommendations by President Johnson, to change the term to four years.

The four-year term would bring into coincidence the terms of representatives and the president, potentially increasing the power of the president over his party in Congress. This would occur because of the coattail effect of the president, and consequently the greater reliance of party candidates upon him to be elected. During presidential election years, the focus of attention is upon presidential rather than congressional candidates, and presidential issues and personalities dominate the electoral scene. This in turn has a spill-over effect upon congressional candidates, who seek to identify with popular presidential candidates of their own party and who must be concerned with the issues raised by the contenders for the White House.

The net effect of coincidental terms for president and congressmen would be that the president would be far more likely to have a majority of his own party in Congress, increasing his relative power over the legislature; nevertheless, he would not have total domination because of the parties' undisciplined nature. Some indication of the significance of presidential campaigns in placing members of the party of the victorious candidate into Congress is seen in the fact that President Nixon was the first president in 120 years who failed to bring a majority of his own party into Congress when he was initially elected.

Generally there is significantly greater success for presidential requests made during Congresses that are elected with the president than those chosen in mid-term elections.[3] There is little doubt that if the four-year term were adopted to coincide with the election of the president, Congress as a whole would act less independently and would be more likely to support the legislative requests of the White House. Congress as a whole, even though under presidential control, would become a more active policy force. It would be more capable of acting on policy issues because its majority would have clearer leadership than is presently the case.

Continuation of the off-year election will buttress the independence of congressmen, who in order to get reelected, will seek issues that often oppose the White House. In fact, it seems to be characteristic of American politics that in off-year elections large numbers of voters will desert the party in power, and thereby increase the opposition party in Congress. Only once in the twentieth century, in 1934, did the president's party increase its margin in the House. The record in the Senate is somewhat better, but in most off-year elections the opposition party increases its strength. In contrast, during presidential election years the party in power almost always increases its numbers in both the House and the Senate.

---

[3] See Charles O. Jones, *Every Second Year: Congressional Behavior in the Two-Year Term* (Washington, D. C.: The Brookings Institution, 1967), pp. 72–95.

Presumably if a four-year term of office is going to have an impact in making Congress more responsive to presidential demands, the Senate as well as the House will have to have a four-year tenure. Although this has been suggested, in reality it is impractical since there is no motivation within the Senate to reduce the six-year term. On the other hand, the four-year term of office receives a great amount of support in the House because it would make life less difficult for representatives by reducing the demands upon their time taken up in constant bids for reelection.

The drain upon the energy and financial resources of the average congressman is extraordinary. As one congressman recently pointed out:

Some of the members in the cloakroom were talking about the recent flock of retirement announcements by our senior colleagues. It's without precedent for nine ranking minority members to call it quits voluntarily over the span of several months. . . . Included in this group are the ranking Republicans on the Appropriations, Ways and Means, and Judiciary Committees as well as the Senior Republicans on Rules, Interstate and Foreign Commerce and Merchant Marine and Fisheries. This exodus surely reflects a collective belief that the party has no chance to capture control of the Congress in the foreseeable future. Otherwise, these men would be determined to hang on until they received a chance to serve as chairmen of their respective committees. It reflects other factors as well: the pressures of redistricting, the higher pension benefits available for retiring members—it's possible now for some of them to draw as much as $34,000 per year; the frequency with which senior members are being stricken fatally while in office here; the longer sessions of Congress and the growing assertiveness of the newer members.

In recent years a congressman's job has changed dramatically, and this has imposed a new set of pressures on the old soldiers of both parties. Fifteen years ago the House was largely an island unto itself. Few Americans knew or seemed to care very much about what happened here. That's not true any longer. Today the country is peering directly over our shoulder. It's Ralph Nader who is watching over us, and Common Cause and the League of Women Voters. It's newly politicized groups of blacks, women, young people and Chicanos. It's groups such as SOS, NAG and Vietnam Veterans Against the War. They've learned that Congress determines our national priorities; that we provide the men and money to fight undeclared wars; that we have the power to clean up the environment; restore the cities and help old people. They're letting us know their demands and lobbying aggressively to make sure we act. The pressures on members, already intense, are multiplying rapidly. As [Congressman] Cederberg said to me, "it's just not as much fun to be here anymore." [4]

The establishment of a four-year term would at least reduce slightly these pressures from the outside, although it can be argued that such pressure upon congressmen is beneficial for it keeps them responsive to the voters.

It is almost impossible to determine accurately the real impact of the two-year term, or what increasing it to four years would produce. The most recent debate of importance on the issue came after President Johnson recommended the four-year term to Congress in 1966. The major reasons he cited were the increasing volume of legislation and the complexity of the problems confronting the legislature. He noted that representatives have to:

. . . be familiar with an immense range of fact and opinion. It is no longer sufficient to develop solutions for an agricultural nation with few foreign responsibilities; now a man or a woman chosen to represent his people in the House of Representatives must understand the consequences of our spiraling population growth, and urbanization, of the new scientific revolution, of our welfare and education requirements, and of our responsibilities as the world's most powerful democracy. [5]

President Johnson also cited the longer sessions of Congress, which made it necessary for representatives to stay in Washington for long periods of time to attend the public business, and making it virtually impossible for them to both campaign effectively and meet their legislative responsibilities. Finally, he noted the increasing costs of political campaigns which place an unequal burden upon representatives from closely contested districts. [6]

Following President Johnson's proposal for the four-year term, *Congressional Quarterly* conducted a poll of House and Senate Members on the issue. Of the 195 representatives responding to the poll, the vote was 105–90 in favor of increasing the House term to

---

[4] Donald Riegle, with Trevor Armbrister, *O' Congress* (New York: Doubleday and Company, 1972), pp. 284–85.
[5] *Congressional Quarterly Weekly Report*, January 28, 1966, p. 306.
[6] Ibid.

four years. In the Senate, of the 39 respondents, the vote was 20–19 opposed to the change.[7] Many Senators fear House members running against them without sacrificing their seats. Typical comments of representatives were:

"In favor, if four year terms do not run concurrent with the election of the president."

"In favor, if half of membership runs alternately each two years."

"To tie the entire House to the coattails of the president would destroy the independence of Congress."

"Running each two years is expensive and wearisome."

"Will enable me to escape further fund raising chores, something I find particularly obnoxious."

"Being a congressman has now become a full-time, twelve-month a year job. . . . I believe the proposed change would give a congressman more time to be a statesman rather than a politician, and would be in the national interest."

"Two years is long enough for a bad congressman or a bad Congress."

"Until members of the House are willing to accept or impose some voluntary self-restraint and fringe benefits and recognize that their office is a full-time job, and not a feeder for lucrative law practice, which encourages the Tuesday–Thursday club, they do not deserve further confidence. The Framers of the Constitution were right."

"Yes, but I would more strongly support a resolution that elected representatives in odd-numbered years. . . . This would help rid the country of coattail riders and rubber-stamp representatives."[8]

Size of the Legislature The context within which Congress functions is defined not only by the formal characteristics of the Constitution but also by a variety of

---

[7] *Congressional Quarterly Weekly Report*, February 11, 1966, p. 364.
[8] Ibid., pp. 364–65.

informal factors, most of which were unforeseen by the Framers of the Constitution. Congress has greatly increased in size since the early days of the Republic. In *The Federalist, No. 58,* James Madison warned against increasing the size of the House of Representatives, because he felt that this would make it more liable to domination by an elite, capable of swaying the mass membership by appeals to passion rather than reason. He felt that "in all legislative assemblies, the greater the number composing them may be, the fewer will be the men who will in fact direct their proceedings." The increased size of both the House and the Senate has in fact produced the result Madison feared, but not for the reasons he suggested. As the size of the legislature has grown, no one has been able to control a majority by manipulating emotions. But elites do control the legislative process. Because of the necessary division of labor and consequently the delegation of legislative tasks to specialized committees, the nature of legislation passed by Congress is generally determined by the relatively few senior members that dominate the committee system. The elite control over the legislative process in both the House and the Senate exists because of the fragmentation of Congress and its inability to operate as a unit. Congress is not characterized by demagoguery, but by power that is often hidden from the average legislator.

Volume and Complexity of Legislation

The volume of legislation coming before Congress has increased simply because of the vast expansion of government. This, in turn, has occurred because of increased demands for governmental action to meet a variety of problems once considered in the private realm. Although legislation has never been a simple process, since it always involves complex legal technicalities, the nature of problems confronting Congress in the twentieth century has demanded a wider range of knowledge on the part of legislators than in the past.

Through specialization in committees, congressmen with long seniority have often been able to gain deeper knowledge of the policy fields under their jurisdiction. It is difficult for most legislators to achieve a sufficient level of comprehension of policy problems to exert individual impact.

In discussing the problem that Congress has in developing the requisite knowledge to influence the policy process, Ernest S. Griffith has stated that:

The principal difficulty faced by Congress in carrying out its contemplated functions may be put in question form. How can a group of non-specialists, elected as representatives of the electorate, really function in a specialized and technological age? For surely no one will deny the overwhelming majority of the great problems facing the government are complex to such a degree that the most skilled specialization and the most profound wisdom are none too great to deal with them.[9]

Insofar as Congress is inexpert, or does not have an adequate expert staff, it will be under the domination of those on the outside who do have the required expertise.

Attempts to Improve the Policy-Making Machinery of Congress

One major attempt that was made to bolster the resources of Congress was the passage of the Legislative Reorganization Act of 1946. The Act attempted to increase the expertise of Congress by providing more staff aides for committees, and by setting up the Legislative Reference Service as a separate branch of the Library of Congress to provide information to legislators. It attempted to reduce the workload of Congressmen by reducing the number of committees on which they could serve, and by eliminating certain categories of private bills from congressional jurisdiction. Under the provisions of the Act, congressmen could no longer introduce private bills to pay pensions or certain types of tort claims (those where, under the Federal Tort Claims Act of 1946, the government can be sued directly), to construct bridges, or to correct military records. Congressional supervision over policy formulation was to be strengthened by having standing committees continuously overseeing the activities of administrative agencies operating in the same substantive policy field.

In effect, the 1946 Act accomplished very little. The increase in staff aids to congressmen—four professional and six clerical staff members for each standing committee, with the exception of two Appropriations Committees which were given the authority to appoint any number of professional staff people agreed upon by the majority of the committees—could hardly counteract the expertise of literally thousands of professional persons working in the

---

[9] Ernest S. Griffith, *Congress: Its Contemporary Role* (New York: New York University Press, 1961), p. 67.

bureaucracy. The Legislative Reference Service had very few professional staff people to supplement those within Congress. After the Act the essential problem remained: most congressmen were generalists rather than specialists.

It was not until 1970 that any further attempts were made to streamline congressional procedures. The Legislative Reorganization Act of 1970 was directed primarily at making the procedures of Congress less secret and permitting greater access to decision-making within Congress both by legislators themselves and by outsiders. The Act also contained provisions to help Congress gain more fiscal and budgetary information, expand committee staffs, and increase the aid given to congressmen by the Congressional Research Service in the Library of Congress. Given the tremendous increase in the volume and complexity of legislation considered by Congress since World War II, the provisions of the Act were designed as a minimum to place Congress on a footing equal to what it had been over two decades before. The Act of 1970, like that of 1946, helped to alleviate a very difficult situation, but it did not cure the basic inadequacy of the legislature in coping with the complexities of policy today.

In 1972 Congress established the Office of Technological Assessment, under the sponsorship of Senator Edward Kennedy. The OTA has enormous potential to develop expertise, since its mandate gives it the authority to assign whatever experts it wants from the bureaucracy to work for Congress. Once OTA begins to function the vast reservoir of expert talent within the bureaucracy will be more readily available to Congress under the auspieces of OTA than is now the case. The OTA can use bureaucratic experts to work for congressional goals, established independently of the bureaucracy. Administrative experts generally push for programs that are consistent with the goals of the agency for which they work. Working for OTA, however, will broaden the horizons of these experts and make them more useful to Congress. Moreover, the president can not, as President Nixon has consistently attempted to do, control the policy inputs that bureaucratic experts make upon Congress if they work for OTA. The OTA is also a way of getting around the present requirement that all legislative and budgetary proposals coming from the bureaucracy must first be channeled through the OMB. Administrative experts working for OTA will not be subject to this requirement in their legislative or budgetary proposals.

In the complicated labyrinth of the contemporary Congress,

legislators attempt to find their way by adhering to certain procedures that have been devised to bring order out of what would
otherwise be chaos. The committee system and the seniority rule,
while commonly looked upon as antiquated and undemocratic,
actually are a necessity given the lack of any central focal point of
direction for Congress. The legislature attempts to cope with intricate problems of public policy by operating through specialized
committees, thus gaining the necessary continuity and understanding to shape policy in a rational way. The seniority rule avoids
bloodshed by selecting committee chairmen on a seniority basis,
which is the most acceptable procedure in the absence of disciplined
parties whose leaders would allocate committee seats.

Electoral and
Policy Constituencies

Just as the presidency is rarely
given concrete mandates by the electorate, congressmen also must
deal with constituencies where relatively few individuals and interest groups are dealing with public policy issues. It is with the inputs
from these sources that congressmen must concern themselves in
their behavior in relation to issues of public policy.

Warren E. Miller and Donald E. Stokes have pointed out in one
study of constituency influence in Congress that less than 20 percent of the electorate had even read or heard anything about candidates running in their district.[10] Being ignorant of representatives'
policy positions means that the electorate is not concerned with
what policy preferences candidates or incumbents have. As a result:

. . . The communication most congressmen have with their districts
inevitably puts them in touch with organized groups and with individuals
who are relatively well-informed about politics. The representative knows
his constituents mostly from dealing with people *who do* write letters,
who will attend meetings, *who have* an interest in his legislative stance.
As a result, his sample of contacts with a constituency of several hundred
thousand people is heavily biased; even the contacts he apparently makes
at random are likely to be with people who grossly overrepresent the
degree of political information and interest in the constituency as a
whole.[11]

---

[10] Warren E. Miller and Donald E. Stokes, "Constituency Influence in Congress," *The American Political Science Review* 57 (March 1963): 45–56.
[11] Ibid., pp. 54–55.

Constituency influence, then, may help the congressman with respect to a narrow set of issues, but it does not provide him with a well-charted guide for his legislative actions. In many of his votes on legislation he will have to act as a Burkean trustee for the interests of his constituency. He will vote in accordance with his perceptions of the needs of the district he represents.

Charles O. Jones has developed the concept of a "policy constituency" to explain how congressmen behave in the policy process.[12] This consists of substantial interests within the legislator's constituency that have knowledge of and are concerned with particular issues of public policy. Jones found in one case study of the House Agriculture Committee that legislators having clearly defined policy interests in their districts sought and usually succeeded in getting assignments to committees having jurisdiction over those interests. For example, a representative who had substantial interests in tobacco would be assigned to the Tobacco Subcommittee of the House Agriculture Committee. At the committee stage the representative would work hard to take into account the demands of pressure groups in his district. Since most legislation is given final shape within committees, a representative who is on the relevant policy committee or committees for his district is in a good position to serve private interests within his constituency.

Legislative Parties as Policy Inputs

Where there are no constituency forces to guide legislators, they will be more likely to turn to their political party within Congress for guidance. They will not always necessarily follow the dictates of party leaders within Congress or the White House, but the party will be used as a reference point when other considerations are less relevant.

Following the party line within the House or Senate means adhering to the position of "the legislative party." However, such phraseology assumes that there is a unified legislative party that has a position on policy matters. But there is no formal party position on public policy issues simply because there is no "party" that operates as a collective unit within the legislature. There is no one party member or group that a congressman

---

[12] Charles O. Jones, "Representation in Congress: The Case of the House Agricultural Committee," *The American Political Science Review* 55 (June 1961): 358–67.

can call when trying to decide how to vote or act within a committee in reference to a particular issue. This may seem puzzling at first, since the legislative parties do have leaders, and one of the parties has an incumbent in the White House. Both legislative leaders and presidents take positions on many issues of policy. However, unless the stands taken by the leaders reflect the views of a majority of party members in the legislature, they do not by definition represent "the party."

Frequently the leaders of legislative parties will differ among themselves on policy issues, and record contrasting votes. On the basis of observing the behavior of Congress during the years 1949 and 1950, David B. Truman noted:

> . . . The legislative parties are marked by a paradoxical set of attributes: fractionation and, in some instances, structural fluidity, but also a tendency towards shared attitudes and expectations, even in substantive policy matters, and an apparent interdependence of role among the members, both of which testify to their persistence as groups. These attributes have been summarily described in these pages by designating the congressional parties as "mediate" groups, meaning that the relations constituting the groups are distinctively affected but not wholly determined by their members' affiliations with and dependence upon other groups. The latter would include primarily interest groups and constituency parties, but would of course not be confined to these.[13]

The legislative party's cohesion is based upon the existence of shared attitudes on a variety of matters, including substantive policy. It does not result from the dictates of the leaders. Effective leadership, on the contrary, depends upon the ability to articulate the shared attitudes of party members.

The *Congressional Quarterly* has compiled statistics that reveal the extent to which congressional parties hold together on roll-calls in the Senate and recorded Teller votes in the House. Defining "party unity votes" as those where a majority of voting Republicans and Democrats follow party lines, Table 6:1 reveals the percentage of total roll calls where parties acted in a relatively cohesive fashion during the years 1968–1972.

---

[13] David B. Truman, *The Congressional Party* (New York: John Wiley & Sons, 1959), p. 292.

Table 6:1
Party Unity Scoreboard, 1968–1972

	Total Roll Calls	Party Unity Roll Calls	Percent of Total
1972			
Both Chambers	861	283	33%
Senate	532	194	36
House	329	89	27
1971			
Both Chambers	743	297	40
Senate	423	176	42
House	320	121	38
1970			
Both Chambers	684	219	32
Senate	418	147	35
House	266	72	27
1969			
Both Chambers	422	144	34
Senate	245	89	36
House	177	55	31
1968			
Both Chambers	514	172	33
Senate	281	90	32
House	233	82	35

Source: *Congressional Quarterly Weekly Report*, January 15, 1972, pp. 87–88; Nov. 18, 1972, p. 3018.

Table 6:1 reveals the relatively low number of party unity votes, and therefore by implication the large number of votes on which congressional parties do not reflect significant differences. In only one year, and in only one body of Congress—the Senate—was there party unity on more than 40 percent of the roll-call votes. Generally speaking, party members hold together on between 30 and 40 percent of the roll-calls. These figures reveal the disparity of viewpoints within congressional parties on most legislative issues.

Since roll-call voting is only one aspect of policy-making by the legislature, lack of party unity in this area does not necessarily mean that the legislative parties are insignificant in terms of other aspects of the operation of Congress that can have an important bearing upon the course of public policy. But just as parties do not operate as a collective force influencing the voting behavior of legislators, they do not determine the views of congressmen as they function on committees, or in relation to parliamentary procedure. Such issues as the general power of committees, the role of the House Rules Committee, and the seniority system, all of which have an important influence upon the policy outputs of the legislature, are not debated along party lines. When these issues are raised from time to time, and changes sought in congressional procedures, the contrasting positions that are taken split along liberal–conservative rather than party lines.

Because Table 6:1 reveals only quantitative data, there is the possibility that if one could construct a scale of importance of legislative issues then party cohesion might be greater as one moves from the less to the more important roll-call votes. However, the construction of such a scale would have to be an entirely subjective matter, for it is impossible to measure objectively the significance or impact that most legislative proposals will have. And, from a general examination of roll-call votes, it is clear that there is no consistently greater party cohesion that is solely tied into the magnitude of the legislation under consideration. There are simply too many intervening variables to make this avenue of analysis profitable.

The kinds of issues that give rise to party unity votes vary from one session of Congress to another. The extent to which party "ideologies" are reflected in these votes will depend upon the extent to which the issues have been defined in party terms. For example, after the landslide victory of President Johnson in 1964, votes in Congress in 1965 along party lines emphasized the contrasting ideologies of the Republicans and Democrats. This resulted because President Johnson in his campaign had highlighted a number of rather clear-cut issues that reflected traditional party differences, specifically the proper role of the government in fostering economic development and in meeting pressing social needs.

Johnson's landslide victory gave him tremendous clout with many legislators of his own party because of the obvious coattail effect of his candidacy. At the same time that the overwhelming Democratic victory laid the groundwork for greater than usual cohesion within the congressional Democratic Party, it motivated the diminished ranks of the Republicans to hold together for survival. Legislators became more aware of the significance of party identification. In 1965 in the House of Representatives and the Senate, respectively, 52 percent and 42 percent of the total roll-calls were split along party lines. This is an unusually high percentage of party unity votes, although it should be noted that from 1962 to 1964 in the House the lowest number of party unity roll-calls was 46 percent in 1962, and the highest was 54.9 percent in 1964. These figures are set forth in Table 6:2.

The issues that most frequently split the parties in 1964 and 1965 centered upon the core of the "great society" program of President Johnson. The congressional parties were sharply divided

Table 6:2
Party Voting in Congress,
1962–1965

	Total Roll Calls	Party Unity Roll Calls	Percent of Total
1965			
Both Chambers	459	213	46%
Senate	258	108	42
House	201	105	52
1964			
Both Chambers	418	171	40.9
Senate	305	109	35.7
House	113	62	54.9
1963			
Both Chambers	348	166	47.7
Senate	229	108	47
House	119	58	49
1962			
Both Chambers	348	149	43
Senate	224	92	41
House	124	57	46

Source: *Congressional Quarterly Weekly Report*, November 5, 1965, p. 2246.

on such issues, with Democrats favoring and Republicans opposing expanded medical care under Social Security, anti-poverty programs, increased government aid for housing and urban development, and other policies increasing the involvement of the federal government in economic and social programs.

In contrasting Tables 6:1 and 6:2, it is quite clear that between the period of the early and middle sixties, and that commencing with President Nixon's administration in 1968, party unity roll-call votes in Congress became significantly less frequent. Does this indicate that the influence of congressional parties, always weak, has become a less important factor in shaping legislative behavior? The data is far too sparse to indicate any trend. The number of party unity roll-calls depends upon a variety of factors, including the extent and skill of the White House in presenting issues to Congress that result in coalescence rather than diffusion of party voting in the legislature.

Congress, the Bureaucracy, and Policy Formulation

The bureaucracy is a major input in congressional policy formulation. The close cooperation that exists between many parts of Congress and the bureaucracy is a vital component of the context of congressional policy-making. Such cooperation gives administrative agencies special access to Congress to influence the legislative process. And, at the same time, it gives congressional committees special avenues of influence to the bureaucracy so that they can influence administrative decision making and thereby shape public policy that is often in its final form determined by administrators rather than legislators. Admittedly, the scope of governmental activities and the necessary specialization tends to reduce the influence of Congress as a whole in administrative policy-making. Even specialized legislative committees and congressmen of long tenure and great skill in particular areas cannot begin to keep up with the rapidly moving activities of the bureaucracy and the complexities of administrative policy-making. Often the bureaucracy acts in secret, and is responsible to Congress only after the fact.

The extent to which administrators consult congressmen depends upon a variety of political factors and personalities. Sometimes very close ties exist and administrative action is not taken without prior knowledge on the part of key congressmen. In some instances prior congressional authorization is sought. Insofar as Congress does operate through the bureaucracy it is because of the knowledge and power of a small group of senior members who control appropriations committees and committees that oversee particular administrative agencies.

An important aspect of the relationship between the bureaucracy and Congress is that the agencies are often instrumental in shaping the technical details of legislation that they must administer. As early as 1937, the report of the President's Committee on Administrative Management recognized that well over two-thirds of all legislation emanating from Congress originates in and is often drafted by the bureaucracy. This does not mean, of course, that the agencies stand apart as a separate political force dictating the contents of congressional bills.

Special interests within the constituencies of the agencies often help to shape the agencies' positions. However, administrative agencies are not simply pipelines between private interests and Congress. Congress itself hears the views of private interests in the legislative process. Moreover, it is a gross oversimplification to suggest that administrative agencies are always completely dominated by private interests. All agencies must maintain a balance of political support in order to survive, but this does not mean that they must consistently heed the requests of a particular segment of the community that comes under their jurisdiction. Within administrative constituencies there is often conflict and ambiguity, just as in the electoral constituencies of members of Congress. And there are many areas of legislation where special interests are so diffuse and conflicting that the judgment of a powerful department or agency will determine Congress' course of action.

The direct influence of administrative agencies in the legislative process stems from their political clout and expertise. Administrative agencies have more expertise than the average congressman because of long specialization on the part of the staffs of the agencies, although not necessarily at higher levels where political appointees have more frequent turnover. The only approximation of this kind of expertise in Congress is to be found in the senior members who have dealt for considerable periods of time with limited policy spheres. In the give and take between the executive and legislative branches, the expert views of bureaucrats are often determinative in shaping the content of final legislation.

Unlike most congressmen, agencies deal with policy matters under their jurisdiction continually on a day-to-day basis. They have a chance to develop programs and policy positions from the constant inputs of private groups with which they deal and from the settlement of cases and controversies arising within their jurisdiction. Congress is often at a disadvantage in the policy process because it does not receive the constant flow of information available to administrative agencies.

Faced with the ambiguity of constituent attitudes, and the lack of consistent and meaningful party guidance in many areas of public policy, it is natural for key congressmen to pay particularly close attention to the inputs from the agencies in the legislative process. Many agencies, such as the independent regulatory commissions, are formally assigned the responsibility in their enabling statutes to advise Congress on appropriate legislative changes in their respective regulatory fields. These agencies are considered to be "arms of Congress" and they have been given quasi-legislative tasks within the framework of delegated legislation. At the same time, they have continual legitimate access to congressional committees to recommend whatever changes they consider necessary in the formal statutory framework under which they operate.

Formally all bills originating within the bureaucracy must be channeled through the Office of Management and Budget for clearance before going to Capitol Hill. In reality, however, this process is often short-circuited through informal contacts that administrators make with congressional allies. Moreover, OMB is often swayed by the positions of agencies in many legislative areas where the president cannot possibly have a well-defined program. If new legislation does not involve the expenditure of additional funds, OMB is naturally more likely to approve it, provided it does not intrude upon and contradict a presidential policy position.

Historically, the important role of the administrative branch in recommending legislative proposals to Congress is relatively new, dating from the middle New Deal era. The vast expansion of the bureaucracy during the Roosevelt administration, and the increasing responsibilities assumed by the federal government, necessitated the injection of large amounts of expertise and man-hours into the process of formulating legislation for Congress. Congress itself, operating under antiquated rules and without adequate staff, naturally turned to the executive branch as the only source of available help outside of private interest groups. The latter were then as they are now only too willing to supply Congress with information that backed their policy stances; however, most legislators recognized that the bureaucracy was a far more legitimate source of direct influence than private interests since it was, like Congress, part of government and presumably representative of broad interests. This belief remains true today, and gives bureaucrats far easier access to the offices and committee rooms of Congress than is available to the paid lobbyists for private interests.

Congressmen generally recognize that private interests often dominate the agencies, and that the proposals emanating from the administrative branch are in many cases nothing more than a reflection of private concerns. Rarely, however, do agencies simply represent one group; rather, they attempt to balance the needs of the large number of organizations under their jurisdiction. On an industry-wide basis there may be certain common demands that may show up in Congress as a result of a proposal of an administrative agency. However, an agency is highly unlikely to transfer directly to Congress a bill that would benefit only one firm. Since many agencies are delegated responsibilities to foster industry-wide interests, it cannot be claimed that legislative proposals which they make to further this purpose reflect illicit pleading in behalf of private interests.

One of the more paradoxical aspects of our governmental system is that while agencies are continually involved in lobbying Congress, they are proscribed from doing this by law. Various acts prohibit the use of public funds for public relations purposes, which presumably includes attempts to influence legislation pending before Congress. (See Chapter 8.) Administrative agencies don't have to register, as do private groups, under the Federal Regulation of Lobbying Act of 1946. On the unlikely chance that some conscientious administrator might suggest that this is appropriate, given the fact that agencies are powerful lobbies, his proposal would undoubtedly be dismissed on the basis that such activities simply do not exist by definition. "Lobbying" is an activity that can only be undertaken by private interests.

It is important to emphasize that while administrative agencies shape a great deal of legislation (the general current estimate given by congressmen is that 80 percent of the bills coming from Congress are initiated and in large part drafted by the executive branch), the communications that exist between Congress and the agencies inevitably opens up a two-way street of influence. Congressmen have far better access to the agencies because of the lack of separation between the administrative branch and the legislature than would be the case if barriers were erected between these two branches. One such barrier is OMB. Legislative and executive proposals of the executive branch now have to be approved by OMB, therefore reducing the direct influence of congressmen on the agencies while at the same time increasing the power of the executive office. It is more difficult for congressmen to get agencies to develop positions which they favor because of the possibility of a veto from OMB. As long as the legislature is fragmented and operates through specialized committees, power over the bureaucracy will be diminished to the extent that the administrative branch is centralized under the control of the Executive Office of the President.

It is difficult to calculate the extent to which congressional autonomy has been reduced with the growth in the powers of the presidency and the administrative branch. Although administrative agencies may initiate most of the legislation before Congress, congressional inputs upon the legislative process are still important. As a minimum Congress has the power and more often than not the inclination to negate legislative recommendations coming from the White House and the bureaucracy. It is a foolish president indeed who underestimates the irascibility of Congress. While the complexities of the modern policy process may frequently give legislators the feeling that their understanding of most policy issues is very thin, the same is true for bureaucrats, presidents, and judges. Only through specialization, whether within or without the legislature, can knowledge in depth of policy spheres be gained.

CONGRESS IN OPERATION

What is a day, a month, a year like in the life of the average congressman? When analyzing how "the Congress" operates in the policy process, attention must be paid to the institutions, customs, and procedures of the legislature. Only in this way can the necessary generalizations be made. Every congressman functions somewhat differently, depending upon his style, the nature of his electoral constituency, his party, his length of service, his background and general knowledge, outside contacts, and legislative committee memberships.

Most autobiographical books on the life of a congressman seem to be written by legislators before they achieve positions of power within Congress.[14] They describe the hectic life of congressmen, the almost unbearable time pressure placed upon them that inevitably produces physical as well as mental fatigue. We have yet to be

---

[14] For two examples see Donald Riegle, *O Congress;* and Clem Miller, *Member of the House* (New York: Charles Scribner's Sons, 1962).

presented with more than one account of Congress written by senior and powerful leaders.[15] While in office these men clearly lack the time to write their memoirs, and after leaving Capitol Hill they seem to lack the inclination. This is regrettable for there is little doubt that, for example, an account of Congress written by the long-time Speaker John McCormick of Massachusetts would be fascinating and would present insights quite different from those revealed by congressmen at lower echelons.

Policy-making
Through Committees
The committee system remains the focal point of congressional involvement in policy-making. Both through legislation, and through oversight of administrative activities, committees and more specifically their chairmen are constantly molding the way in which public policy is developed and implemented.

Appropriations and Subject Matter Committees There are two types of committees in Congress —appropriations and subject matter committees—that possess different kinds of authority over the policy process. Appropriations committees, as the name implies, have the responsibility of actually designating how much money will be spent to implement legislation that has been passed by the subject matters committees. Subject matter committees have jurisdiction over particular areas of policy, such as agriculture, defense, and veterans affairs. They may *authorize* money to be spent in the areas over which they have jurisdiction, but they cannot in any way guarantee that the levels of authorization will be the same as the budgets finally approved by the appropriations committees.

The appropriations committees can stymie the implementation of any legislation simply by refusing to appropriate adequate funds for administration. Of what use is it for Congress to pass a law that guarantees equality in voting rights and hiring practices if insufficient funding is given to administrative agencies to enforce such policies? There is little doubt that the vigor with which administrative agencies are capable of developing and implementing policies is profoundly affected by their financial resources. The

---

[15] Joe Martin (R. Pa.) was the only prominent member of Congress in recent decades who wrote his memoirs. See Joe Martin, *My First Fifty Years in Politics* (New York: McGraw Hill, 1960).

appropriations committees of both the House and the Senate have a large say in the way in which the revenues flowing to government will be distributed among the various components of the executive branch, and therefore among different policy objectives.

The Ways and Means Committee
The power of the purse, which the Constitution so carefully delegates to Congress, not only encompasses authorization and appropriation of funds, but also the raising of revenue. The House Ways and Means Committee along with its Senate counterpart, the Finance Committee, have a great deal of clout both within and outside of the legislature because they have jurisdiction over tax measures. Nothing affects the government and the people more than taxation. Overburdening taxes may destroy individuals, and inadequate taxation cuts off the lifeblood of government.

Wilbur Mills, the Chairman of the House Ways and Means Committee, is one of the most powerful individuals in Congress, due not only to his committee position, but also to his skill as a politician. Because House rules generally exclude amendments to revenue bills, tax legislation hammered out by the Ways and Means Committee is final as far as the House is concerned. It is subject to approval by the Senate Finance Committee and the Senate itself, so that often the ultimate shape of tax legislation derives from compromises reached at the conference stage. In conference, however, the House Conferees, led by Chairman Mills and drawn from the Ways and Means Committee, generally pull greater weight than their Senate counterparts. This is due to the position of the Ways and Means Committee as an initiator of tax legislation, based on the constitutional provision that the power of the purse originates in the House rather than the Senate.

Problems of Committee Coordination One of the major difficulties facing Congress in dealing with appropriations matters is the lack of coordination among the various committees that authorize and provide money. This makes it virtually impossible for Congress as a whole to set a limit upon the amount of money appropriated. As each special committee authorizes or appropriates money, it is not aware of what other committees are doing.

Since Congress was unable to set overall spending limits, President Nixon, in 1972, pushed hard to secure enactment of legislation that would authorize him to make whatever cuts in new programs he felt were necessary in order to place a $250 billion limit upon federal spending. In the Fall of 1972 the House Ways and Means Committee, in a surprise move, voted to delegate broad discretionary authority to the president to set a budget ceiling. Such legislation is "revenue legislation" and normally not subject to debate on the floor of the House. However, the House Rules Committee in this instance voted to allow floor debate because of the magnitude of the issue involved. By giving the president total discretion to bring federal spending within a predetermined limit, Congress was abdicating a large part of its traditional power of the purse. Strong pressure, from such powerful House Democrats as Speaker Carl Albert of Oklahoma, was brought to bear upon the Rules Committee to change the ordinary way in which revenue bills are considered. In the fight Albert was backed by the Majority Leader Hale Boggs (D. La.), and George Mahon (D. Texas), Chairman of the House Appropriations Committee. The Nixon administration strongly supported the Bill as reported by the House Ways and Means Committee. However, disagreements between the House and the Senate over the amount of discretion that should be granted to the president to cut budgetary allocations defeated the bill. In 1973, Congress was working to establish new House and Senate budget committees that would have the authority to set broad budgetary allocations in specific policy areas, such as defense, agriculture, and health, education, and welfare. The appropriations committees would have the responsibility of allocating budgetary priorities within the broad goals set by the budget committees.[16] In general Congress is attempting to establish more effective overall budgetary planning by strengthening the hands of the appropriations committees and by creating new budget committees to engage in broad budgetary planning.

Policy-making
Without Legislation

The influence of legislators upon the policy process is not limited to the passage of legislation. Indeed, it can be argued that Congress influences policy most effectively outside of the legislative process. Remember that most legislation is vaguely stated, leaving the power to fill in the details

[16] For a description of the 1973 efforts towards congressional budgetary reform, see *Congressional Quarterly Weekly Report*, November 24, 1973, pp. 3092–3094.

to administrative agencies. It is in the continuous interaction between congressional committees and agencies that policy decisions
are often made. Committees, particularly the appropriations committees in the House and Senate, use various formal and informal
means of communication between themselves and administrative
policy-makers to make sure that the latter do not have total
discretion in policy-making.[17] As Michael Kirst has reported:

> . . . the appropriations committees use their reports and hearings to
> advance suggestions on policy that they would hesitate to legislate. Or,
> take the case where the appropriations committees wish to expand pro-
> grams but are unable to translate their desires into specific money terms.
> Here they can employ non-statutory directives that urge expansion at as
> fast a rate as the administrator feels is optimal. In these and many other
> situations non-statutory techniques enhance the scope and depth of
> appropriations control over broad policy and thereby better enable the
> appropriations committees to fulfill one facet of their proper role.[18]

Through "non-statutory" techniques, legislative committees can
control the policy process without submitting their actions to the
scrutiny of Congress as a whole. This continuous interaction between agencies and committees partially limits the authority of the
bureaucracy to fill up the details of vague statutes. Kirst points out
that "non-statutory devices provide an important supplement to
statutory regulation of executive implementation. Numerous details
of personnel, procedure, procurement, and organizations not suited
to statutory control are regulated through hearings and reports.
Also the committees frequently earmark money for specific purposes
in the reports rather than the statutes." [19]

A partial indication of the way in which non-statutory techniques
work can be seen through observing the comments of congressmen
in reports and hearings. Legislators on the appropriations committees will frequently let it be known to administrators by their
questions and comments how they want money to be spent, how
particular programs should be carried out, and generally how
policy should be shaped and implemented by the agencies. Subject

---

[17] For a provocative study of "non-statutory" techniques influencing policy-
making by Congress see Michael W. Kirst, *Government Without Passing Laws*
(Chapel Hill: University of North Carolina Press, 1969).
[18] Ibid., p. 153.
[19] Ibid., p. 155.

matter committees use the same techniques, although since they do not have the same clout as the appropriations committees they are not as effective in controlling administrative policy.

"Congressional Intent"

Since Congress is divided into what amounts to feudal fiefdoms, it is difficult to develop a meaningful definition of "congressional intent" that goes beyond the intent of committees and powerful congressmen. This is why administrative agencies and courts, in attempting to assess the intent of Congress, are forced to concentrate upon the hearings and reports of committees more than debate on the floor of the House. The "debates" that take place over particular pieces of legislation are so unstructured and ambiguous that they are useless as evidence of the nature of the pulse of Congress. Obtaining a majority of the House and Senate requires a broad consensus of the membership, which reflects diverse constituencies. The necessity of division of labor means that the legislation emanating from committees is respected, and congressmen will vote either for or against it without making any serious attempts to change it on the floor.

In the House of Representatives much of the legislation is not subject to floor amendments under the rules. The extent to which legislation will specifically spell out the terms of policies to be implemented depends upon the drafting of the bill by committee. Legislation is more often than not expressed in terms that leave wide discretion in the implementation of programs to administrative agencies. A cursory reading of legislation may seem to indicate that it is fairly specific, but upon careful analysis the exact meaning of the legislation is not revealed by the text. For example, regulatory agencies that have rate-making authority are directed to act in the "public interest, convenience, and necessity," and to establish "just and reasonable" rates. But these legislative standards are anything but exact, and must be defined further by those who have the responsibility of carrying out the programs. The real definition of policy, then, is made both by legislators and administrators outside of the formal legislative process itself.

Since congressional committees receive specific inputs from private interest groups and government agencies, and are themselves composed of legislators who often have had long contact with the policy field under their jurisdiction, why is it a common practice to use what amounts to vague generalities in writing legislative standards to guide administrators charged with carrying out legislative intent? One reason is that sometimes legislators pass the burden of reconciling group conflict on to the bureaucracy by drafting legislation with vague standards, thus getting themselves off the hook and placing the final decision-making responsibilities upon outside administrative agents. For example, everyone may agree that regulation of railroads is in the "public interest," but there may be intense differences between consumer-oriented groups and railroads concerning what constitutes appropriate kinds of regulation. Should railroad mergers be encouraged or discouraged? Should the railroads be allowed to drop passenger train service simply because it is unprofitable, or should some effort be made to force the railroads to accept a public responsibility to carry passengers even if this activity is not as profitable as the freight business? Should railroad rates be structured to eliminate or to foster competition within the industry, and with competing modes of transportation? These are important issues of public policy, and their resolution is required. However, it is impossible to satisfy all of the competing interests with any single decision on such complex matters.

Congressmen may best feel that they should avoid getting involved in the actual decision-making process, which they can safely do simply by creating a regulatory agency to deal with such controversial issues. But it is far too simple to suggest that the ambiguity of legislative standards is due solely to the desire on the part of congressmen to avoid unnecessary political conflict. The need for continuity and specialization in the policy-making process is also required if issues are to be understood and dealt with adequately. No congressional committee can devote as much time to specific areas of public policy as can an administrative agency, whose sole responsibility may be established within a fairly limited policy sphere. The agencies supply the continuity and expertise that Congress necessarily lacks.

A Sample Congressional Policy— Water Pollution Control

Although legislation does not determine the final shape of public policy, it is certainly a central component of the policy process. Without congressional authorization no administrative agency would have the authority to act. The major function that legislation fulfills is to authorize administrative agencies to enter particular policy spheres. The boundaries within which agencies can formulate public policy are set by Congress, although these boundaries are very broad. Consider, for example, the water pollution control bill which was passed by Congress on October 4, 1972, vetoed by the president, and subsequently passed over his veto in a congressional act of defiance on October 18. The bill provided for the establishment of a comprehensive water pollution program, to be created by the administrator of the Environmental Protection Agency (EPA), who was given the responsibility to develop regulations under the terms of the statute.

In almost every respect, the guiding standards of the Water Pollution Control Act, to be followed by the administrator, were expressed in such vague terms that virtually total discretion resided in the hands of the agency. The objective of the Act was "to restore and maintain the chemical, physical, and biological integrity of the nation's waters." [20] To accomplish this purpose, the statute directed the administrator to develop research programs relating to the problems of water pollution. Construction grants were to be authorized by the administrator, at his discretion, to state and local agencies for treatment works, with the federal government picking up a maximum of 75 percent of the cost. Title III of the statute defined the "standards" to be followed by the EPA and how the Act was to be enforced. This section clearly illustrates the nature of a typical delegation of legislative authority to an administrative agency. The standards and enforcement provisions of the Water Pollution Control statute include the following:

1. Required by July 1, 1977, effluent limitations for point sources (mostly factories) which used the "best practicable control technology currently available" *as defined by the EPA administrator.*

2. Required by July 1, 1983, effluent limitations based on the "best available technology economically achievable" *as determined by the administrator.*

3. *Authorized the administrator* to set water quality related effluent limitations, after holding public hearings.

4. *Directed the administrator* to develop and publish detailed water quality information and guidelines.

5. *Directed the administrator* to list categories of industrial pollution sources and set national performance standards for each new source. States were authorized to take over enforcement if their laws were as strict as the federal standards.

---

[20] *Congressional Quarterly Weekly Report,* October 14, 1972, p. 2692.

6. *Directed the administrator* to list toxic pollutants and prohibit their discharge and to set effluent limitations providing "an ample margin of safety."

7. *Required the administrator* to set pre-treatment standards for discharges into publicly owned treatment plants.

8. Gave the EPA the right of entry to pollution sources and the right to inspect records and monitoring equipment, and to make the data public (except trade secrets).

9. *Authorized the administrator* to hold public hearings and take other necessary action to stop international pollution originating in the United States if requested by the secretary of state.

10. *Directed the administrator* to set federal performance standards for marine sanitation equipment.

11. *Required the administrator* to set effluent limitations for thermal discharges that would ensure a balanced population of fish, shellfish and wild life.[21]

The EPA administrator was authorized to issue federal discharge permits if they met the requirements of the Act. He was authorized to suspend state programs that did not meet federal guidelines. Although the amount of discretion this statute conferred upon the administrator of the Environmental Protection Agency may seem excessive, it is actually a typical statute establishing a federal regulatory program. Aside from providing for certain procedural checks upon the administrator, as in its requirement for public hearings before certain administrative actions could be taken, the content of the rules and regulations that will "fill in the details" of the statute will be entirely at the discretion of the administrator, as will be the enforcement of the Act. The "discretionary enforcement" provisions of the Bill drew strong objections from some environmental groups and Ralph Nader's Task Force on Water Pollution Control. A joint statement of the Environmental Policy Center and the Nader Task Force stated in part that "Congress has failed to repair the most serious loophole in the old [water pollution control] law—discretionary enforcement. By leaving the government free not to prosecute politically powerful polluters, the Bill virtually guarantees abusive under-enforcement."[22]

---

[21] Ibid., pp. 2693–2694. (Italics added.)
[22] Ibid., p. 2692.

One can see that Congress affects regulatory policy-making through legislation by determining the boundaries of administrative action rather than by the specific content of policy outputs. Although legislation does not determine the final shape of public policy, it is a central component of the policy process. Except where the presidency and the courts can take action under the Constitution and thereby shape policy, no part of the government can formulate policy without congressional authorization. Congressional action is a necessary first step in the policy process. The failure of Congress to be responsive to demands for new policies has always been a major roadblock in the path of policy innovation. Of course both the president and the bureaucracy are capable of initiating new policies under the broad delegations of authority usually given to them by the legislature. However, major changes in public policy must be approved by Congress, for without legislative ratification not only would the executive branch be liable to accusations of usurpation of power, but it would also be unlikely to receive the funds necessary for continuous support of new programs.

Congress as a Negative Force

During the era of the 1960's all of the major legislative innovations of President Johnson's Great Society program were enacted by Congress. The major source of inputs for these programs came from the president and the bureaucracy. Before the Johnson era, the plight of President Kennedy in his dealings with Congress illustrates the key negative role that a recalcitrant legislature plays. James L. Sundquist points out that the Democratic "presidential party" led by President Kennedy in the election of 1960 lived up to its commitment to the party program as it had been developed by various sections of the party over the preceding decade, including endorsement by various party organs and members of the party in the Senate and House.[23] The first Kennedy Congress effectively emasculated the measures supported by the Democratic Party, as Table 6:3 illustrates.

---

[23] The process of definition of a "party program" is very difficult. As we have pointed out frequently, what constitutes the "party" is almost impossible to define. However, Sundquist uses certain measures as indicators of "party support." For example, if most of the party members in the House or Senate vote for a particular measure, this constitutes an indicator of party backing. Support by the Democratic Study Group, and the Democratic Advisory Council also indicate party endorsement. See James L. Sundquist, *Politics and Policy* (Washington, D. C.: *The Brookings Institution*, 1968), pp. 412–13.

TABLE 6:3
Disposition of Major Democratic
Party Measures by the
Eighty-Seventh Congress, 1961–62

Issue and measure	Date adopted as party measure	Date recommended by President Kennedy	Disposition
Unemployment			
Area redevelopment	1956	January 1961	Enacted
Youth Conservation Corps	1959	June 1961	Killed by House Rules Committee
Manpower development and training	1959	May 1961	Enacted
Education			
Aid for elementary and secondary schools	1955, 1960	February 1961	Killed by House Rules Committee
Aid for college construction	1958	February 1961	Killed by House Rules Committee in 1961, by House in 1962
Civil rights			
Power to initiate civil rights enforcement (Part III)	1958	Not recommended	—
Fair employment practices; elimination of poll taxes and literacy tests	1960	Not recommended	—
Medicare	1958	February 1961	Defeated in Senate; killed by House Ways and Means Committee
Outdoor environment			
Expansion of water pollution control grants	1959	February 1961	Enacted
Wilderness preservation	1959	February 1961	Died in House
National seashores	1959	a	a

a Each seashore acquisition was handled as an individual bill; three were enacted in 1961–62.

SOURCE: Sundquist, *Politics and Policy*, p. 475.

The reason for congressional failure to act on the Kennedy program centered around the control of powerful committees, particularly the House Rules Committee and Ways and Means Committee, by conservative rather than liberal congressmen. President Kennedy was not elected by a landslide, as was President Johnson four years later. Moreover, his majorities in Congress were far slimmer than those of President Johnson. This made it much more difficult for him to persuade Congress to go along with his programs. The effect of his death, in addition to the landslide victory of President Johnson which drew into Congress large Democratic majorities, accounted for the relative success of Johnson compared to Kennedy in Congress.

CONCLUSION

It is clear that both legislation and the non-statutory communications made between Congress and the bureaucracy shape the nature of policy outputs of government. In the case of the water pollution legislation mentioned above, the real details of water pollution policy will be shaped by the administrator of the Environmental Protection Agency. It is only through the exertion of influence after the passage of legislation that Congress can determine the details of public policy. This raises a very important dilemma, because insofar as Congress exerts influence over policy through non-statutory means it is reflecting highly specialized inputs. At least the entire membership of the legislature has a chance to vote when legislation is brought before Congress, whereas the interaction between legislative committees and administrative agencies excludes even the possibility of majority control over the nature of the legislative outputs.

Congress is supposed to be representative of the people, and when it does act in a collective capacity it is supposed to reflect, even in a disorganized way, a loose consensus of popular opinion that is concerned with the policy issues at stake. Legislation is a matter of public record, which can be judged by the electorate in deciding whether or not to vote for a particular congressman. A broader sense of accountability, therefore, exists with respect to congressional legislation than prevails in the dialogue between powerful congressmen and particular policy-makers in the executive branch. Where non-statutory influence is exerted through formal communications, as in congressional hearings, voters who are aware of the hearings can make a judgment. However, except in the case of congressmen who wish national publicity by holding spectacular hearings investigating such areas of crime, drug abuse, and the Watergate affair, most hearings escape the scrutiny of a majority of voters. In essence, much of what Congress does to influence public policy is hidden from the public, although not from relevant interest groups.

Those who have the authority and power to make public policy within our system must not have uncontrolled discretion. Because of the way Congress functions, there is little evidence that it acts more responsibly and within tighter boundaries than the other branches of the government. Because of the constant publicity surrounding the presidency, presidential actions are far more likely to be scrutinized by the press and revealed to the public. The electorate is far more conscious of who occupies the White House and what policies are being formulated there than in the legislature. Since the public rarely knows how its own congressmen vote on particular public policy issues, it is even less aware of what actions outside of voting are taken by congressmen to affect the course of policy. These considerations may suggest that the enormous increment in the power of the presidency and the bureaucracy in the policy-making sphere, as well as the dominance of the courts in many areas, is not at all contrary to the underlying theories of our constitutional democracy. Perhaps, for example, the exercise of the war power by the president produces more rather than less governmental responsibility and limitation. Given the disinterest of many voters in whom they choose to send to Congress, and the less than superior caliber of many legislators, perhaps it is desirable to reduce rather than increase congressional influence in the policy-making process.

7

Policy–Making

Through the Courts

When Chief Justice John Marshall stated in the historic case *Marbury* v. *Madison* (1803), that the last word on interpretation of the Constitution resides in the hands of the Supreme Court, an important precedent was established: the High Court was given the power and responsibility to define constitutional law. The entire federal judiciary as well as the Supreme Court had this power and responsibility, according to Marshall. Throughout American history the judiciary has from time to time rendered decisions that have had a major impact upon the community at large. In this and many other ways, the judiciary has played a central role in defining public policy.

THE JUDICIARY AS A
POLICY-MAKING INSTRUMENT

Courts are involved in the policy-making process in several ways. The federal courts have the authority to declare both state and federal legislation unconstitutional. Less than a hundred congressional enactments have contained provisions held to be unconstitutional by the Supreme Court, out of a total of over 70,000 public and private bills that have been passed. However, it has been estimated that 750 state laws and provisions of state Constitutions have been overturned by the Supreme Court since 1789.[1] This illustrates the greater impact of judicial review of statutory legislation at the state level. Courts, however, reach constitutional issues only if they feel it is necessary. Over 99 percent of all cases are settled without having to resort to the Constitution. Courts are significantly involved in the policy-making process through interpretations of statutory and administrative law

---

[1] See Henry J. Abraham, *The Judicial Process* (New York: Oxford University Press, 1968), p. 284.

independently of the Constitution. For example, when the courts decide that the attorney general does not have unreviewable discretion to deport aliens an important policy decision is being made. But the issue is not decided on the basis of the Constitution, but rather upon interpretation of legislation and administrative practice, as well as prior judicial precedent.[2]

Final determinations of constitutional law are made by the Supreme Court. Lower courts, by deciding federal constitutional questions, may force the Supreme Court to exercise its appellate authority to either ratify or nullify the action that has already been taken. When the Supreme Court refuses to grant review of a lower court decision, it does not necessarily mean that the Court agrees with the reasoning and decision of the lower body. A primary task of the Supreme Court is to foster consistency of legal interpretation of the Constitution and federal laws. Conflicting judicial opinions of the lower courts are reviewed by the Supreme Court in order to establish uniform legal principles.

One of the most remarkable facts about judicial policy-making in the last several decades is the extent to which it has been innovative and has exceeded in this respect the outputs of the other branches of the government—Congress, the presidency, and the bureaucracy. Whether the outputs of the Supreme Court are "liberal" or "conservative," one fact about its operation stands out in stark contrast to most domestic policy-making by coordinate branches—its independence. Of course no court is an ivory tower, and judges have been accused of everything from "following the election returns," to being the captives of the dominant economic interests of the nation.

Courts have often exercised judicial self-restraint to avoid becoming embroiled in political controversies that would threaten their independent status. Certainly the Supreme Court of the latter nineteenth century was not a bold innovator, upholding as it did vested property rights and ingeniously inventing the "separate but equal" doctrine to avoid altering the institution of segregation. No one would argue that the Supreme Court was being particularly independent of at least the dominant political interests of society in ruling as it did during this period. The judiciary often seems to have a built-in conservative bias, reflecting the age and training of most judges. A. V. Dicey, that great English scholar of the common

---

[2] See, for example, *Wong Wing Hang* v. *Immigration and Naturalization Service*, 360 F. 2d 715 (1966).

law who extolled the virtues of the common law courts and the need for maintaining their independence in opposition to the parliament and the king, noted that:

. . . [W]e may, at any rate as regards the nineteenth century, lay it down as a rule that judge-made law has, owing to the training and age of our judges, tended at any given moment to represent the convictions of an earlier era than the ideas represented by parliamentary legislation. If a statute, as already stated, is apt to reproduce the public opinion not so much of today as of yesterday, judge-made law occasionally represents the opinion of the day before yesterday.[3]

One of the major reasons for creating administrative agencies with adjudicative authority was to bypass the conservative biases of the judiciary. Judges all too frequently were nullifying the intent of legislative enactments by interpreting them to conform to conservative common law doctrines.

Regardless of what labels are affixed to the decisions of the Supreme Court, whether "liberal" or "conservative," the fact remains that at critical times in our history the Supreme Court has helped to shape our destiny by bold and independent interpretations of constitutional and statutory law. It was the Marshall Court that established such important principles as the supremacy of the authority of the national government over the states, and the doctrine of implied powers permitting Congress to expand its constitutional authority far beyond the strictures of Article I of the Constitution.

The fact that John Marshall succeeded in getting the Supreme Court to uphold the Federalist interpretation of the Constitution gave to the new Republic the necessary legal authority to withstand the attacks from proponents of state sovereignty that would have seriously undermined the national government. Marshall's decisions certainly did not demonstrate judicial servility to the president or Congress, from which numerous threats of impeachment issued because of the course of action taken by the Court. With the possible exception of the Warren Court, the Supreme Court has never been as innovative over such an extended period of time as it was during Marshall's tenure.

---

[3] A. V. Dicey, *Law and Opinion in England*, 2nd ed. (1926), p. 369. Quoted in James M. Landis, *The Administrative Process* (New Haven: Yale University Press, 1938), pp. 96–97.

THE CONTEXT OF
JUDICIAL POLICY-MAKING

The judiciary operates within much more closely defined procedural limits than the other branches of government. The president can operate secretly, and does not have to give reasons for his actions. Congress can obscure its decision-making processes and avoid placing direct responsibility upon any one part of the legislature. The bureaucracy too is more flexible procedurally than the courts. Judges must adhere to written standards. Initial decisions must be reasoned, and in writing, available to the parties involved and subject to appeal.

Constitutional Courts and
Policy-making

Constitutional courts consist of the Supreme Court and other courts created by Congress under the Supreme Court pursuant to Article III. The stipulations of Article III limit these courts to the consideration of concrete cases and controversies arising under the Constitution, laws, or treaties. Congress cannot delegate "non-judicial" authority to these courts without violating the Constitution. Historically judges have been careful to avoid the acceptance of non-judicial responsibilities, when Congress has, from time to time, attempted to lodge such functions in the judicial branch.

The very first Congress, in 1791, passed a statute that delegated to the circuit courts the responsibility for settling claims of disabled veterans of the Revolutionary War. Circuit judges examined proofs submitted by the veterans regarding the extent of their disabilities, and on the basis of such submissions the judges determined levels of disability and the amount of benefits the veterans would receive. Such judicial determinations under the statute were subject to the supervision of the secretary of war, who could overrule the decisions of the circuit courts. This statute clearly delegated non-judicial authority to the courts, and in 1792 in *Hayburn's* case the Act was held to be an unconstitutional delegation of authority to the judiciary. Chief Justice Jay declared the statute unconstitutional because:

. . . neither the legislative nor the executive branches can constitutionally assign to the judicial [branch] any duties but such as are properly judicial, and to be performed in a judicial manner.

. . . the duties assigned to the circuit courts by this Act are not of that description, and . . . the Act itself does not appear to contemplate them as such, inasmuch as it subjects the decisions of these courts, made pursuant to those duties, first to the consideration and suspension of the secretary of war, and then to the revision of the legislature; . . . by the Constitution, neither the secretary of war, nor any other executive officer, nor even the legislature, are authorized to sit as a court of errors on the judicial acts or opinions of this court.[4]

Hayburn's case was the first in which the Supreme Court held an act of Congress to be unconstitutional.

A key attribute of judicial power is that it is final, subject only to review within the judicial system itself. Congress cannot confer authority upon the judiciary which subsequently can be reviewed by an administrative officer or other outside party. Another important restriction upon judicial power is that it can be applied only within the framework of cases and controversies. In *Muskrat* v. *United States* (1911) the Supreme Court refused to accept jurisdiction that Congress had conferred upon it to rule upon the constitutionality of certain congressional statutes in an advisory capacity, that is, in the absence of specific cases and controversies. The congressional statute in question clearly violated the case and controversy requirement of Article III. [5]

Standing, Justiciability, and the Case and Controversy Rule

The courts can and often have used the provisions of Article III to limit the reach of their authority and thereby to restrict the realm of questions that can be brought before them for consideration. For example, before the Supreme Court ruled the Connecticut birth control law unconstitutional in 1965 (*Griswold* v. *Connecticut*), it had refused in other challenges to the law to rule on the statute. The Court held that a concrete case and controversy was not present until Connecticut officials enforced the statute, which they finally did in the *Griswold* case. The law could not be challenged if it was moot. Whether "hypothetical" cases are justiciable, meaning concrete and adversary cases and

---

[4] This case and the entire matter of the proper scope of judicial authority are discussed in the landmark case *Muskrat* v. *United States*, 219 U.S. 346 (1911).
[5] Ibid.

controversies exist, is largely a subjective matter. For example, in the Connecticut birth control case it would have been possible even before enforcement for the Supreme Court to hold that there was a concrete threat of prosecution for alleged violation of the old Connecticut law banning the use of contraceptives. But the Court's majority, by adhering to the line that such a matter was not "ripe" for judicial determination, avoided the necessity of ruling on a very delicate case. The majority was not holding that such a question was "political," and therefore not properly within the jurisdiction of the Court, but rather that the parties had not presented a real case and controversy.

The concepts of standing (the right to sue), justiciability, and the case and controversy requirement of Article III are really fused. A matter is justiciable when there is a case and controversy, which in turn automatically gives the parties standing. In general terms, in order for the courts to exercise jurisdiction, opposing interests must present the issues of the case, and a petitioner for court review must be adversely affected in a personal way which sets him apart from the community as a whole. If Congress has provided by statute that the Courts are to have jurisdiction over certain matters, then recourse to the judiciary is far easier than where no statute grants the right to judicial review. The Courts will not hear cases unless "legal" interests are at stake, that is, interests protected by statutory or constitutional law. Because these conditions must be met before the Courts will hear a case, access to the judiciary is extremely limited.

In recent years, as environmental groups in particular have sought judicial help to stall governmental and private actions that they consider to be detrimental to long-range environmental interests, the Courts have developed and expanded the traditional doctrine of standing. Generally they have opened their doors to greater participation on the part of legitimate environmental and other public interest pressure groups. But the courts still demand that groups or individuals seeking judicial review must have a personal interest at stake distinguishable from the interests of the public at large. They must show some injury from the government action they are challenging.

The current doctrine of standing is well illustrated by the case of *Sierra Club* v. *Morton* (1972). In this case, the Sierra Club challenged a Forest Service decision that permitted a Disney development in the Mineral King Valley, adjacent to the Sequoia National Park in the Sierra Nevada mountains of California. The

Disney Corporation had submitted a plan to the Forest Service to develop a $35 million complex for recreational purposes in the valley, under a 30-year use permit from the government. Access to the resort was to be gained by a 20-mile highway, a part of which traversed Sequoia National Park. The Forest Service approved the plan and the Sierra Club in June of 1969 filed a suit in the district court for the Northern District of California seeking a judgment that certain aspects of the proposed development were not authorized by federal laws.

Before the courts can reach the "merits" of the case—that is, the issues upon which the petitioner is basing his case—standing to sue must be granted. Although the district court granted standing to the Sierra Club in this case, its decision was reversed by the Ninth Circuit Court of Appeals on the basis that the Sierra Club had not indicated in its complaint that its members would in any way be specifically affected by the Disney Development. The Sierra Club then appealed this decision to the Supreme Court, which granted review and upheld the court of appeals. Like the appellate court, the Supreme Court noted that the Sierra Club had failed in its complaint to indicate how the Disney Development would affect its membership:

The Sierra Club failed to allege that it or its members would be affected in any of their activities or pasttimes by the Disney Development. Nowhere in the pleadings or affidavits did the Club state that its members used Mineral King for any purpose, much less that they use it in any way that would be significantly affected by the proposed actions of the respondents.

The Club apparently regarded any allegations of individualized injury as superfluous, on the theory that this was a "public" action involving questions as to the use of natural resources, and that the Club's long-standing concern with and expertise in such matters was sufficient to give it standing as a "representative of the public."

The Court held that it was not enough for the Sierra Club merely to assert that the proposed development was contrary to their value preferences, without alleging specific injury.

The Court's decision in *Sierra Club* v. *Morton* should not be taken to indicate judicial intention to construct new obstacles in the way of environmental groups seeking to use the courts. But the decision did set *some* limits, and it required that at least minimum conditions of the case and controversy criteria be met. In reaction to the Supreme Court's decision, the Sierra Club merely rewrote its brief, claiming individualized injury to its membership, which was readily supportable, and refiled its complaint in the case.

Judicial Independence in Policy-making

Since the courts interpret both constitutional and statutory law, in a sense they stand above the law. When the courts are determined even the clearest mandates of Congress can be interpreted out of existence by a clever stroke of the judicial pen. For example, in the late 1960's heated controversy arose over the operation of the selective service system. The selective service system was attempting to punish as "delinquents" under the terms of the Selective Service Act individuals who were involved in demonstrations against the draft and the Vietnam war. The Selective Service Act at that time clearly stated that *pre-induction* judicial review of classifications by draft boards was precluded. The only channels of review were within the selective service system itself. This was written into law to prevent mass appeals of classifications, which could have had the effect of impeding the operation of the selective service system.

Regardless of the specific statutory preclusion of judicial review, the courts when presented with cases involving the reclassifications of demonstrators and other acts by selective service boards that judges considered *ultra vires* did not hesitate to step in and exercise judicial review. For example, in the case of *Wolff* v. *Selective Service Local Board No. 16*,[6] two New York selective service boards, at the request of the New York City Director of Selective Service, reclassified two University of Michigan students for their demonstration at the offices of the Selective Service local board in Ann Arbor, Michigan, in October of 1965 to protest the Vietnam war. The district court held that it did not have jurisdiction because of the legislative preclusion of judicial review, but on appeal the circuit court held that the action of the selective service system threatened constitutional rights. The court declared that, "the threat to first amendment rights is of such immediate and irreparable consequence not simply to these students but to others as to require prompt action by the courts to avoid an erosion of these precious constitutional rights."

Holding that the selective service boards acted *ultra vires*, the

---

[6] 372 F. 2d 817 (1967).

circuit court in the *Wolff* case reversed the lower court's decision. The court found that although the Selective Service Act provides explicitly that the decisions of local boards shall be final, subject only to review within the selective service system, what this really means is that local board decisions are final provided the boards have acted within their legal jurisdiction. When boards act beyond their jurisdiction the courts can intervene even before administrative remedies have been exhausted (which is usually required before judicial review can be obtained). Remember that the real issue in the *Wolff* case concerned the proper stage at which courts would be involved. The statute clearly stated that if a registrant refused to be inducted, and criminal proceedings were brought against him, he would be initially tried in the federal district courts as is customary in federal criminal proceedings. But this is quite a different matter from authorizing *pre-induction* judicial review of classifications.

Congressional response to the *Wolff* case was swift and straightforward. Congress passed a new law that provided:

No judicial review shall be made of the classification or processing of any registrant by local boards, appeal boards or the president, except as a defense to a criminal prosecution instituted under Section 12 of this Title *after* the registrant has responded either affirmatively or negatively to an order to report for induction, or for civilian work in the case of a registrant determined to be opposed to participation in war in any form.[7]

The explicitness of this language was such that no one could possibly mistake the intent of Congress. Indeed, the Armed Services Committee of the House of Representatives in recommending this change stated:

The Committee was disturbed by the apparent inclination of some courts to review the classification action of local or appeal boards before the registrant had exhausted his administrative remedies. Existing law quite clearly precludes such a judicial review until after a registrant has been ordered to report for induction. . . . In view of this inclination of the courts to prematurely inquire into the classification action of local boards, the Committee has rewritten this provision of the law so as to more

---

[7] 50 U.S. C. Section 460 (b) (3). 81 Stat. 100, Section 10(b) (3) (1967). Italics added.

clearly enunciate this principle. The Committee was prompted to take this action since continued disregard of this principle of the law by various courts could seriously affect the administration of the selective service system.[8]

Similar expressions of dissatisfaction came from the Senate.

How would the courts respond to this new law that so clearly precluded judicial review of selective service determinations before an order for induction? The issue was immediately raised in *Oestereich v. Selective Service System Local Board No. 11*,[9] involving the reclassification of a theological school student from 4D which granted exemption, to 1A. Oestereich had returned his registration certificate to the government to express his dissent from United States participation in the Vietnam war. In response to this action, his board changed his classification from 4D to 1A. After his administrative appeal failed, he was ordered to report for induction and at that point he sought to restrain his induction by a suit in a district court. Section 10(b)(3) clearly stated that there should be no judicial review of a registrant's classification at this stage, but only as part of his defense to a criminal prosecution (which was not the case here). The Supreme Court, overruling the lower courts, held that judicial review was appropriate because the action of the board was *ultra vires*. Speaking for the majority, Justice William Douglas stated in part that:

. . . to hold that a person deprived of his statutory exemption in such a blatantly lawless manner must either be inducted and raise his protest through habeas corpus or defy induction and defend his refusal in a criminal prosecution is to construe the act with unnecessary harshness.

These selective service cases are examples of how the judiciary can override clearly stated preferences of Congress simply by interpreting statutory language and the "intent of Congress" to be something other than what it is. This means that even though Congress has the constitutional authority to control the appellate jurisdiction of the Supreme Court, and both the original and appellate jurisdiction of lower courts, under the terms of Article III, the courts can and have exerted their independence and overridden congressional wishes. This is particularly true where the courts

---

[8] H.R. Rep. No. 267, 90th Congress 1st Sess. 30–31 (1967).
[9] 393 U.S. 233 (1968).

consider that constitutional rights are involved, or that clear *ultra vires* action has been taken by administrative agencies.

Judicial Self-Restraint in Policy-making

The selective service cases illustrate one aspect of the independence of the judiciary. The courts can be subject to political control and influenced by the demands of Congress. The classic retreat of the New Deal Court in the face of vehement opposition by President Roosevelt, who in turn represented a large majority of the people, is a case in point. The fact that courts do not always retreat, however, in the face of strong political opposition is illustrated by the decisions of the Warren Court. All of the innovative decisions of that Court, from *Brown v. Board of Education* (school desegregation), *Baker v. Carr* (one man–one vote), through the School Prayer Decision and the cases that incorporated the Bill of Rights under the due process clause of the fourteenth amendment, raised strong opposition from various sections of the country. Nevertheless, the Court did not retreat, but continued its innovative policy-making.

It is clear that the Supreme Court can pick and choose what cases it wants to hear within its appellate jurisdiction, under the provisions of the Judiciary Act of 1925, which was passed to allow the Court discretion in choosing when to grant writs of *certiorari* (writs to review the record of lower court decisions). The Court had become overburdened under the old rules, which required the granting of most appeals for writs of *certiorari*. In practice, then, the Supreme Court can choose to hear a case or not as it wishes. This is not true of lower courts, which must hear cases if jurisdiction is established.

Aside from appellate jurisdiction, the Supreme Court exercises original jurisdiction "in all cases affecting ambassadors, other public ministers and consuls, and those in which a state shall be a party . . ." (Article III.) An interesting and generally unknown dimension to judicial self-restraint is the fact that the Court can and often has refused to hear cases (particularly involving political questions) that clearly arise within its original jurisdiction. Although Chief Justice Marshall stated in *Cohen v. Virginia* (1821) that "we have no more right to decline the exercise of jurisdiction which is given than to usurp that which is not given," the Supreme Court has not hesitated to decline to hear cases which it does not consider appropriate.

An interesting recent case illustrates refusal by the Supreme Court to exercise its original jurisdiction. In *Ohio* v. *Wyandotte Chemicals Corp.* (1971), the Supreme Court refused to go to the merits of an appeal by the state of Ohio, that sought to bring the case within the original jurisdiction of the Court. The state sought a Court order that would prevent two out-of-state corporations, as well as a Canadian corporation that was owned by one of the domestic corporations, from polluting Lake Erie by dumping mercury into its tributaries outside of Ohio. In addition, Ohio sought monetary payments for damages that had already been done to fish, wildlife, and vegetation within its borders. Clearly, this was a case between a state and citizens of another state, as well as between a state and foreign citizens, and therefore within the original jurisdiction of the Court. Nevertheless, the Court concluded that:

While we consider that Ohio's complaint does state a cause of action that falls within the compass of our original jurisdiction, we have concluded that this Court should nevertheless decline to exercise that jurisdiction.

Various reasons were given by the Court for refusing to exercise its jurisdiction in the *Wyandotte* case. The "difficulties" of the case were cited, and the "sense of futility that has accompanied this Court's attempts to treat with the complex technical and political matters that inhere in all disputes of the kind at hand." The Court believed that this was a matter for resolution by other parts of the government, whether federal, state, or local. It did not exclude the possibility of jurisdiction being exercised by lower courts. In concluding its opinion, the Court stated:

To sum up, this Court has found even the simplest sort of interstate pollution case an extremely awkward vehicle to manage. And this case is an extremely complex one, both because of the novel scientific issues of fact inherent in it and the multiplicity of governmental agencies already involved. Its successful resolution would require primarily skills of fact finding, conciliation, detailed coordination with—and perhaps not infrequent deference to—other adjudicatory bodies, and close supervision of the technical performance of local industry. We have no claim to such expertise, nor reason to believe that, were we to adjudicate this case, and others like it, we would not have to reduce drastically our attention to those controversies for which this Court is a proper and necessary forum. Such a serious intrusion of society's interest in our most deliberate and considerate performance of our paramount role as the supreme federal appellate court could, in our view, be justified only by the strictest necessity, an element which is evidently totally lacking in this instance.

This is a clear-cut example of the way in which the Court can avoid involvement in a major policy-making area, even though it has jurisdiction and could set the directions of policy if it wanted to become involved.

The Procedural Context of Judicial Decision-making

The case and controversy requirement of Article III, and questions of appellate and original jurisdiction are all part of the procedural context within which the federal judiciary functions. Beyond formal constitutional requirements and judicial interpretations of them, the courts have established elaborate procedures for the determination of cases that profoundly affect their policy-making role. Nowhere is there a more rigid chain of command in the ultimate sense than in the federal judiciary, as well as in state judiciaries. Lower courts must operate within the framework of policies set forth by the Supreme Court or face almost certainly being overturned on appeal. The lower the level of court, the less likely it is to establish broad policy principles. Trial courts, in the federal system of the district courts, must render their decisions based upon the record that is developed by the immediate parties to the proceedings.

In broad terms, judicial policy-making takes place within the context of the following procedural boundaries:

1. Cases are initiated by parties outside of the judiciary. The courts are helpless to take the initiative to rule and enunciate principles of public policy if an outside agent does not bring a legitimate case and controversy.

2. Assuming that the parties meet the rigid conditions of the case and controversy rule, once the case is before the court at the trial level the judge (and jury if one is involved) at least theoretically is bound by the factual record developed by the parties themselves, and cannot take "judicial notice" of matters beyond the record unless they are of common knowledge or involve points of law. Judicial proceedings, unlike many congressional hearings, are not merely rhetorical exercises, but establish records that often deter-

mine the outcome of the case. On appeal, judges are limited to the factual record of the trial court, although they can of course over-rule points of law that have been established by lower courts.

3. The process of judicial decision-making is to be impartial insofar as the interests of judges are not to conflict or to be directly connected with the interests of the parties to the proceeding. Judges can have general policy biases, but cannot have a personal stake in the outcome of a decision.

4. Unless points of law have been improperly applied by lower courts, generally their decisions are upheld if there is substantial factual evidence in the record to support their opinion.

5. Where constitutional issues are involved in federal cases, at the trial level three-judge district courts are convened to hear them. Direct appeals may be made from these courts to the Supreme Court.

The case-by-case approach of the judiciary means that policy is established only insofar as cases set precedents. Since courts do not have to follow the rule of *stare decisis* (adherence to precedent), there is no way to tell how far precedents will extend, although decisions of the Supreme Court clearly bind all lower courts until the Supreme Court itself decides to overrule its prior decision.

Judicial Administration

Part of the procedural context of the judiciary involves the way in which courts are administered. This is a rarely discussed and generally misunderstood field. Who are the administrative agents of the courts? To what extent is the federal judiciary influenced by the inputs of those who are involved in various ways in administering what the courts do but are not themselves judges? Mark Cannon, speaking as administrative assistant to the Chief Justice of the United States, has pointed out that the number of cases and their complexity has vastly increased over the last decade, but the use of managerial techniques by the judiciary has not kept pace. While complexity and volume of business have necessitated the growth of bureaucracy in other branches of the government, the federal judiciary has not followed suit. The same number of judges in the district courts now are handling approximately 50,000 more cases per year than they did five years ago. Before the courts of appeal, cases have almost quadrupled, growing from 4,200 to 14,500 over the last decade, while in the same period the docketed cases before the Supreme Court have doubled from 2,585 to 4,533.[10]

The inevitable result of the increasing burdens upon the judiciary has been delay and frustration for both judges and those involved in the judicial process. Judicial procedure emphasizes the central role of the independent and impartial judge, making it difficult, if not impossible, to delegate judicial tasks of any significance to lower level administrators. The most common recommendation that is made to aid the judiciary in meeting its increased responsibilities is simply to expand the number of judgeships. At the same time, there is widespread recognition within the judiciary that the simple expansion of numbers of judges will not by itself solve the problems that they face. In 1968 the Federal Judicial Center was established to conduct research into special problems of the judiciary.

One of the most far-reaching recommendations that came from a study group sponsored by the Judicial Center is for the establishment of an intermediate court of appeals between the regular appellate courts and the Supreme Court. At the present time the Supreme Court is operating with a staff that is minuscule relative to the scope of its responsibilities. The Chief Justice now has an administrative assistant, four law clerks, an executive secretary, and last but not least, a chauffeur. The Associate Justices have staffs of five—three law clerks, one secretary, and a messenger. In addition to the personal staffs of the Chief Justices, the Supreme Court employs some professional staff to aid it in handling its case loads. However, Supreme Court Justices as well as their counterparts in the lower federal judiciary always personally peruse cases that come before them, because by the very nature of the judicial process it is impossible to delegate this task.

The staff of the office of the Clerk of the Supreme Court, less than a dozen career employees, handles the formal requirements for applications of cases coming before the court. Of course, the clerk's staff in no way affects or participates in the decisions of the high tribunal. It is the law clerks to the Justices themselves that are thought to influence the preparation and writing of decisions, both in the Supreme Court and in the lower echelons. However, in reality the Justices do not delegate final decision-making authority in any way to their clerks, and on cases appealed to them they do not even establish a division of labor among themselves. Both in

---

[10] Mark W. Cannon, "Can the Federal Judiciary Be an Innovative System?" *Public Administration Review* 33, no. 1 (1973): 74–79, at 74.

handling appeals for writs of *certiorari* and other appellate writs, and in the writing of final opinions, each Justice takes part. Anthony Lewis has described the role of the clerks in the following terms:

. . . Law clerks assist in research and may write drafts of material for the Justice. They also perform the function of keeping him in touch with current trends of legal scholarship, especially the often critical views of the law schools about the Supreme Court. That is an important role in a court which could so easily get isolated in its ivory tower. But the law clerks do not judge, they can only suggest. As a practical matter, a young man who is there only briefly is unlikely to make any significant change in the actual votes cast on cases by a Judge who has been considering these problems for years.[11]

The current proposal for a new intermediate appellate court just below the Supreme Court to screen out, hear, and decide certain cases involving conflicting rulings among the circuit courts would have the effect of reducing the work load of the Supreme Court. However, in no way would it change the non-bureaucratic approach of the Court to judicial decision-making. The effect of such a Court would certainly be to deny appellees the consideration that is now given to their cases by all of the Supreme Court Justices. Some significant cases might never reach the Supreme Court, although it is not the intention of those proposing the intermediate appellate body to give to it any final authority should the Supreme Court wish to act in a particular case. Moreover, the new court is not supposed to decide cases involving significant issues of constitutional and statutory law, but is to pass such cases along to the Supreme Court. Although there is a possibility that such an intermediate appellate court might reduce the policy-making role of the Supreme Court, this is anything but certain.[12]

Although an increasing emphasis is being placed upon the need to improve judicial administration, there is little doubt that judicial efficiency will always depend largely upon the actions of judges rather than administrators. The judges ultimately have to make the

---

[11] Anthony Lewis, *Gideon's Trumpet* (New York: Random House, Vintage Edition, 1966), p. 32.

[12] See Nathan Lewin, "Helping the Court with its Work," *New Republic*, March 3, 1973, for a discussion of the intermediate court proposal.

decisions. Case disposition may be improved by the increasing use of lower level quasi-judges, such as magistrates (formerly U. S. Commissioners) who aid district courts in processing civil and criminal litigation. Magistrates conduct trials of individuals who have been accused of minor offenses, and they can impose sentences of up to one year in jail or fines up to $1,000. They conduct pre-trial conferences for cases that are pending on the civil and criminal dockets of the district courts, screen pre-trial motions and recommend disposition of them. They also review social security appeals, screen prisoner petitions, review petitions under the Narcotic Addict Rehabilitation Act, conduct first indictment arraignments of defendants in felony cases, serve as special masters under the appointment of district judges, issue search and arrest warrants, fix bail for persons charged with criminal offenses, and issue commitment and release orders for persons charged with criminal offenses. These are not insignificant judicial responsibilities. They obviously affect the procedural policies of the courts, although they do not influence major judicial policy-making decisions.

The major task of judicial administrators and judges in the future will be to render the court system more responsible both in terms of the standards that the judges in the legal profession themselves have established, and in response to broader demands from the community. For example, the speedy disposition of cases is a major goal of the judiciary, and current procedural rules may have to be changed to expedite case disposition. Speed in the handling of cases must always be complemented by fair procedures in accordance with due process of law as defined by the judiciary itself.

One of the greatest needs in judicial policy-making is for consistency and uniformity of standards that are applied within the federal court system and among the states in the adjudication of individual cases. Standards enunciated by the Supreme Court are not always followed. In cases that do not raise important issues of constitutional and statutory law, and therefore are in practice excluded from the purview of the Supreme Court, it is even more difficult to maintain consistency. This is particularly true in those areas where "quasi-judges," magistrates and referees in bankruptcy, handle a large volume of cases that are not for practical purposes generally appealed and where they are appealed do not usually raise issues that the Supreme Court feels the need to resolve. Referees in bankruptcy, for example, although agents of district courts and operating under the authority of the federal bankruptcy law, often handle cases quite differently in different sections of the country.[13]

The problems of judicial discretion and inconsistency in policy implementation is analogous to the problem of administrative discretion that arises within the bureaucracy. Wherever subordinate officials are given the responsibility and power to interpret law, even though avenues of appeal may be present, their decisions are often in fact final. Maintenance of uniformity and consistency of legal interpretation within given jurisdictions is difficult to achieve.

EXAMPLES OF
JUDICIAL POLICY-MAKING

Although courts cannot set policy on their own initiative, and must operate within the framework of the case and controversy requirement, the number and variety of appeals give judges ample opportunity to shape public policy in many fields. Even a brief glance at American history demonstrates the profound impact that judicial policy-making has had upon our society.

Economic Policy

Sometimes the courts shape policy by negating acts of Congress and state legislatures. In the period from approximately 1890 to 1920, the Supreme Court imposed its own views on state legislators with regard to the scope and content of economic regulations that were permissible under the due process clause of the fourteenth amendment. Acting in an entirely subjective manner, the Court defined "due process" as requiring "reasonable" state action in the regulation of economic interests.

It was impossible to predict the subjective feelings of the Court regarding what constituted reasonable action, and therefore exactly how it would hold in particular cases. Sometimes the Court upheld state statutes that regulated economic activity and on other occasions it did not. In *Holden* v. *Hardy* (1898), the Court by a 7 to 2 vote held constitutional a Utah statute limiting the hours of workmen in mines, smelters, and ore refineries, to a maximum of eight

---

[13] See David T. Stanley, Marjorie Girth et al., *Bankruptcy; Problem, Process, Reform* (Washington, D. C.: The Brookings Institution, 1971), for a description of how the referee system works and the attending problems.

hours a day. In that case the Court found that the state should have discretion to regulate the hours of workmen. This ruling seemed to negate the "right of free contract" (part of "liberty of due process") that had been previously established by the Court, which limited the authority of states to interfere in contractual arrangements between employers and employees. In its opinion in the *Holden* case the Court upheld state regulation because of the existence of hazardous working conditions, and also because of the unequal bargaining power of employers and employees.

Shortly after the *Holden* ruling, in the historic case of *Lochner v. New York* (1905), the Court in a 5 to 4 decision declared unconstitutional a New York statute that limited the hours of labor in bakery shops to sixty per week, or ten in any one day. The statute, the Court said, violated the right of free contract. Employers should be free to purchase or to sell labor. The contradiction between the *Holden* and *Lochner* decisions illustrates that during this period the Court was not adhering to strict principles of the law. Rather, the Court was going beyond even its own interpretations of the Constitution in previous cases to look at the conditions under which the cases arose, and on this basis trying to make the appropriate decision. This type of substantive decision-making extended into all areas of social legislation at that time, with the Court freely imposing its own values upon state legislatures and Congress alike. Where economic regulations involved hours of labor, public utility rates, taxation, or other aspects of economic activity, the Court felt itself obliged to act as the final arbiter of the reasonableness of the substantive content of the laws. When the Court acted in this way under the due process clause of the fourteenth amendment, it was essentially defining due process in substantive rather than in procedural terms, and its doctrines became known as "substantive due process" in the economic realm.

Just as the courts during the latter nineteenth and early twentieth centuries were reluctant to grant much leeway to legislatures to make economic policy without careful judicial scrutiny, they were unwilling to allow the infant administrative process to act in an independent fashion. The Interstate Commerce Commission (ICC) was created in 1887, and Congress delegated to it "quasi-legislative" and "quasi-judicial" functions. At the beginning, the authority of the ICC was not as great in the exercise of legislative and judicial powers as it was to become in later years. At first the courts carefully supervised the agency, and did not hesitate to overrule it when its decisions did not agree with judicial opinion. The initial confusion over whether the agency had the power to fix rates, which seemed to be implied in its enabling statute, was resolved by the Supreme Court in 1896 in a decision holding unequivocally that the ICC could not determine reasonable rates, but only establish facts with regard to rates already in effect.[14] This meant that the ICC was limited to declaring *existing* rates unreasonable. It had no positive power to set new rates.

In 1897, the Supreme Court declared again emphatically in *ICC v. Cincinnati, New Orleans, and Texas Pacific Railway Co.*, that the Commission could not determine and enforce new rates upon a railroad after having first determined that the existing rate structure was unreasonable. Rate making, said the Court, is essentially a legislative function, and the separation of powers doctrine requires that if it is to be exercised by government at all it must be carried out within the legislative branch. In another decision the Court held that, although the Interstate Commerce Act of 1887 clearly declared that the findings of fact of the ICC were to be taken as conclusive by the courts when they exercised judicial review, the circuit courts of appeals that reviewed the decisions of the ICC were not to be restricted to the agency's factual record, but could accept additional evidence presented by the parties and act upon it.[15] Railroads wishing to circumvent the authority of the ICC were encouraged to withhold information purposely during the agency proceedings so that it might be later introduced before a reviewing court in such a way as to make the decision of the Commission appear unreasonable.

Legislatures and administrative agencies became less beholden to subjective judicial opinions as the twentieth century progressed. The judiciary never completely retreated into a doctrine of judicial self-restraint. It tended to become more cautious about involving itself in political disputes with Congress or state legislatures on the one hand, and administrative agencies that were the chosen agents of the legislatures on the other. The invocation of the doctrine of substantive due process in the economic sphere to overrule legislative action was not abandoned by the Supreme Court until after the bitter struggle over the scheme of President Franklin Roosevelt to "pack" the Court in an attempt to overcome its opposition to the key legislative proposals of the New Deal.

---

[14] *Cincinnati, New Orleans, and Texas Pacific Railway Company* v. *ICC* (1896).
[15] *ICC* v. *Alabama Midland Ry. Co.* (1897).

The Court in the
New Deal Period

The early New Deal period witnessed a conservative and activist Supreme Court holding unconstitutional major legislation designed to curb the economic ills of the country. The Supreme Court, standing alone within government but reflecting the viewpoints of powerful economic interests on the outside, was single-handedly negating presidential and congressional policy proposals. While some of President Roosevelt's advisors—for example, Secretary of the Interior Harold Ickes—felt that a constitutional amendment should be pushed that would revoke the authority of the Supreme Court to declare acts of Congress unconstitutional, the president took a less drastic course. He recommended to Congress that he be allowed to appoint one new Justice for each Justice on the Supreme Court over seventy years of age. In 1937 this would have meant that he would have been able to appoint up to six new Supreme Court Justices, and thereby have switched the Court from a conservative to a liberal position, assuming his appointees continued to adhere to the policy preferences of the president (which would have by no means been a certainty).

Roosevelt's court packing plan was doomed from the very beginning. Beginning in 1937 the Supreme Court, due to the crossing over of Justice Roberts from the conservative to the liberal side of the bench, changed its position and began to support New Deal programs. The historic case in which the Supreme Court began to shift its position from the conservative to the liberal side was *West Coast Hotel Co. v. Parrish* (1937). In this case the Court upheld a minimum wage statute for women in the state of Washington, overruling its former opinion in *Adkins v. Children's Hospital* (1923).

In the *Adkins* case the court had invalidated a minimum wage statute of the District of Columbia because it violated the principle of "freedom of contract" implied, it said, in the due process clause of the fifth amendment. "Freedom of contract" was an important principle that was also applied by the Supreme Court under the due process clause of the fourteenth amendment to invalidate a number of state statutes that regulated employer-employee relationships.

In the *West Coast Hotel* case the Court pointed out that its prior decisions upholding freedom of contract did not imply an absolute right to contract. For example, in *Muller v. Oregon* (1908), the

Court upheld the constitutional authority of the state to limit working hours for women. Holding the *Adkins* case to be specifically
overruled, the Court found in *West Coast Hotel* that the public
interest justified the regulation of working hours for women. Moreover, it pointed out that workers placed in an unequal position
vis à vis employers can be exploited, and denied a living wage
which places a burden upon the community to support them. Taking judicial notice of the Depression, the Court reasoned that states
can take into account social problems and legislate accordingly. By
implication this applied to the federal government also. Secretary of
the Interior Ickes noted in his diary the day after the decision that,
"Chief Justice Hughes delivered the opinion and he used language,
which, if it had been adopted earlier by the Supreme Court and
consistently followed, would probably have prevented the strained
relationship that now exists between the Supreme Court on
the one side and the legislative and executive branches on the
other." [16]

In a series of cases after *West Coast Hotel*, the Supreme Court
held that the federal government had the authority to extend its
power over the states in a number of fields, and thereby upheld the
core of the New Deal program. In April of 1937, a month after the
West Coast Hotel decision, the Supreme Court upheld the National
Labor Relations Act in *NLRB* v. *Jones and Laughlin Steel Corporation* (1937). The issue was whether or not Congress had the
authority under the Commerce Clause to regulate labor conditions
in industries that were "indirectly" involved in interstate commerce. In prior decisions the Supreme Court had held that manufacturing operations were only "indirectly" involved in interstate
commerce because, although their goods were later shipped out of
state and therefore were in interstate commerce, the actual manufacturing took place within a particular state and therefore did not
involve interstate commerce. For example, in *Hammer* v. *Dagenhart*
(1918), the Court posed the following question:

. . . Is it within the authority of Congress in regulating commerce
among the states to prohibit the transportation in interstate commerce
of a manufactured good, the product of a factory in which, within thirty
days prior to their removal therefrom, children under the age of fourteen
have been employed or permitted to work, or children between the ages

---

[16] Harold L. Ickes, *The Inside Struggle* (New York: Simon and Schuster, 1954),
p. 106.

of fourteen and sixteen years have been employed or permitted to work more than eight hours in any day, or more than six days in any week, or after the hour of 7 p.m. or before the hour of 6 a.m.?

The Court pointed out, "the thing intended to be accomplished by this statute is the denial of the facilities of interstate commerce to those manufacturers in the states who employ children within the prohibited ages." But, the Court held, only if the goods produced by the children were inherently harmful would it be legally justified to close the channels of interstate commerce to their shipment. This limited view of the commerce power of Congress strictly limited the permissible scope of federal legislation.

The National Labor Relations Act of 1935, like the child labor statute involved in *Hammer* v. *Dagenhart*, sought to regulate the relationships between labor and employers in all firms engaged in "interstate commerce." The National Labor Relations Board was given jurisdiction over all labor disputes that burdened or threatened to burden interstate commerce. Specifically, the Board was to prevent "unfair labor practices" through the issuance of cease and desist orders, enforceable in the courts. The way the Act was framed clearly indicated that it was intended to extend governmental authority over manufacturing industries that were only "indirectly" involved in interstate commerce under the terms of prior Supreme Court decisions. Nevertheless, in upholding the Act, the Supreme Court overruled its previous distinction between direct and indirect interstate commerce with the statement that:

. . . The congressional authority to protect interstate commerce from burdens and obstructions is not limited to transactions which can be deemed to be an essential part of a "flow" of interstate or foreign commerce. Burdens and obstructions may be due to injurious actions springing from other sources. The fundamental principle is that the power to regulate commerce is the power to enact "all appropriate legislation" for "its protection and advancement . . ."; to adopt measures "to promote its growth and insure its safety . . ."; "to foster, protect, control and restrain. . . ." That power is plenary and may be exerted to protect interstate commerce "no matter what the source of the dangers which threaten it. . . ." Although activities may be intrastate in character when separately considered, if they have such a close and substantial relation to interstate commerce that their control is essential or appropriate to protect that commerce from burdens and obstructions, Congress cannot be denied the power to exercise that control.

NLRB v. Jones and Laughlin Steel opened the way to extensive government regulations based upon the Commerce Clause of Article I. Virtually any economic activity can be, and generally has been, interpreted to be part of interstate commerce because it is in some way connected. Any firm that either draws its materials from interstate commerce or ships its products back into that commerce is subject to federal regulation. Most of the federal regulatory apparatus has been legally based upon the authority of Congress under the liberally interpreted Commerce Clause.

Immediately following the decision in *NLRB v. Jones and Laughlin Steel*, the Supreme Court overruled the doctrine of "dual federalism" which had stated that the constitutional authority of Congress was limited by the reserved powers of the states. For example, the Court had declared the first Agricultural Adjustment Act of 1933 unconstitutional on the grounds that its purpose was the regulation of agriculture, which lay within the reserved powers of the states.[17] Chief Justice John Marshall would have been horrified at the doctrine of dual federalism for it repudiated his clear-cut decisions that established the principle of national supremacy over states in cases where there was any conflict of laws. Moreover, dual federalism contradicted the doctrine of federal preemption of a policy field where uniformity is demanded and Congress can imply policy authority from its enumerated powers. Under the doctrine of dual federalism it would have been impossible for the federal government to expand its programs sufficiently to meet the emergencies of the Depression era. Eventually the Supreme Court recognized this reality and abandoned the principle of dual federalism in upholding the Social Security Act of 1935.[18] Although Justice Cardozo, who wrote the majority opinion, did not explicitly overrule the dual federalism doctrine he nevertheless strongly supported national supremacy and by implication held that the reserved powers of the states under the tenth amendment could not be used to negate needed national legislation. Cardozo took judicial notice of the Depression, pointing out its disastrous effects upon the economy and employment. National action was needed, he said, and it would be intolerable for the Supreme Court to negate legislation such as the Social Security Act on the basis of abstract and questionable constitutional principles.

The shift in the position of the Supreme Court in the latter

---

[17] *United States v. Butler*, 297 U.S. 1 (1936).
[18] *Stewart Machine Company v. Davis Case*, 301 U.S. 548 (1937).

1930's towards judicial self-restraint and a respect for the initiatives of the executive and legislature in public policy-making reflected a recognition that courts cannot stand in the way of legislation that is politically supported and clearly in the public interest. The role of the courts as negators of public policy passed by Congress ended with the New Deal, and there has been no law dealing with economic problems that has been declared unconstitutional since 1936.

Post New Deal Period

Between the New Deal Court and the Warren Court there was no significant policy innovation by the federal judiciary. The doctrine of judicial self-restraint in political questions was the rule of the day. In the areas of civil liberties and civil rights the Supreme Court was extremely reluctant to "nationalize" any more provisions of the Bill of Rights than it had during the 1920's and 1930's. The Supreme Court was perfectly willing to overrule state actions on an *ad hoc* basis where it felt that state action violated "fair" procedures in criminal proceedings. However, it was unwilling to upset the federal–state balance of power by holding that all of the rights accorded to defendants in federal courts were applied to the states under the due process clause of the fourteenth amendment.

The Supreme Court might have entered the "political thicket" of electoral reapportionment in *Colegrove* v. *Green* (1946), a case in which the congressional electoral districts in Illinois were challenged as a violation of the equal protection clause of the fourteenth amendment because of tremendous disparity in the number of voters from district to district. Urban voters in the city of Chicago were placed at a tremendous disadvantage in relation to down-state rural voters. One Chicago congressional district had nine times more voters than one of the down-state districts. Illinois had not been reapportioned since 1901, a time when the rural areas of the state were in balance with the urban sections. The Supreme Court voted by a 4 to 3 margin not to give the courts jurisdiction over electoral reapportionment in the state of Illinois because such "political questions" are non-justiciable. However, Justice Rutledge, who voted with the majority, did not accept this argument. He held that the issue was justiciable, but nevertheless decided to vote with the majority on other grounds. The nominees for the Illinois congressional districts had already been chosen when *Colegrove* was before the Court. Rutledge felt that judicial intervention at that time would unduly upset the forthcoming general election in Illinois. Therefore, although Justice Frankfurter's opinion for the majority is widely cited as an example of the Court's avoidance of a tricky political issue, the majority voting in that case did not accept Frankfurter's reasoning.

The Court confronted the reapportionment issue again in 1962, in *Baker* v. *Carr*, and held the case justiciable. The majority of the Court in the *Baker* case noted that in *Colegrove* a majority did in fact hold the issue of electoral reapportionment to be a proper matter of judicial concern. The former position of the Court was ambiguous, however; in 1950 a firm majority of the Court held in *South* v. *Peters* the distribution of voters in state electoral districts to be a political question and therefore beyond the jurisdiction of the courts. In that case the infamous County Unit System of Georgia was challenged as being a violation of the equal protection clause of the fourteenth amendment.

Additional policy areas in the late 1940's and early 1950's in which the Supreme Court refused to innovate included the loyalty and security policies of federal and state governments. This was one of the major political issues of the time. Just as Senator Joe McCarthy was embarking upon his career to ferret out Communists in government, which was soon to terrorize many elements of the community, particularly federal employees, the Supreme Court was confronted with the question of the validity of the Smith Act in *Dennis* v. *United States* (1951). The Court upheld the 1940 statute on the basis that Congress has a right to proscribe first amendment freedoms where there is a "clear and present danger" to the security of the nation.

There is little doubt that the era of the Supreme Court from 1937 to 1954 was characterized by judicial self-restraint. As the Court abandoned the doctrine of substantive due process in the economic realm, it also retreated from active involvement in policy formulation in other areas. Judicial deference to the wishes of government was carried over into such policy fields as civil liberties and civil rights. The Supreme Court became a ratifier of government decisions, rather than an innovator in policy-making.

The Warren Court
The profound impact that courts can have upon public policy was illustrated during the era of the Warren Court. The Court injected a new spirit of activism throughout the federal judiciary, which had a spillover effect upon state courts as well. Of particular importance was the use by the Court of

the due process and equal protection clauses of the fourteenth amendment to rationalize the establishment of federal standards requiring equal educational opportunity by abandonment of the "separate but equal" doctrine; the "one man–one vote" rule that revolutionized electoral apportionment in both congressional and state legislative districts; and the extension of most of the provisions of the Bill of Rights as prohibitions upon state action.

CONTEMPORARY
JUDICIAL POLICY-MAKING

Although President Nixon has made a concerted attempt to appoint "strict constructionists" or conservatives to the Supreme Court and the lower federal judiciary, the legacy of the Warren Court is too firmly ingrained in our law to be overturned completely. The Burger Court is not taking bold policy initiatives, which means that it is not reversing the precedents of the Warren Court. It is, however, diluting some of the policies of that Court, particularly by granting greater leeway to the states to forge independent policies.

The Warren Court had required that state legislative districts be apportioned as closely as possible to insure that the one man–one vote rule would prevail. Ideally, each district electing a state or congressional representative should have an equal population. The Court allowed slight variances from this rule, but in general it and the lower federal judiciary in reviewing apportionment plans strictly prohibited even small variations within a state from one district to another.

The state of Virginia approved a plan in 1971 that allowed for a variation between the most populous and least populous districts electing representatives to the State House of Delegates and the State Senate that clearly was greater than had been previously permitted by the Court. The Supreme Court in *Mahan* v. *Howell* (1973) upheld the plan on the basis that it was advancing a rational state policy, a criteria generally used by the Supreme Court to uphold state variations from the general principles that it enunciates to govern state action. In the words of the Court:

The policy of maintaining the integrity of political subdivision lines in the process of reapportioning a state legislature, the policy consistently advanced by Virginia as a justification for disparities in population among districts that elect members to the House of Delegates, is a rational one. It can reasonably be said, upon examination of the legislative plan, that it does in fact advance that policy. The population disparities which are permitted thereunder result in a maximum percentage deviation which we hold to be in tolerable constitutional limits.

Under the plan for the Virginia House of Delegates the maximum deviation—the difference between the most overrepresented and the most underrepresented districts—was between 16.4 percent and 23.6 percent, depending upon the method of calculation. This clearly constitutes a retreat on the part of the Court from the strict one man–one vote rule adhered to in the past.

Equality in
Public Service Delivery

Potentially the most far-reaching judicial policy-making in the 1970's came from the extension of the equal protection clause to require that governmental services delivered to citizens be equal. For example, in *Hawkins* v. *Shaw*, a class action suit brought by black residents of the town of Shaw, Mississippi, the Court held that the town services could not be distributed on a discriminatory basis without violating the equal protection clause of the fourteenth amendment.[19] The town had failed to provide such services as street lighting and paving equally to its white and black residents, the black districts being denied these twentieth century amenities of urban living. The Court required the town to submit a plan detailing how it proposed to eliminate discrimination in the distribution of its services. In its opinion, the Court noted that there were various precedents for its decision:

When confronted with a similar case, the court in *Hadnot* v. *City of Prattville*, 307 F. Supp. 967 (D.C. ALA. 1970), found discrimination in the provision of various facilities in municipal parks. The Court ordered the city to equalize the "equipment, facilities and services" provided in a park located in a black neighborhood with those provided in parks located in white neighborhoods. In *Gautreaux* v. *Chicago Housing Authority*, 304 F. Supp. 736 (N.D. Ill. 1969), the Court found discrimination in the administration of the Public Housing Program and assumed a major role in implementing desegregation by issuing a comprehensive and specific order for integrating a public housing system.

---

[19] 437 F. 2d 1286 (5th Cir., 1971).

The question that the *Hawkins* and similar cases raised was the extent to which the courts would insist upon equal services not only between blacks and whites, but between rich and poor neighborhoods and communities within states. If states and municipalities are required to adhere to "equal protection" in the administration of public programs, everything from street lighting to police protection would have to be given equal financial support within every governmental jurisdiction. More and more the courts are beginning to require equal treatment in the delivery of public services, particularly social services, although the doctrine has not yet been extended to include all state and municipal services.

One example of the extension of the equal protection doctrine in social services beyond the area of racial discrimination is education that is provided by states and communities to handicapped children. In state after state, beginning in the early 1970's, the courts have forced public authorities to provide reasonably equal facilities for handicapped children and for normal children. Abandoning traditional doctrines of judicial self-restraint, the courts have carefully scrutinized the services that states and local governments provide, including institutional care, and have required adequate educational opportunities and institutional treatment of the handicapped (most of whom are retarded children).

What appeared to be the most significant trend in the direction of equal delivery of public services resulted from decisions of federal and state courts regarding the financing of public education. The first important decision setting this new policy was *Serrano v. Priest* (1971), in which the California state supreme court held that the state must maintain "fiscal neutrality" with respect to expenditures for schools, which meant it could not allow school financing to be dependent upon the wealth of local school districts. Following the *Serrano* decision, federal district courts in Minnesota and Texas ruled that the financing of public school pupils cannot reflect local wealth, but only the wealth of the state as a whole. Each district within a state must receive equal financial support. The New Jersey supreme court also agreed with these precedents in a decision in April, 1973. However, before the New Jersey court acted, interestingly enough, the Supreme Court had retreated from the doctrine of equality in the financing of public education when it reviewed the decision of a three-judge federal panel that had declared the financing of public education in San Antonio to be a violation of the equal protection clause.

In *San Antonio v. Rodriguez* (1963), the Supreme Court in a 5 to

4 decision held that the Constitution does not require "absolute equality or precisely equal advantages" where the issue is discrimination based upon wealth. Reintroducing a policy of judicial self-restraint in federal–state relationships, the Court was reluctant to intrude into state educational policies. The Court held that the right to public education is not among the "fundamental" rights protected by the fourteenth amendment, and therefore, the strict judicial requirements that pertain in areas where such rights are involved, such as the right to vote, need not be applied in the educational field. Admitting that there were substantial disparities between the affluent and poor school districts of San Antonio, the Court nevertheless found that the lack of clear constitutional proscriptions upon such inequality prevented judicial intervention. There is little doubt that the *San Antonio* case will set back efforts in most states to bring about not only equality in education, but also equality in the delivery of public services generally. At the time of the decision there were fifty-two school equalization cases pending in thirty-one states.

Although a more conservative and restrained tone is being set by the Supreme Court now than during the Warren Court era, it is unlikely that the judiciary as a whole will become simply a ratifier of policies formulated by other governmental branches. The "Nixon Court" of 1973, in the *San Antonio* case, showed itself to be more conservative than federal and state courts that had rendered opposite opinions. Federal and state judges alike have been imbued with the need to adhere to strict standards of equal protection of the laws, and hundreds of cases have been decided in the last several decades requiring equal protection in education, voting, and the delivery of governmental services. Courts have become increasingly interested not merely in legal procedures, but in the substance of law. Whether as ratifiers or as innovators in public policy, the courts will always play a key role. At the same time that their independence may produce a stance of isolation from the political process as a whole, it may also enable the judiciary to take initiatives that the elected branches of the government and the bureaucracy would not take because of their sensitivity to political interests.

The vigor and independence of the lower federal judiciary was illustrated in 1973. While Congress was struggling to regain the initiative in its head-on clash with President Nixon in 1973 over such issues as impoundment of legislatively authorized funds, and independent presidential initiatives to reorganize the executive branch in a way the Congress had not approved, it was the courts that were willing to support Congress and put a stop to presidential actions that they considered to be *ultra vires*. President Nixon's impoundments of funds appropriated for a variety of federal programs were struck down by federal district and appellate courts because of the lack of explicit or implicit provisions in congressional legislation authorizing the president to impound such funds. President Nixon's dismantling of the Office of Economic Opportunity was barred by a federal district judge, who held that it was unauthorized by law and *ultra vires* the authority conferred upon the president by statute.

The actions of courts in the 1970's in thwarting presidential policies is a reminder that even though FDR won the New Deal battle against the Supreme Court, extreme presidential actions in clear violation of congressional intent are unlikely to be tolerated by the judiciary. As was intended by the Constitution, the judiciary remains today a vital check upon the exercise of excessive power by coordinate branches, including the bureaucracy.

8

The Bureaucracy

as a Policy Force

In most policy areas the burden of refining and enforcing public policy rests upon the bureaucracy. Administrative agencies are the delegates of both Congress and the president to fulfill the broad policy purposes of the legislative and executive branches. Since most of the legislation passed by Congress sets policy guidelines only in very broad terms, it is the bureaucracy that must fill in the details of legislation and make the concrete decisions that give meaning to government policy.

The scope of activities of administrative agencies, their generally large size, and the complexity of issues with which they deal often precludes accountability for administrative actions to any of the original three branches of the government. Although created by Congress, and unable to act without congressional authority, agencies often tend to dominate the legislative process that gave them birth. The expertise of Congress is often no match for that of the bureaucracy, and most of the subject matter with which modern legislation deals is highly technical and requires specialized skills for proper formulation. The inputs of the bureaucracy upon Congress often determine congressional output. Moreover, through its rulemaking powers the bureaucracy legislates independently of Congress, although of course always within the framework of congressional delegations of authority. The content of our laws is often determined more by administrative legislation than by statutory law.

THE CONSTITUTIONAL AND POLITICAL CONTEXT OF THE BUREAUCRACY

The Constitution makes no specific provision for the bureaucracy, although the administrative branch is a central component of our government. The Framers of the Constitution envisioned that the functions of government would be neatly divided into three categories—legislative, executive and judicial. These functions were to be exercised respectively, of course, by Congress, the president, and the judiciary. No one branch of the government was to have exclusive control over public policy. Implicit in the constitutional system was the idea that public policy was not to be solely identified with legislation, execution, or adjudication. It involved the merger of all three functions of government. That is, the Framers of the Constitution fully recognized that once Congress announced its intentions, the concurrence of both the executive and the Supreme Court would be necessary to implement the intent of Congress.

The Constitutional Context
of the Bureaucracy

The administrative branch exercises, under delegations of authority from Congress, the functions of each of the original branches. In its performance of legislative, executive, and judicial responsibilities it should be accountable to some degree to the original branches having primary responsibility in these respective areas. In the legislative sphere the bureaucracy can be considered an agent of Congress; in the executive and judicial spheres it is accountable to the president and the judiciary, respectively.

However, under the separation of powers system, each of the branches of government was to exercise to some degree the functions of coordinate branches. Congress was given the ability to interfere in the operation of the executive branch, and the president is given legislative responsibilities under Article II, which grants him authority to veto legislation and to recommend proposals to Congress. This means that Congress can and does interfere in the exercise of executive functions by the bureaucracy, just as the president in the performance of his legislative responsibilities seeks to supervise the legislative functions of administrative agencies. The constitutional picture is far from clear regarding control over the administrative branch.

Even though the Constitution does not explicitly provide for the bureaucracy, the system it sets up has a profound impact upon the structure, functions, and general place that the administrative branch occupies in the scheme of government. At the time of the framing of the Constitution there was no discussion of the administrative process as we know it today. Rather, the concept of "administration" was incorporated under the heading of "the executive branch." Executive agencies were to be adjuncts of the presidency, and were to be involved in the "mere execution" of "executive details," to use the words of Hamilton in *The Federalist*.

The Hamiltonian view, which admittedly favored a stronger presidency, was simply that the president as chief executive would have the responsibility and power to control the small executive branch that would be established. Hamilton himself foresaw a vigorous and independent role for the president and the executive branch, and was not adverse to having the executive dominate the legislature, a practice he later encouraged when he became secretary of the treasury. Nevertheless in *The Federalist* Hamilton advanced the theory that the executive branch would not exercise independent political power but would be politically neutral under the domination of the president, and the executive branch acting as a unit would carry out the mandates of the legislature. In *The Federalist No. 72*, Hamilton clearly stated what was to be the relationship between the president and the administrative branch:

. . . The persons, therefore, to whose immediate management the different administrative matters are committed ought to be considered as assistants or deputies of the Chief Magistrate, and on this account, they ought to derive their offices from his appointment, at least from his nomination, and ought to be subject to his superintendence.

Since Hamilton did not foresee the role of the administrative branch in legislation and adjudication, he felt it should properly be under the control of the president. In the classical constitutional model, the bureaucracy was not to be a primary policy-making branch.

Presidential vs. Congressional Control of the Bureaucracy

Although Hamiltonian theory suggested that the administrative branch should be incorporated into the presidency, the constitutional system itself in many ways supported an independent bureaucracy. Comparing the powers of Congress and the president over the administrative branch, it becomes clear that both have important constitutional responsibilities. Congress retains primary control over administrative organization. It alone creates and destroys agencies and determines whether they are to be located within the executive branch and responsible to the president, or outside of it and independent. Congress has created a large number of independent agencies and placed many of their operations outside of presidential control. Presidential powers to reorganize the executive are delegated to him by Congress.

Originally Congress was to have the authority to control appropriations, and the power of the purse was critical in exercising control over administrative agencies. Today the Office of Management and Budget and the president have assumed the initiative in this area, although the centralization of the budgetary process within Congress may restore legislative initiative.

Other ways in which Congress controls the bureaucracy include setting forth the "intent of Congress" to be followed by agencies in exercising policy-making powers. Moreover, Congress can and does interfere in the appointment and removal process for top level officials. Ministerial appointments are to be "by and with the advice and consent of the Senate" under the terms of the Constitution, and this stipulation has been extended by Congress to include a large number of administrators. Congress also may establish conditions for removal, granting administrators such as those on the independent regulatory commissions "tenure" for specified periods of time during which they cannot be removed except for specific causes stated in legislation. In such cases, Congress excludes "political" reasons as a justifiable basis for removal, and usually provides that removal may only be for "malfeasance" or "moral turpitude."

The antagonism between Congress and the president often results in the legislature placing numerous road blocks in the path of presidential domination of the administrative branch. This counters a strong trend in public administration circles to have the president assume more and more power over administrative agencies to produce greater efficiency through coordination and planning from a central point. President Nixon's expansion of the Executive Office of the President and his attempts to centralize control over the bureaucracy in the White House reflect a long tradition emphasizing the need for integration of administrative agencies under presidential supervision. The President's Committee on Administrative Management in 1937, and later the Hoover Commissions of 1949 and 1954, called upon Congress to initiate a series of reforms to increase presidential authority over the bureaucracy. These groups particularly did not like the independent authority that Congress often grants to administrative agencies, which gives them the means to defy presidential wishes.

It is in the independent agencies of government, particularly the independent regulatory commissions, that one finds congressional attempts to insure agencies capable of acting in some respects, if not in all, independently of the White House. For example, Congress has delegated to the ICC final authority to approve or disapprove railroad mergers. The president has no power to veto a decision of the ICC. Should the president and the Commission disagree, the ICC has the legal authority to ignore presidential wishes. Under such circumstances the president must rely upon his political clout to dissuade the agency from contradicting his wishes.

Rise of Administrative Law

The exercise of judicial functions by the bureaucracy means that the courts have constitutional responsibilities to review administrative action in this sphere. The rule of law is a central component of our constitutional system. If the separation of powers were accepted in its purest form, judicial functions could not be performed outside of the realm of the ordinary court system. Of necessity, however, Congress has delegated judicial functions to administrative agencies, which may or may not be subject to review in the courts. This has been done because of the vast expansion of the regulatory functions of government, which require not only the establishment of rules and regulations governing various private groups, but also the ability to adjudicate individual cases and controversies arising under such rules.

Why were the courts not given the responsibility to adjudicate these newly created cases that arose as governmental regulation expanded? Would it have been profitable to create a series of new courts and many more judges to absorb the increased workload? Certainly this would have been possible in theory. However, a number of special reasons, some rational and some not so rational, led to the establishment of specialized administrative agencies that combined all three functions of government.

First, administrative agencies were given what effectively amounted to legislative power because Congress was both unable, and on many occasions unwilling, to bear the burden of passing concrete legislation to deal with the myriad problems that began to confront government in the late nineteenth century. A mere glance at the Code of Federal Regulations, which comprises the law developed by administrative agencies on the basis of broad congressional delegations of authority, illustrates the magnitude of the legislative tasks that confront government. Particularly, in recent decades, commencing with the rapid increase in governmental activities during the New Deal, Congress has been scarcely able to deal even with major problems confronting it. A fragmented and dispersed body, without powerful presidential leadership, it finds the passage of legislation a very tedious and time consuming task indeed. On a purely technical basis Congress must rely upon outside agencies to fill in the details of the legislation that Congress passes in broad outline. Congress can still be specific in legislation; but it does not have the time today, for example, to write the regulations that are formulated by departments such as HEW or agencies such as the Interstate Commerce Commission

In the regulatory field, when the Civil Aeronautics Board sets air fares, it is filling in the details of legislation. No congressional committee, let alone Congress as a whole, has time to analyze and debate the appropriateness of various fares for the hundreds of national airline routes. This is the type of task that must be delegated to a specialized agency with a staff that continually analyzes the problems and makes adjustments in the fare structure on the basis of inputs from the airline industry and the interested public. Air fares policy is almost exclusively within the jurisdiction of the CAB. This is, of course, *de facto*, not *de jure*. Should Congress wish to overrule a decision of the CAB it could do so. But it would take an unusually controversial decision, raising strong opposition to which Congress would be sensitive, in order to bring this about.

In 1973 the CAB decided to abolish all special fares, including the youth fare. Strong pressure was brought upon Congress to overrule the decision of the CAB in the youth fare area, but the agency prevailed. Here we see Congress being asked to act to veto a legislative decision of an administrative agency whose legislative authority was given to it by Congress initially. It is extremely difficult to muster the necessary political clout to get Congress to intervene in the affairs of its legislative delegates. *De jure* under the Constitution, Congress has the primary legislative authority. *De facto* this authority often resides in the hands of administrative agencies.

Another important reason that administrative agencies are given such extensive legislative responsibilities is that in politically sensitive areas Congress is motivated to transfer the burden of reconciling intensive group conflict onto the shoulders of bureaucrats, thus relieving congressmen from having to take stands on controversial issues. Until the advent of Ralph Nader and the consumer movement, Congress was more responsive to the inputs of powerful private pressure groups in formulating legislation. At the same time, it was buffeted by a certain amount of public pressure which often came to it under the auspices of the president as a representative of the nation at large. Administrative agencies during the New Deal period were largely created from recommendations of President Roosevelt and his staff. Many of these agencies were created to regulate business enterprises. In such cases, recognizing that crisis conditions, presidential demands, and public pressure necessitated the extension of the regulatory authority of government, Congress nevertheless did not have to get into the even more tricky political and technical issues of the content of such regulatory policies. It avoided this simply by delegating legislative authority to administrative agencies under very broad standards. It mandates the agencies, for example, to act in the "public interest, convenience, and necessity," or to establish "just and reasonable rates." This essentially gives the agencies carte blanche in the legislative field. Under such circumstances, the agencies become the centers of political controversy, subject to the most intense pressure from regulated groups to secure policies favorable to their interests.

Since administrative legislation is generally highly complex and technical in nature, the adjudication of disputes arising under it requires expertise and a specialized knowledge of the subject for proper resolution. This is an important reason that Congress has assigned judicial responsibilities to administrative agencies to decide cases and controversies arising under their jurisdiction, rather than giving the courts original jurisdiction. However, Congress has provided for judicial review after agency decisions are rendered in many areas, and this does provide a judicial check upon administrative discretion.

In the early twentieth century a major cause for giving agencies adjudicative responsibilities in regulatory and welfare fields was the lack of a sympathetic attitude on the part of the courts to the purposes of federal and state legislation. The courts, generally conservative in nature, were essentially nullifying regulatory statutes by their decisions. For example, when the ICC was originally created in 1887 the courts had to act affirmatively before ICC decisions could go into effect. The Commission was given no independent judicial powers. A conservative judiciary rendered the ICC a totally ineffective regulatory body during the first decade of its existence, until Congress recognized its plight and granted it judicial power subject only to later court review.

In the workman's compensation area it was common practice for the courts to nullify workmen's compensation laws in states where the legislatures had failed to provide for independent workmen's compensation commissions. The courts simply applied old common law rules to workmen's compensation cases, essentially substituting substantive common law standards for those contained in legislation that was in fact passed for the sole purpose of granting more extensive rights to workmen than prevailed under the common law. The only way to get around the courts in such instances was to grant independent judicial authority to the workmen's compensation commissions; this violated traditional concepts of the rule of law that required all adjudication to be handled by regular (common law) courts.

Although conservative legal scholars considered the development of administrative adjudication to be unconstitutional, the courts, faced with the responsibility of having to confront political necessities, eventually invented easy rationalizations for the exercise of both legislative and judicial functions by administrative agencies. This occurred despite the fact that there was no constitutional provision for an administrative branch with such powers. Basically, the courts found that as long as the "primary" legislative and judicial powers remained in the hands of the Congress and the judiciary, respectively, the exercise of "quasi-legislative" and "quasi-judicial" functions by administrative agencies would not undermine the constitutional separation of powers. In the legislative field, as long as Congress clearly states its intent, it is the responsibility of agencies to follow legislative mandates. Filling in the details of legislation is not the same as formulating the legislation in the first place.

Rationalizing the placement of judicial functions in the hands of administrators was somewhat more difficult than justifying administrative exercise of legislative functions. The courts essentially solved this problem rhetorically. They held that "real" judicial power is exercised only by constitutional courts, which must conform to the conditions stated in Article III. In reality, of course, although administrative agencies do not meet the various requirements of Article III, they are of course extensively involved in adjudication.

Agency Response to Political Support

Agencies often develop distinguishable characteristics that shape their orientation toward public policy. Most important is the primary basis of their political support. "Clientele" agencies, such as Agriculture, Labor, and

Commerce, were originally created to serve special interests, not the public interest. It is the job of the Department of Agriculture to protect farmers, not to lower food prices in the cities. The Department of Labor was established as an organization to represent the interests of workers directly, as was the Department of Commerce established to give business interests a voice in government. The public policy outputs of such departments tend to reflect clientele inputs. Moreover, even agencies that were not originally established on a clientele basis tend to develop in such a manner as to serve a narrow set of interests from which they draw political support. Independent regulatory agencies are often characterized as being captives of the groups that they regulate. There is little doubt that the railroad industry has found a strong voice in government in the Interstate Commerce Commission, and similarly the airline industry in the Civil Aeronautics Board, the securities industry in the SEC, labor unions in the NLRB, broadcasters in the FCC, and natural gas companies and electric utilities in the FPC. Regulatory agencies were not originally to be representatives of clientele interests, but were to serve the public interest in implementing regulatory policies.

THE POLICY PROCESS
IN ADMINISTRATION

Administrative agencies affect public policy not only by helping to write legislation, but also through rule-making and the adjudication of cases and controversies arising under their jurisdiction.

Administrative Rule-making

Administrative rule-making is the establishment of prospective rules. Under the requirements of the Federal Administrative Procedure Act, general notice of proposed rule-making must be published in the Federal Register. The notice must indicate clearly where the proceedings are to be held, under what legal authority rules are being proposed, and the substance of the proposed rules. After such notice is given, interested parties are to be provided with the opportunity to participate in the rule-making proceedings through the presentation of written data. At the discretion of the agency, oral presentation may be permitted. Unless notice or hearing is required by the statutes governing the agency's operation, notice of rule-making can be withheld if the agency considers it to be "impracticable, unnecessary, or contrary to the public interest." This exemption potentially excludes a large body of rule-making proceedings from any possibility of public participation; however, in practice, agencies do attempt to conform to the general requirements of the APA which are designed to allow public participation in rule-making.

Agency flexibility in rule-making procedures is far greater than in formal administrative adjudication. Formal hearings are not held in rule-making unless required by statute. Administrators are free to consult informally with interested parties, and are not bound by the more rigid requirements of adjudicative hearings. The number of parties that may participate is also potentially far greater than in adjudicative proceedings where only those directly and immediately affected by an administrative order have standing, although the strict definitions of standing that prevailed in the past have been loosened up in recent years to allow for a greater range of parties to intervene in administrative adjudication.

Most of the voluminous code of federal regulations is composed of the substantive rules of administrative agencies. Collectively these rules comprise a large part of the formal public policy of the federal government. The Internal Revenue Code, for example, is part of this compendium of regulations. It consists of a seemingly endless number of rules interpreting the internal revenue statutes passed by Congress. Regulatory agencies, both those that are independent and those that reside within formal departments of government, state many of their regulatory policies through rule-making. The Civil Aeronautics Board announces its airline fare policy through rule-making proceedings. The Food and Drug Administration similarly determines policies governing the labeling, availability and safety of drugs by rule-making. Rate-making proceedings of regulatory bodies are considered to be rule-making. Outside of the regulatory realm, departments such as HEW, Interior, and Defense are constantly stating their general policies through the issuance of rules. In the past, the selective service policy of the United States was given final form by the interpretations of statutory law on the part of the selective service system.

Administrative Adjudication and Policy-making

A second important way in which agencies formulate policy is through their adjudicative powers, given to them by congressional grants of authority. Adjudication differs from rule-making in that it applies only to a specific, limited number of parties involved in an individual case and controversy before the agency. Administrative orders have retroactive effect, contrasting with the prospective effect of rule-making. In rule-making the agency is apprising in advance those under its jurisdiction of what the law is. When an agency opens proceedings with a view to the issuance of an order, however, it must eventually interpret existing policy or define new policy to apply to the case at hand. The parties involved do not know how the policy is going to be applied until after the order is issued, giving the agency decision retroactive effect. Deciding policy through adjudication necessarily means that it will be decided on a case by case basis, which tends to produce inconsistencies. The rule of *stare decisis* (requiring precedent to be followed) does not prevail, and the rapid turnover of the top level policy-makers often results in a lack of continuity.

Substantive and Procedural Guidelines for Administrative Action

Very little of the voluminous writing in administrative law or court opinions concentrates upon the need to develop consistent *substantive* as well as procedural law. In the decades preceding the passage of the Administrative Procedure Act of 1946, the American Bar Association and administrative law scholars emphasized the need to pass a statute that would control the *procedures* used by administrative agencies in adjudication and rule-making. The APA says nothing about substantive law. Nor can a general statute really go beyond establishing the general procedures that agencies are to use in adjudication and rule-making. The APA reflects the faith of the legal profession that proper procedures will produce good substantive policy outputs. Through a stretch of the imagination, one might liken the APA to the Constitution, the APA establishing a broad outline of procedures to be followed by administrative agencies while the Constitution does the same for the government as a whole. Insofar as Congress can deal with substantive policy it must do so through the specific statutes establishing and controlling the agencies, rather than through a general instrument such as the APA.

A major change resulting from the APA was the expansion of judicial review of agency decisions. Although subject to varying interpretations, and in some cases severely limited through judicial decisions, the intent of Section 10 of the APA was to give to any party "aggrieved" by an agency order (not a rule) the right to judicial review, and to provide that when courts go to the merits of individual cases they are to weigh all the evidence on each side rather than uphold an agency decision that is supported only by adequate evidence on the affirmative side. Before the APA it was common practice for the courts simply to weigh the evidence in favor of an agency's decisions, and overlook or ignore evidence on the other side. If the agency had substantial supporting evidence, the courts would not overturn it. The APA made the courts a potentially stronger force in administrative policy-making. However, this could not come about unless the courts decided to shape substantive policy to be enforced upon the agencies.

Controlling Administrative Discretion

Administrative policy-making through rule-making and adjudication may be compared to formulating policy deductively and inductively respectively. The formulation of general rules requires the deduction of broad policy principles which are then set forth in writing. On the other hand, adjudication is a case by case, inductive (empirical) process whereby policy is built gradually on the basis of each individual decision.

Kenneth Culp Davis, in his work *Discretionary Justice*, has called for a wide use of administrative rule-making powers to reduce the broad discretion now exercised by officials from local police departments to federal policy-makers.[1] Since administrative discretion in policy-making is inevitable, it is largely up to the agencies themselves to place reasonable boundaries upon their authority. Although more precise guidance by Congress, the president, and the courts might limit administrative discretion far more than is now the case, it is unrealistic to expect that these branches can sufficiently control the vast array of responsibilities exercised by bureaucrats. Davis is particularly concerned, like Henry Friendly,[2] that agencies develop some standards to guide their quasi-judicial determinations.

---

[1] Kenneth Culp Davis, *Discretionary Justice* (Baton Rouge: Louisiana State University Press, 1969; Urbana: University of Illinois Press, 1971, paperback edition).

[2] Henry J. Friendly, *The Federal Administrative Agencies* (Cambridge: Harvard University Press, 1962).

At all levels of government hundreds of thousands of individual decisions are made each year that interpret policy and apply it to individuals. At local levels, for example, the actions of police officers give meaning to state statutes governing criminal and civil offenses. And these statutes are often far more specific than a great deal of federal statutory law in regulatory and other areas. Even in the face of precise legislative definition of policy, police officials have been known to interpret it in a way that they find convenient and practical. Davis cites a number of interesting examples in this regard. In 1958, the city of Chicago passed an ordinance providing that "no pedestrian shall cross a roadway other than in a cross-walk in any business district."[3] In 1966 a Chicago newspaper stated flatly:

Chicago police Supt. Orlando W. Wilson said Tuesday that city policemen will continue to ignore jaywalking. On the basis of a two-month study of cities that enforce jaywalking laws, he explained, his men will leave well-enough alone. He said that Chicago's pedestrian death rate is substantially lower than in cities that have had enforcement programs for years.[4]

Whether it is jaywalking, gambling, or other criminal or civil offenses, each police department interprets for itself how it is going to enforce the law in individual cases. The average citizen never knows how the law will be enforced in his particular case. Differential justice is a common condition in all states, and those who are poor or in minority groups well know the uneven hand of the law. Anyone seeking to determine the nature of government policy in areas involving the police would be totally frustrated in seeking a formal definition of policy enforcement. Rather it is through the informal, often inconsistent and sporadic actions of the police that policies first enacted by legislatures are given concrete meaning.

Police officials in Massachusetts were confronted with an extraordinarily complex situation in 1973, when the legislature passed a "liberal" bill that removed drunkenness from the list of crimes for which arrests and jail detention could result. The bill originated in the attorney general's office, and was written by a legal staff that was well versed in legal theory but not in police administration. The law states that when the police determine that a person is

---

[3] Davis, p. 85 (University of Illinois Press edition).
[4] Ibid., p. 85.

drunk, he is to be taken home or placed in an "appropriate facility" for detoxification. But the police cannot arrest a person for drunkenness and hold him overnight in jail as was the common practice for decades.

Interviews with local police officials have demonstrated that they are faced with an impossible dilemma from their point of view. The state has an inadequate number of detoxification centers. "Appropriate facilities" include hospitals, but the hospital emergency rooms are not prepared or willing to receive at any hour of the day or night individuals who may be violently drunk. Although the law specifies that at the discretion of the policeman a drunken individual may be taken home, experience has shown that this does not work very well. His spouse may be far from willing to see him, and he may be in a violent mood which makes some kind of detention necessary. Indeed, in the past most arrests for drunkenness, aside from the common derelict, have been for violent behavior.

As of this writing police officials are busy issuing guidelines for the enforcement of the new law. In some communities police policy will nullify the intent of the legislature, by arresting drunks for a cause subject to detention, such as "disorderly conduct," requiring a court appearance. Here is a complicated situation in which a well-intentioned legislative policy will be totally shaped, or misshaped, by police action. The police, for their part, feel they have no other alternative because if interpreted strictly the law imposes impossible burdens not only upon police administration, but also upon community facilities and individual citizens. The police feel that the community will not accept what the legislature has mandated!

Suppose police departments were to issue guiding rules that would explicitly state their policy with regard to statutes governing criminal and civil behavior? Davis gives an excellent hypothetical example of a realistic rule:

Whereas, various statutes make distribution of narcotics a crime; whereas, the federal and state constitutions guarantee equal protection of the laws; and whereas, the police department of the city of X finds that law enforcement with resources at its disposal is inadequate when the statutes and constitutions are complied with; now therefore, the police department of the city of X, pursuant to power which it necessarily assumes but which no statute or ordinance has granted to it, does hereby promulgate the following rules, which shall supersede all constitutional provisions, statutes, and ordinances to the contrary:

1. The arresting officer may release a violator of a narcotics statute, no matter how clear the evidence against him, upon making a finding that he may become an informer.

2. Upon releasing such a violator, no officer shall interfere with his further purchase or sale of narcotics, so long as a finding is made that he is supplying information to the police or may be about to do so.

3. All transactions by which an officer trades non-enforcement for information shall be kept secret, so that the absolute discretion of the officer will be immune to check or review by any other governmental authority and immune to criticism by the public.

4. When two violators of the narcotics laws have committed the same offense in the same circumstances, no principle concerning equal justice under law or equal protection of the laws shall control when an officer chooses to trade non-enforcement for information; all provisions of constitutions, statutes, and ordinances to the contrary are hereby superseded.

5. Whenever an informer becomes recognized as such by the underworld, the officer who has made promises of immunity from arrest shall request another officer to arrest and prosecute the informer, and the second officer shall falsely pretend to have no knowledge of such promises of immunity; as soon as an informer's effectiveness has been spent, considerations of decency and fairness about keeping promises shall be given no weight.[5]

Similar "realistic" rules could be promulgated by police departments in virtually every field they administer.

Why is it that police departments cannot write such explicit rules for law enforcement? Primarily because most communities seem to prefer that the rhetoric of formal law-making conform to acceptable constitutional, political, and moral standards. At the same time citizens do not expect, and often would not tolerate, the rhetoric of the law being enforced explicitly. Informal community standards are often quite different from formal law. And the informal standards followed by administrators in enforcing law may diverge sharply from the formal language of the law.

Perhaps administrators would not mind making the informal

---

[5] Ibid., p. 96.

rules by which they operate available to the public, but it is doubtful that a realistic rule such as that proposed by Davis would ever see the light of day. First, it is illegal by the standard norms of the system. Administrators cannot usurp authority from the legislature and ignore the Constitution. Second, while these police practices are going on citizens do not necessarily want to be formally apprised of such activity. The vast majority of people simply want the police to do their job, and are not particularly concerned about individual rights or about whether or not the police are adhering strictly to the law. Although it is difficult to bring rhetoric and reality into line, it is in the interests of all citizens that this should be done. Police enforcement affects everyone's life, not simply that of the common criminal. All law enforcement and interpretation affects individual rights and obligations; therefore, every attempt should be made to limit totally unstructured and unlimited administrative discretion.

Whether exercising legislative, judicial, or executive functions or some combination of the three, administrators are constantly involved in the formulation of policy. And administrative discretion is a fact of life. Administrators can negate the policies established by legislatures, the directives of chief executives, and even circumvent the dictates of the judiciary. This can be done by administrative action or inaction. As the bureaucracy began to expand and flourish under the administration of Franklin Roosevelt, conservative critics stated that the central problem of administrative expansion was the delegation of too much power to the agencies. In Britain the Lord Chief Justice referred to the powers of the burgeoning British bureaucracy as "the new despotism." In the United States this cry was echoed by Herbert Hoover, Roscoe Pound, and numerous other conservative thinkers.

In another context, to men such as Ralph Nader, the problem of the bureaucracy is not that it possesses too much power but too little. And, that where it does possess power it often refuses to exercise it, making the bureaucracy as an effective instrument of regulation and policy-making inadequate.

What should be the proper role of the administrative branch in the formulation and execution of public policy? How does it fit into our system of constitutional democracy? If it can negate the will of the other branches of the government, can it make the democratic process a sham? Where does the responsibility of the bureaucracy lie?

THE PROBLEM OF
ADMINISTRATIVE
RESPONSIBILITY AND
POLICY-MAKING

"Administrative responsibility" means adhering to standards that are considered to be legitimate within the political system. Administrators who act responsibly are, by definition, acting in conformity with certain criteria. Administrative discretion, and the power of agencies in the policy-making process, complicates administrative responsibility immensely. For example, if administrators exercise discretion then the only meaningful checks are self-imposed. For decades, since the growth of the bureaucracy as a significant political force, political scientists, politicians, and lawyers have attempted to devise ways of insuring that the administrative branch is made accountable to standards developed by branches outside of the bureaucracy itself. The myth that Congress does not delegate primary legislative authority to the agencies, but only creates agencies to act as agents of the legislature, conforms to the folklore of our constitutional system. In this way the problem of administrative responsibility is solved rhetorically.

Those who feel that the essence of responsibility lies in establishing administrative accountability to each of the original three branches of the government in their respective spheres want to eliminate administrative discretion. Administrators are not to create their own standards of responsibility. Herman Finer, the classical spokesman for creating administrative accountability to legislatures, states the problem as follows:

Are the servants of the public to decide their own course, or is their course of action to be decided by a body outside themselves? My answer is that the servants of the public are not to decide their own course; they are to be responsible to the elected representatives of the public, and these are to determine the course of action of the public servants to the most minute degree that is technically feasible. . . . This kind of responsibility is what democracy means; and though there may be other devices which provide "good" government, I cannot yield on the cardinal issue of democratic government. In the ensuing discussion I have in mind that there is the dual problem of securing the responsibility of officials, (a) through the courts and disciplinary controls within the hierarchy of the administrative departments, and also (b) through the authority exercised over officials by responsible ministers based on sanctions exercised by the representative assembly.[6]

Administrative accountability to the legislature can be maintained through continuing legislative surveillance of administrative activity. Such legislative surveillance can be through close committee supervision of administrative actions, budgetary controls, and the development of sources of expertise for the legislature outside of the bureaucracy. In varying degrees Congress has formally attempted to strengthen itself in all of these ways in the hopes that it can better control the administrative branch. The Legislative Reorganization Act of 1946, and that of 1970, were designed to increase the technical proficiency of the legislature and to establish a more streamlined committee network to supervise administrative activities. Today, the new Office of Technological Assessment, a staff arm of Congress with potentially enormous staff capabilities, may develop into a major counterbalance to the expertise of administrative agencies. If Congress is to control the bureaucracy it must have its own independent sources of information and, what is even more important, independent motivation to check and balance the power of the bureaucracy.

One of the principal devices in the checks and balances system of the Constitution was the establishment of separate constituencies for the three branches of the government, so that they would be motivated to act in opposition to each other. If the bureaucracy is to be checked within this system, the branches of government that are to control it must also have contrasting interests to those of the agencies. With regard to Congress, administrative agencies and congressional committees are often in close alliance rather than in opposition. The same inputs that affect the committees operate as well upon the agencies. In order for legislative oversight to be meaningful, congressional committees must be able to oversee administrative action on an independent basis. Accountability to the legislature must mean accountability to an independent organization. Congress must reflect a public interest that goes beyond the spheres of specialized interest groups.

Another way in which the legislature can insure administrative accountability is to write strict laws, in which the delegations of authority are clear-cut and provide guidelines for administrative

---

[6] Herman Finer, "Administrative Responsibility in Democratic Government," *Public Administration Review* 1, no. 4 (1941): 335–50, at 336.

action. This has been recommended by Lowi in *The End of Liberalism*, who advocates that we return to the *Schechter* rule, which prohibits broad delegations of legislative authority to the president or administrative agencies. Such a solution is impossible, however, because the *raison d'être* of the administrative process is the need for agencies to fill in the details of legislation passed by Congress, applying their expertise and professional skills to areas where Congress does not have the necessary resources to develop public policy.

The bureaucracy and administrative discretion go together. Of course Congress should strive to make its intent as clear as possible, and both the president and administrators can be kept within the boundaries of this intent through judicial review. But responsibility to Congress can never realistically be achieved by the clearer expression of statutory language. Not only has Congress generally been unwilling to be specific in the enabling statutes of administrative agencies, but once passed it is difficult to get the legislature to amend these statutes to deal with new problems that may arise.

The independent regulatory agencies are considered to be statutory arms of Congress, with responsibilities to recommend legislative proposals to meet regulatory needs in their respective areas. However, Marver Bernstein and others have pointed out that congressional committees rarely respond to the legislative recommendations of these agencies.[7] Judge Henry J. Friendly amusingly cites the writings of the French writer Dean Rippert in referring to why legislators, regardless of their nationality, prefer not to legislate:

. . . What Dean Rippert has written of the Palais Bourbon could have been written of the Capitol just as well. I commend the entire discussion; here I can extract only a few plums: every man with a privileged position tries to keep it; "when the legislator is asked to legislate, he knows the benefits he will be conferring on some will be matched by burdens on others; he will have his eye fixed on the relative number of his constituents on one side or the other." Moreover, he realizes that "the benefit accorded to some will bring less ingratitude than the loss suffered by others will in resentment"; the optimum is thus to do nothing, since failure will be understood by those desiring the legislation whereas success will not be forgiven by those opposing it. If legislation there must be, the very necessity of a test arouses further opposition, hence

---

[7] Marver H. Bernstein, *Regulating Business by Independent Commission* (Princeton: Princeton University Press, 1955).

the tendency to soften it in the sense of compromise or even of unintelligibility.[8]

In public administration circles the most frequently heard recommendation for curtailing administrative discretion is to place the executive branch under the control of the president. Since the development of the scientific management school in the early part of the twentieth century, "principles of public administration" have been fostered in varying forms, one of the most tenacious being that administrative efficiency requires hierarchical control, with one man (in the case of the federal bureaucracy, the president) at the top capable of commanding those below him, and therefore accepting responsibility for what is done. A classic statement of the scientific management position is that of W. F. Willoughby in his *Principles of Public Administration* (1927):

It can be stated without any hesitation that a prime requisite of any proper administrative system is that . . . the Chief Executive shall be given all the duties and powers of a general manager and be made in fact, as well as in theory, the head of the administration.[9]

Why does it go without saying that the president is to be, to use Clinton Rossiter's term, "chief administrator"? As Willoughby states, certain advantages flow from this arrangement:

Fundamentally these advantages consist in making of the administrative branch, both as regards its organization and its practical operations, a single, integrated piece of administrative machinery, one in which its several parts, instead of being disjointed and unrelated, will be brought into adjustment with each other and together make a harmonious whole; one that possesses the capacity of formulating a general program and of subsequently seeing that such program as is formulated is properly carried out; one in which means are provided by which duplication of organization, plant, personnel, or operations may be eliminated, conflicts of jurisdiction avoided or promptly settled, and standardization of methods of procedure secured; and finally, one in which responsibility is definitely located and means for enforcing this responsibility provided.[10]

---

[8] Friendly, *The Federal Administrative Agencies,* p. 167.
[9] W. F. Willoughby, *Principles of Public Administration* (Baltimore: Johns Hopkins University Press, 1927), p. 36.
[10] Ibid., p. 51.

The recommendations of Willoughby and the scientific management school were directly translated into the proposals of the President's Committee on Administrative Management in 1937, and later in the recommendations of the Hoover Commission of 1949.

Many of the same factors that limit the control of Congress over the bureaucracy also serve to prevent presidential domination. The size, complexity, and scope of activities of the agencies preclude control by the president, even with the assistance of the staff of the Executive Office of the President which was specifically created in 1939 to aid White House supervision of the bureaucracy.

Scientific management theorists supported the idea of presidential control of the bureaucracy for the purposes of administrative efficiency. During the New Deal, liberal Democrats supported the same idea in order to insure that the programs of President Roosevelt would be carried out. This gave a political coloration to the concept of presidential control. The same liberal supporters of the New Deal and later Democratic presidents who endlessly sought increased presidential power over the bureaucracy and a general strengthening of the presidency were not overly concerned to see the legacy of their efforts pass to President Eisenhower, whom they considered a responsible if somewhat ineffective president. Before Eisenhower came into office, President Truman had been careful to "blanket" the New Deal–Fair Deal bureaucrats under civil service regulations, so that they could not be removed by any incoming president. This had always been a common practice of presidents before presidential elections, to prevent the possibility of the opposition party firing unsympathetic administrators.

The Nixon presidency has shed a new and disturbing light upon the role of the president as Chief Administrator. More than any other president before him, President Nixon attempted to centralize power in the White House and dominate the executive branch. He vastly expanded the personnel of the Executive Office of the President, and created a Super-Cabinet in January of 1973—abandoned in May of that year—designed to centralize control over administrative activities in the White House. Administrative agencies were bluntly ordered to impound funds appropriated for programs that did not meet with the approval of the president.

Opposition to the Nixon program led many former supporters of presidential supremacy within the executive branch to reassess their ideas. Because of the Watergate scandals, prospects of total control over the executive branch by a potentially ruthless presidential staff raised the specter of a police state. It was the opposition of independent bureaucrats, such as J. Edgar Hoover and the FBI, as well as the CIA, that prevented President Nixon from carrying out an extensive plan, devised in 1970, of spying upon his political adversaries. And, the Internal Revenue Service refused Nixon's request to harass those on his "enemy list" by conducting special audits of their returns. In order to carry out the break-in on Ellsberg's psychiatrist, Nixon's staff had to employ a special group known as the "plumbers" who operated outside of the official bureaucracy. Administrative efficiency under the control of the president can mean carrying out legitimate programs and, in the words of the President's Committee on Administrative Management of 1937, "making democracy work." But, ironically, at the same time such efficiency can give to the president tools to eliminate political opposition, and thereby to undo the carefully woven design of our democratic government.

Among other things, the Watergate scandals illustrated that an independent bureaucracy is necessary for the maintenance of a system of governmental responsibility. The powers of the executive branch are far too extensive to be controlled by any one of the primary branches of government without upsetting the delicate balance of powers in the Constitution. The bureaucracy must be maintained as a semi-autonomous fourth branch of the government to check any potential excesses on the part of the president or Congress. Administrators are always subject to partial control by coordinate branches. Over the long run administrative discretion is never absolute, but the fact of discretion will remain with us. Administrative discretion in policy-making cannot be eliminated entirely.

Carl Friedrich has forcefully put forward the argument that in a wide area of administrative action the only way to insure responsibility is through auto-limitation, that is, administrative adherence to professional standards.[11] Where the administrator is faced with no guidance from the legislature, the people, or the president, what is he to do when the task of making public policy has been delegated to him? Friedrich suggests that he is to be responsible to "technical standards" that have been developed in the particular policy-making area. He places a great deal of emphasis upon the scientific community and its development of standards of professional conduct. A major problem with Friedrich's argument is that

---

[11] Carl J. Friedrich, "The Nature of Administrative Responsibility," *Public Policy* (1940): 3–24.

there does not exist for the most part agreement within any profession on what is the best public policy in novel areas. Current debates over environmental policy reflect sharp splits within the scientific community, to use one example. When the Secretary of the Interior is confronted with deciding whether or not to authorize the trans-Alaskan pipeline, or to push for the development of a trans-Canadian pipeline, he cannot refer to clear-cut professional or scientific standards for guidance. The issues are simply too complex, with conservationists arguing vehemently against the trans-Alaskan plan at the same time that energy specialists, equally reputable within the scientific community, argue for its rapid development. How does an administrator balance the conservation costs of such an energy policy with the benefits to the nation that will accrue from greater energy resources? This is the kind of decision that administrators are again and again forced to make on their own, although not without inputs from all of the other branches of government.

The most important source of administrative responsibility lies in the acceptance by administrators themselves of those procedural standards that have been developed as an integral part of our system of constitutional democracy. These standards require respect for the rights of individuals and the support of procedural due process as that has been defined with regard to administrative adjudication and rule-making proceedings. It means respect for the mandates of Congress if they have been clearly stated. All points of view should be weighed and carefully considered before policy-making decisions are made. Above all, the bureaucracy must not be politically neutral when it comes to supporting the values of the system. Fortunately these values have been clearly articulated, and there is no excuse for administrative arbitrariness, unreasonableness, or blind obedience to distorted authority, whether it is the White House or the legislature.

Index